Perfect Copies

Perfect Copies

Reproduction and the Contemporary Comic

SHIAMIN KWA

Rutgers University Press

New Brunswick, Camden, and Newark; New Jersey, and London and Oxford, UK

Library of Congress Cataloging-in-Publication Data

Names: Kwa, Shiamin, author.
Title: Perfect copies : reproduction and the contemporary comic / Shiamin Kwa.
Description: New Brunswick : Rutgers University Press, [2023] |
    Includes bibliographical references and index.
Identifiers: LCCN 2022012371 | ISBN 9781978826571 (paperback ; alk. paper) |
    ISBN 9781978826533 (hardback ; alk. paper) | ISBN 9781978826540 (epub) |
    ISBN 9781978826557 (mobi) | ISBN 9781978826564 (pdf)
Subjects: LCSH: Comic books, strips, etc.—History and criticism. |
    Comic books, strips, etc.—Technique. | Graphic novels—History and
    criticism. | Repetition (Aesthetics) | Repetition in literature. | Copying processes. |
    Discourse analysis, Narrative.
Classification: LCC PN6714 .K93 2023 | DDC 741.5/9—dc23/eng/20220628
LC record available at https://lccn.loc.gov/2022012371

A British Cataloging-in-Publication record for this book is available from the British Library.

www.rutgersuniversitypress.org

Manufactured in the United States of America

This book is dedicated
to Us

Beauty brings copies of itself into being. It makes us draw it, take photographs of it, or describe it to other people. Sometimes it gives rise to exact replication and other times to resemblances and still other times to things whose connection to the original site of inspiration is unrecognizable.

—ELAINE SCARRY, *On Beauty and Being Just*

To distribute material possessions is to divide them
to distribute spiritual possessions is to multiply them.

—JOSEF ALBERS, "MMA-1"

三十辐共一毂当其无有车之用埏埴以为器当其无有器之用凿户牖以为室当其无有室之用

(The thirty spokes unite in the one nave; but it is on the empty space, that the use of the wheel depends. Clay is fashioned into vessels; but it is on their empty hollowness that their use depends. The door and windows are cut out to form an apartment; but it is on the empty space that its use depends.)

—LAOZI, *Daodejing* (trans. James Legge)

Contents

Perfect Copies

Introduction

The 2019 self-published booklet *Threadbare* bears a subtitle printed on its back cover: "A conversation about love . . . overheard and embroidered by Gareth Brookes." The front and back cover show, respectively, a nude woman and a nude man, each holding a black, oblong, and palm-sized object. It is the kind of object that has become ubiquitous in our contemporary lives, and the portal through which we shop, learn, date, work, play games, watch our front doors when we are inside, watch the goings-on inside the house when we are away, research the lives and doings of those long gone, and watch events as they unfurl in real time. The object watches us, too, noting how much time we spend doing such things, predicting what we want to see and what we don't want to see, but that we pay attention to anyway. *Threadbare* is also oblong in shape, compact and easily held, smooth and cool in the hand.

The difference is that the images on *Threadbare* are static. And in their representations, they are different, too. The image is created with embroidery, and the black thread of the handheld device in each figure's hand is wound around and under the stitches that delineate their bodies, showing beneath the pale peach stitches, traversing the chest, following the outer edge of thigh, calf, and ankle. Upon opening the book, the reader finds the back of the embroidery reproduced on the inside cover; the shapes of the figure correspond exactly, but the backs of the title and author's name are missing. The raised shapes of these stitches suggest their cushiony softness; the wispy ends of the black thread spring apart and as if outward from the page. The page, however, is obstinately smooth. The promise of the haptic and the sensual is an illusion, and it is no coincidence that the story *Threadbare* is itself a found object, an exchange of stories about lost love, recorded by a self-consciously cynical eavesdropper on a train who initially reports the conversation on Twitter, copies it down on his smartphone's "Notes" app,

1

and then goes home and embroiders it. Before it reaches booklet form, the embroidery is scanned, aligned, and laid out on a computer, and printed in multiple copies. Books like *Threadbare* emphasize the mode of their production and the manner in which we perceive them, the image and text are presented in such a way that we recognize them as reproductions, and that recognition makes us feel a sense of loss. We know from the *look* of things how they are supposed to *feel*, and we know, from looking and feeling, that looking and feeling are incompatible. The page will never be what we think it should be. This kind of book, where the way it is made and the way it is read are critical aspects of the story itself, is the subject of the chapters that follow in *Perfect Copies: Reproduction and the Contemporary Comic.*

Perfect Copies analyzes how some recent works of graphic narrative use the sequential word-image comics form to engage with ideas of reproduction, both mechanical and biological. Mechanical reproduction is a critical defining characteristic of the comic, and yet it is a characteristic that has not been properly discussed as a meaning-making phenomenon. Many artist-authors have been creating hybrid works of text and image that lay claim to the productive possibilities of this connection. These works are by no means limited to the comics form alone. Works like the illuminated texts of William Blake, the posthumously published painting text narrative *Life? Or Theatre?* by Charlotte Salomon, and the books of Maira Kalman and Laura Redniss that range across memoir to essay and reporting are a few examples of text-image books that are not categorized as comics but that, practically speaking, are indistinguishable from many books that are categorized as comics or graphic novels today. I look at books where image and text combine to tell a story sequentially, and that generally have been categorized as graphic novels, although they need not be. What connects them together for me are the fact that they are each the product of a singular vision that combines mind and hand and, further, are united by the fact that both in vision and in facture they are committed with an awareness that the final "work" exists as multiple copies of a print run. For the purposes of this book, that aspect of the reproduction as final work is the common denominator that unifies these works as comics. I consider how comics, which have fundamentally incorporated this aspect of print culture as part of its order of things, increasingly draw attention to this aspect by commenting on it in the work itself. To that end, the analyses that follow stay with works where reproduction as end product, content, and form is a critical and defining feature.

Comics are natively objects of repetition. The idea of an original is not a necessary factor in our understanding of the comics form; indeed, one might argue that the opposite case has traditionally held as its defining mode. Acknowledging that there will be, as with any form, particular exceptions, the comic, whether newspaper serial, zine, or graphic novel, is generally conceived with multiple, identical, reproductions as its intended final product. Taken biologically, reproduction also communicates the means of production of offspring. Because, rather strikingly, the comics form also fosters a preponderance of family narratives, past, present, or future, as its actual subject matter, I consider these two notions of reproduction—technological and biological—together. The biological aspect, played out in considerations of ideas of family as given and made, is as visible in daily or weekly print and web comics as it is to a seemingly limitless and growing range of longer form graphic memoirs. The history of assisted reproduction, itself a late twentieth-century phenomenon, focuses our attention on the boundaries and capacities of family building.

The limits of human reproduction have been challenged and redefined by technological innovations, but so have the conventionally accepted views that have long attached to such categories as marital status, age, gender, and sexuality. The technological reproducibility of comics corrals into view our broader, more pervasive, ambient anxieties that define our contemporary culture as one tethered to an aesthetic and social paradigm rooted in the copy. From the second half of the twentieth century well into our times, theories about the copy have been fraught with ideas of theft and inauthenticity. But is a shift coming, guided by creative spheres, that redefines the way that the monetizing impulses of the business world interacts with notions of the copy? If our interactions with the copy are intrinsic to our habits of consumption, where it is commonplace to accept copies, more and more in completely nonmaterial form—music streaming, for example, has nearly obviated the CD and its anterior concrete forms of delivery—as equivalences that allow for a "being there," in what ways may our categories of judgment have changed as well?

Each chapter of *Perfect Copies* analyzes the creative strategies involving reproduction by a different artist as a method for interrogating that paradigm. These individual artistic works engage creative practices that critically foreground the broadly rooted questions in our culture about reproduction in all its complicated and entangled meanings. Theodor Adorno, in writing about the essay as form, postulated that "if technique is made absolute in the work of art; if construction becomes total and eradicates expression, its opposite and its motivating force; if art thus claims to be direct scientific knowledge and correct by scientific standards, it is sanctioning a preartistic manipulation of materials as devoid of meaning. . . . It is fraternizing with reification—against which it has been and still is the function of what is functionless, of art, to protest, however mute and reified that protest itself may be."[1] Embedded in my own investigation is a curiosity about whether closely looking at the "mute protest" present in these works might facilitate our ability to read and perhaps even live differently.

In her analysis of the forensic, archaeological investigations of the nature of family, Marianne Hirsch writes about the way that the idea of family itself has become the object of scrutiny that has laid bare the fragile structures that disguise themselves as firm and impenetrable integuments. In fact, Hirsch writes, "There is nothing about the notion of family that can be assumed or in any way taken for granted."[2] The notion of family is always open and contingent, defined in ways that extend beyond biological boundaries. She continues,

> When we look at one another within what we think of as our families, we are also the objects of an external gaze, whether sociological, psychological, historical, or nostalgic and mythical. The dominant ideology of family, in whatever shapes it takes within a specific social context, superposes itself as an overlay over our more located, mutual, and vulnerable individual looks, looks which always exist in relation to this "familial gaze"—the powerful gaze of familiality which imposes and perpetuates certain conventional images of the familial and which "frames" the family in both senses of the term. The particular nature of the familial gaze, the image of an ideal family and of acceptable family relations, may differ culturally and evolve historically, but every culture and historical moment can identify its own "familial gaze." Its content and even its mode of operating may be variable, but what doesn't change is that this ideal image exists and can be identified, and that it has determining influence.[3]

The works analyzed in these chapters are directly or indirectly the inheritors of Hirsch's scrutiny of the exchange of glances of the familial gaze. Whether or not they intend to do so, they engage and articulate this back-and-forth gaze that frames the subject of family through the eyes of the artist, the surface of the printed page, and the eyes of the reader.

It is notable that one of the most compelling readings in Hirsch's 1997 book *Family Frames* centers on the interpretation of Art Spiegelman's *Maus*, and in particular the inclusion of family photographs in its steadfastly cartoonish rendering of people as animals on its pages.[4] Spiegelman's text, about families and the burdens of telling a family story, has itself become a progenitor of the family graphic novel: Spiegelman's direct influence on Emil Ferris's *My Favorite Thing Is Monsters* is discussed later in this book. Some of the most exemplary works of graphic narrative, and certainly the most popularly welcomed, have been those that present examinations of family. Alison Bechdel's preoccupation with the development of her individual identity in her "family tragicomic" memoir *Fun Home* suggests that family is one part the genetic material and disposition she inherits from her parents, and one part the explicative mechanisms that she applies to that process. Book titles and quotations litter the panels of her book, as she enacts the detached archival and critical research she pursues while redrawing the personal and intimate lives of her family.[5] Marjane Sartrapi's *Persepolis* is a detailed examination of her own personal journey toward adulthood, but always within the context of her family and its embeddedness in the history of Iran.[6] Lynda Barry's work presses the comics form so that it does not simply document families "as they are" but presents them as a constructed artifact composed of memory and the retrospectively guided hand of the artist. Her pages are compositions of text and image that are surrounded by the ornamenting and gestural marginalia and collage effects that define her style in the world of Marlys, Freddie, and Maybonne as well as in her recent books on making comics. Indeed, comics have offered a welcome harbor not only for sincere explorations of family structures, but also for playful ones.[7]

How do comics reconcile their material status as objects of mass reproduction with the intimate units they examine? We all learn eventually that biological families, to which we initially ascribe so many assumed functions of the natural and the original, often fail, in the concrete, the promises that they make in the abstract. Are the "products" in a family that they examine in fact assumed to be "originals"? In less than a decade, some compelling examples have emerged from the comics publishing community that define the limits and strengths of these two dominant, but seemingly unrelated, characteristics of comics, highlighting ideas of reproduction that are deeply connected and mutually constructing. The five contemporary comics artists chosen here suggest why a medium that is defined by reproduction is the perfect medium to explore the limits and failures of reproduction. The works of Emil Ferris, Gareth Brookes, Conor Stechschulte, Nick Drnaso, and Brecht Evens negotiate the boundaries of reproduction in strikingly different ways. In the most facile terms, one might suggest that the first three suggest the limits of and the second two suggest the failures of reproduction; yet, it might be better to conceive of them as concerning the same web of problems of reproduction, but with different and particular balances. What they do share is an engagement with the formal capacities of comics for expressing these philosophical questions. These artists knowingly engage the form to explore some of our deepest anxieties and desires about belonging and proximity, in an age when proliferation is often equated with overwhelming loneliness and isolation. That they do this through explorations of the domestic and narratives of the family can hardly be coincidental.

Perfect Copies explores works for and of reproduction that embed within them a question about reproduction itself. I argue that this is a question that inspires in the reader a desire to engage with the animistic medium engendered between the author, the reproduced page, and the reader. In this way it facilitates a relationship with the material text that invokes the materiality of the maker and the consumer as well that is well acknowledged in scholarship on the comics form. For example, Eszter Szép notes the kind of trinity accomplished by the interaction with the comics text as particularly corporeal: "Engagement with comics takes place, on the one hand, by the involvement of the drawer's and reader's bodies, and on the other hand, by interacting with the materiality of the actual comics that is mediating the interaction. Comics can thus be thought of as a mediated interaction between three bodies: those of the drawer, reader, and object (the actual comic)."[8] That relationship is engendered precisely because the reader is made aware, with the problems of reproduction explored in each work, of the limited capacities of the reproduced page. They do this while also relying on this flawed reproduced text to deeply create that awareness. It is precisely in this paradox that I believe such texts can compel us, through their aesthetic power, to think differently about what we expect from the world and from each other. *Perfect Copies* argues that this kind of reading can, to borrow a phrase from Jonathan Crary in his book on sleep in an age of 24/7 machinations, "stand for the durability of the social" that may be "analogous to other thresholds at which society could defend or protect itself."[9] Allowing ourselves to be absorbed into this triangulated medium with the text and the imagined maker of the text may also stand for the "durability of the social."

The genre of comics, even those that are created collaboratively and not created as auteur forms like the subjects of this book, allows for a great expression of individual style. This individual style embraces, for example, distinct writing voices, drawing strategies, and the "signature" of handwriting. Scholars focus on the distinctiveness of the comic as a narrative form that is able to create a sense of immediacy and presentness because of these very individual marks that extend beyond the arrangement of words to the line of a drawing and of lettering. Yet comics is also very much a creative medium that is implicitly manufactured for and as reproduction: the artist designs this work with stacks of identical versions in mind. With a few requisite exceptions, this is distinct from approaches in literary studies and visual studies. Variations initiated as handwritten manuscript and then transformed into typeset page are typically considered as simply cases of difference in medium, and therefore practically invisible, unless clarification problems of orthography occur. When particular materials, for instance vellum, are used in the original writing of a text, they can indeed contribute greater density of meaning to the text written on it. Vellum, a writing material made from the skin of animals, could remind one of the finitude of life or the mortification of flesh made literal, emphasizing or challenging the content of the words inscribed on its surface. Nonetheless, when the contents of such a text are reproduced in typeset print, they are generally treated as interchangeable with the original, with perhaps a footnote appended on the historical significance of the materials in which it was originally inscribed. The image-text comic must be reproduced in its entirety; it is not the "same thing" if it is copied with image only, or if it is converted to a text-only document. If pagination is altered, the effect of the narrative can be undone: surprises can be ruined when page turns are changed. Sometimes even the scale in which a comic is printed can affect how it is perceived: converting all frames on a single page to the same size can have drastic and unwanted effects on their impact and function.

Reproductions of images are also understood differently, as evidenced in the way they are handled in catalogue copy and captions. The materials used and the dimensions of the original work are carefully noted, so that the reproduced work of art is understood with the meaning of reproduction construed as difference: a diagram, or a map, of the original. The philosopher Arthur Danto begins with his explication of the work of art in the 1960s by first discussing reproductions of artwork that "fail" because of their inability to reproduce what makes the work of art "art": "Roy Lichtenstein paints comic-strip panels, though ten or twelve feet high. These are reasonably faithful projections onto a gigantesque scale of the homely frames from the daily tabloid, but it is precisely the scale that counts. . . . A *photograph* of a Lichtenstein is indiscernible from a photograph of a counterpart panel from *Steve Canyon*; but the photograph fails to capture the scale, and hence is as inaccurate a reproduction as a black-and-white engraving of Botticelli, scale being essential here as color there. Lichtensteins, then, are not imitations but *new entities*."[10] Danto argues that "to see something as art requires something the eye cannot decry—an atmosphere of artistic theory, a knowledge of the history of art: an artworld."[11] The comic book, on the other hand, is committed through the act of reproduction; its material form is defined by the technologies of its production even as the artists producing these pages may work at scales different from the intended final printed text. Does it still have, or incite a need for recognizing, an atmosphere?

When comics studies has turned to a consideration of the materiality of its texts, the focus has resulted in particularly illuminating results. Jared Gardner investigates the way that reading comics can be understood in the context of the archive fever of the collector.[12] Bart Beaty, in his commentary on the relationship between comics and fine art, notes the ways that the condition of collectors editions constitutes their value.[13] Questions of memory and the relationship of memory to an exploration of "the specific gestures of collection, reproduction, exhibition, imitation, and appropriation that materialize and give shape to their engagement with the past" are at the heart of the work of many contemporary scholars of the comic.[14] Aaron Kashtan attends to the relationship between the codex, or bound printed pages, and the digital or e-document.[15] In writing about "retrograde script" in comics, Thomas Bredehoft persuasively argues that "even the most faithful facsimile cannot escape the logic of the copy: these retrograde texts explicitly challenge the ideological claims of the logic of the copy, regardless of whether they . . . remind us of the necessity of encountering the thing itself or . . . expose certain failures of the logic of the copy from within the paradigm of printed reproduction itself."[16] The material facts of the comic as an object of reproduction, and how that aesthetic characteristic may be used to comment on its particular concerns, are not often discussed or, when they are, more frequently discussed outside the scope of comics studies. The facts of reproduction can be largely taken for granted when discussing thematic connections such as the family structures that are ever-present in these texts. We take them for granted at our peril, for the medium of the reproduced page is a powerful tool for commenting on "reproduction" broadly defined. The readings presented here, therefore, engage specifically with this aspect of the printed (comics) page, showing how these artists interact with the surface of the reproduced page to comment precisely on the state of reproduction in an age anxious about reproduction.

In an earlier book on the comics form, *Regarding Frames: Thinking with Comics in the Twenty-First Century*, I applied a close-reading-based and multidisciplinary methodology developed from visual studies theory, philosophy, and literary criticism to analyze the ways that certain contemporary comics artists create their work while commenting on the comics form.[17] My analysis of the work of Michael DeForge focused on the way that his stories manipulated perspectival shifts on the page to make broader arguments about perspectival shifts on an epistemological level. In my exploration of Dash Shaw's work, I analyzed works that deliberately gestured to the processes associated with layering colors in the printing process and in animation work. I argued that these literary comics makers knowingly engaged with the form as an integral part of their storytelling and put pressure on the form in unique ways that highlighted the narrative issues in the stories themselves. I read the image-text book as performing a particular kind of perlocutionary effect on the reader, causing an active searching response conditioned by one's recognition of the impenetrability of the surface, making the reader into what McCloud calls an accomplice.[18] In the epilogue of *Regarding Frames*, I laid the preliminary work for *Perfect Copies*, singling out the first volume of Emil Ferris's *My Favorite Thing Is Monsters* and its fascination with reproductions and doubles as a working metaphor for thinking with comics in the twenty-first century, the subtitle of that book. Here I continue and build on this argument, focusing on that aspect that encompasses these questions: reproduction.

The question of reproduction, understood as representing part of a parcel of concepts that append to labor and the means of production, has fixed the attention of critical theorists and philosophers for well over a century. Reproduction is a concern in the work of Karl Marx, for whom the means of production and its material effects define our social and psychological lives. For Marx, biological reproduction provided a metaphorical language as well as structural analogue for economic reproduction, by which he meant the conversion of labor into "use values." In a remarkable chapter on "Commodities and Money" in *Capital*, Marx uses the example of the production of a linen coat to express this meaning: "If we subtract the total amount of useful labour of different kinds which is contained in the coat, the linen, etc., a material substratum is always left. This substratum is furnished by nature without human intervention. When man engages in production, he can only proceed as nature does herself, i.e., he can only change the form of the materials."[19] Marx added, in a footnote, a quotation from eighteenth-century political economist Pietro Verri: "Composition and separation are the only elements found by the human mind whenever it analyses the notion of reproduction; and so it is with the reproduction of value . . . and wealth, whether earth, air and water are turned into corn in the fields, or the secretions of an insect are turned into silk by the hand of man, or some small pieces of metal are arranged together to form a repeating watch."[20] This distinction regarding the conversion of natural material elements and human labor to produce use value was thus directed at the commodity, rather than at art, but the connection between concomitant natural and value forms has been influential in analysis of culture as well as social structures, most notably in the work of Pierre Bourdieu.[21] The ideas of composition and separation that Marx, via Verri, identifies as intrinsic to our understanding of reproduction inhere in the processes used to print the comics I discuss in these chapters, as well as the ways they are animated as ontological questions of reproduction within the texts.

Cultural critics, keen to approach Marx's theories of commodity fetishism humanistically, explored ways to employ his theories to interpret the world from a cultural perspective. The comics analyzed in this book function as rejoinders to the "culture industry" critiqued by Adorno and Horkheimer, who pointed out the ways that reproductive technologies could be manipulated to direct the consumption of culture: "Culture today is infecting everything with sameness. Film, radio, and magazines form a system. Each branch of culture is unanimous within itself and all are unanimous together. Even the aesthetic manifestations of political opposites proclaim the same inflexible rhythm."[22] In the "Culture Industry" chapter of *Dialectic of Enlightenment*, Horkheimer and Adorno continued,

> Interested parties like to explain the culture industry in technological terms. Its millions of participants, they argue, demand reproduction processes which inevitably lead to the use of standard products to meet the same needs at countless locations. The technical antithesis between few production centers and widely dispersed reception necessitates organization and planning by those in control. The standardized forms, it is claimed, were originally derived from the needs of the consumers: that is why they are accepted with so little resistance. In reality, a cycle of manipulation and retroactive need is unifying the system ever more tightly. What is not mentioned is that the basis on which technology is gaining power over society is the power of those whose economic position in society is strongest. Technical rationality today is the rationality of domination. It is the compulsive character of a society alienated from itself. . . . For the present the technology of the culture industry confines itself to standardization and mass production and sacrifices what once distinguished the logic of the work from that of society.[23]

In their critique of the communication tools that were relevant at the time of their writing in the 1940s, they identified the telephone and the radio as technological examples of these conceptual rivals. Horkheimer and Adorno took care to point out that it was not the technological means of production themselves that enacted the control of society, but rather their functions.

The differing functions of telephone and radio were significant because of the level of interaction between individual and their means of consuming information: "The step from telephone to radio has clearly distinguished the roles. The former liberally permitted the participant to play the role of the subject. The latter democratically makes everyone equally into listeners, in order to expose them in authoritarian fashion to the same programs put out by different stations. No mechanism of reply has been developed, and private transmissions are condemned to unfreedom."[24] The alienated consumer, interacting with these products of the culture industry, is thus lulled into a sense of spontaneous interaction, whereas they have in fact already been typed, so that "each single manifestation of the culture industry inescapably reproduces human beings as what the whole has made them.... And all its agents ... are on the alert to ensure that the simple reproduction of mind does not lead on to the expansion of mind."[25] Whereas the telephone allowed for a response from the receiver, the radio trafficked in the one-way. How to be liberated from passive receipt? The "Culture Industry" chapter focused on the pernicious ways that technological reproduction accelerates the grasp of the industry on the domination of humans, yet neglected to acknowledge the reliance of the authors themselves on the tools of reproduction: they themselves had circulated these essays in mimeographed form as "Philosophische Fragmente" among their friends and associates.[26] To some degree, "Culture Industry" is a reaction in opposition to ideas developed by Walter Benjamin in the famous 1935 essay "The Work of Art in the Age of Mechanical Reproduction," alternately translated as "The Work of Art in the Age of Its Technological Reproducibility." Adorno's reaction lasted for several decades and certainly through the writing of the *Dialectic of Enlightenment*; but he too eventually returned to and modified that reaction in a later essay.[27]

Walter Benjamin's text has been succinctly described as concerning "the relationship between, on the one hand, the history of artistic production in terms of the history of techniques and technological development, and, on the other, the concomitant effect of that development on the concepts and categories through which art is to be understood."[28] The ideas in his essay are primarily devoted to film. Benjamin identified film as disrupting the aura, or the work of art's "presence in time and space, its unique existence at the place where it happens to be,"[29] that one can access with a live theatrical work. The disruption of the aura was enacted by film's dissemination of the actor to the masses through the intervention of the mediating apparatus of technology. Benjamin's essay, although cautious in its appraisal of technological change and innovation, allows for the productive possibilities of mechanical reproduction as well: "For the first time in world history, mechanical reproduction emancipates the work of art from its parasitical dependence on ritual. To an ever greater degree the work of art reproduced becomes the work of art designed for reproducibility. From a photographic negative, for example, one can make any number of prints; to ask for the 'authentic' print makes no sense."[30]

If we conceive of Benjamin's work of art in terms of the reproduced printed copies of the comics page, we find that pattern more properly in that of the photographic negative. The negative is not the "original" or "actual" but itself a "virtually actual" iteration of the work of art, in Deleuze's sense of the virtual as a state where "the elements, varieties of relations and singular points coexist in the work or the object, in the virtual part of the work or object, without it being possible to designate a point of view privileged over others, a centre which would unify the other centres."[31] The alienation between performer and audience created by the reproduced work of art is foregrounded in recordings of musical and theatrical performance. Accessibility to such forms is afforded by the introduction of film and audio reproduction at the turn of the twentieth century, but the printed book has maintained the distance created by this artifice from its beginnings. The amount of labor and layers of material that go into making a "virtual actual" object that awaits dissemination as its end product is precisely the point, when it comes to discussing reproduction and the comic.

Adorno and Benjamin shared a wariness about the potential of such systems of reproduction to cultivate a passive mass of consuming spectators. Yet within both of their critiques there was also a call to the subject to engage the liberatory impulse available to every subject, a pathway through the stultifying barricades created by the distractions of the reproduction. For Benjamin there was the "gestus" derived from his analyses of Brecht's theater as a moment of "making gestures quotable" in the way that "an actor must be able to space his gestures the way a typesetter produces spaced type."[32] Adorno viewed time as a dialectic between domination and freedom—a future that "is not built on the fantasy of the certain arrival of a better world"[33] but that nonetheless holds the potential for a discriminating subject. This subject was conceived as one who strove to transgress the confines of contemporary existence while maintaining a pragmatic view of the confinement that nonetheless inhered in it. That this future-oriented production can be developed through the close scrutiny of individual objects is particularly captivating to me. As Adorno wrote in "The Essay as Form," "An intellect irrevocably modeled on the domination of nature and material production abandons the recollection of the stage it has overcome, a stage that promises a future one, the transcendence of rigidified relations of production; and this cripples its specialist's approach precisely when it comes to specific objects."[34] There is an articulation here of "stepping out" that I would like to apply to a specific method of reading performed in *Perfect Copies*, whether in Benjamin's attention to gestus, where the actor quotes themselves acting in order to shock the audience into responding, or in the focus on a specific object of cultural criticism that allows the recognition of the stage it has yet to overcome. Both Adorno and Benjamin envision interruption as a key mode of resistance to the apparatus of reproduction. The work of art can still transform the masses from simple hypnotized consumers to active participants through moments of shock, and it is precisely in these moments of stutter or stepping out where I situate my own close readings.

To return to the relationship between original and reproduction in the comics text, I turn to that spiritual or animistic component that complements the material aspects discussed here. This is what Arthur Danto called "a certain theory of art." In his final evaluation of Andy Warhol's Brillo boxes, Danto argues that "what in the end makes the difference between a Brillo box and a work of art consisting of a Brillo Box is a certain theory of art. It is the theory that takes it up into the world of art, and keeps it from collapsing into the real object which it is. . . . Of course, without the theory, one is unlikely to see it as art, and in order to see it as part of the artworld, one must have mastered a good deal of artistic theory as well as a considerable amount of the history of recent New York painting. . . . It is the role of artistic theories, these days as always, to make the artworld, and art, possible."[35] I follow Danto's lead in the necessity of considering the perplexities that arise in our contemplating a certain theory of art with respect to the comics. I also follow this lead in a way that leans more toward the "certain" than to the "theory" of this conception; these chapters are always situated on the side of the text as itself generative of its theory, rather than from a desire to apply a theory to those texts. Where a philosopher, art or literary critic, or cultural theorist has already developed a vocabulary to discuss a certain phenomenon, I gladly follow their lead in using their terms; but the close reading of the primary source always directs the course of this expression.

When I say that I consider the perplexities that arise from contemplating a comics-centered certain theory of art, I mean that there is an affective response that is elicited from the comics discussed in this book that is intrinsic to my readings. I hesitate to call it a theory of art, and see it is more as a kind of calling to attention, as I have discussed above, to the ways in which the thing represented is simultaneously not itself. I point to that moment as the point where we are best able to access the meaning of the work itself. The subject, then, is less the actual objects on the page than the *process* of distinguishing those structural relationships and the meaning that inheres in them; reading these comics is one part registering the image and text on the page, and the other part reading the process inscribed by their presence there. In this way, it is not unlike Foucault's reading of Magritte in *This Is Not a Pipe*, where Magritte's text "sets out to name something that evidently does not need to be named (the form is too well known, the label too familiar). And at the moment when he should reveal the name, Magritte does so by denying that the object is what it is. Whence comes this strange game, if not from the calligram? From the calligram that says things twice . . . from the calligram that shuffles what it says over what it shows to hide them from each other."[36] Foucault's interpretation of the force of Magritte's art as activated by the logic of the reading helps to define the work at hand in the readings that follow. The "perfect copy" makes us aware of what we don't know when we read these texts, which is why they are so important as instruments for showing us how to make our way through worlds of perfect copies. Rather than pretending that they are an easy substitute, and that there is no substantive difference between an original and the deliverables that are its copies, these texts openly acknowledge that there is something crucial about how they are made and that holds the key to our understanding. Simultaneously, they openly acknowledge that it is impossible to access that crucial thing. This leaves the reader with the very important job of attempting to make sense of things all the while accepting that they cannot know. This cultivates a spiritual mode that persists in our digital, agnostic age.

Reading is central to the analyses performed in these texts, and the way that reading can be and is directed by a text is central to the idea that a reproduction qua reproduction is consumed. If we accept that the reproduction can show us only what appears on the surface, how might we conduct our interpretation? I propose in this book to progress with a reading practice that is surface based rather than to claim that one can "get past" a surface. By surface reading, I mean specifically an attention to a reading at the surface of a text of evidence that I have argued is "already there."[37] What it means to claim that the evidence is already there is to assume a deliberate resistance to the authoritative claims of being an expert reader tasked to excavate the "hidden meanings" in texts. Instead, this book approaches the texts from the perspective articulated by art historian Jonathan Hay, as inspired by "the design process that has been incorporated into the material artifact and can be separated out analytically with the help of a two-dimensional diagram, be it a line drawing or a roll-out photograph or a rubbing"[38] or literary critic Heather Love's injunction to read in a way that is "close but not deep."[39] My interpretation of surface reading, lodged as it is within the intersection of reader-response theory and formal structuralist criticism, requires an implied reader who is adequately competent to "concretize" the aesthetic formulations of the author-artist that does require some degree of competence.[40] The curious thing about this competence is that it requires the reader to make sense of what is not there, the "nothing that connects everything," as Joe Milutis captivatingly expresses in the subtitle of his book *Ether*.[41]

I propose a return to—though I myself, along with many others, have hardly been capable of straying very far from it in the first place—formalism in a way that W. J. T. Mitchell has defined it, as "a commitment to emancipatory, progressive political practices united with a scrupulous attention to ethical means. Insofar as formalism insists on paying attention to a way of being in the path rather than to where the path leads, it seems . . . central to any notion of right action."[42] My own approach to reading in general, and to reading comics in particular, has cleaved most firmly to the affective stylistics proposed by Stanley Fish. Fish's particular program of reading allows for the reader's progress through, indeed not just allows but demands, a certain degree of fumbling. This kind of fumbling through a text where mistakes and mistaken anticipation prevail is what I believe to be an integral part of the reading process.[43] An interpretive stance given to the anticipation of failure, and in which the mistake and the interruption is highlighted, allows for a destabilization of even the most competent of readers, who is propelled forward and then called to a stop by the very same set of assumptions that they have brought to the text. In the case of

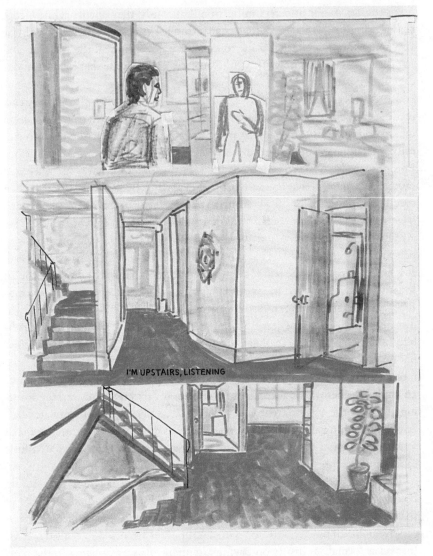

FIGURE I.1 "I'm upstairs, listening." Frank Santoro, *Pittsburgh* (New York: New York Review Comics, 2019), n.p. Copyright © Frank Santoro.

Surprised by Sin, Fish articulated the fallenness of the reader, whose vulnerability to being led astray in Milton mimics that of Adam and Eve falling prey to the rhetoric of the devil. In the case of *Perfect Copies*, we are led as readers through variations on reproduction that both appeal to our sense of touch and resist it.

To that end, these works also actively engage the ideas formulated by Bill Brown in his distinction between things and objects, where things "assert their presence and power" precisely when they stop working: "The story of objects asserting themselves as things . . . is the story of a changed relation to the human subject and thus the story of how the thing really names less an object than a particular subject-object relation."[44] The particular subject-object relations that I am interested in pursuing in this book are those between artist, text, and reader that I see engaged in the kind of merging of material and spiritual that May Adadol Ingawanij has applied to certain filmmakers of Southeast Asia, and especially to the films of Apichatpong Weerasethakul. Ingawanij notes a "similar epistemological grounding" in performances of animistic possessions in Apichatpong's "layering of diegetic worlds in which material immaterialities are perceived as real."[45] This kind of epistemological grounding describes what I see in the balance between reality—of the material printed book—and the animistic possession inculcated by the reading process in certain text-image narratives. And it is precisely the fact that these are text-image narratives, and text-image narratives that often incorporate the way that those text-images have been collated together, that highlights the complex processes of reading that inhere. As Charles Hatfield writes, this is "their great strength: comic art is composed of several kinds of *tension,* in which various ways of reading—various interpretive options and potentialities—must be played against each other. If this is so, then comics readers must call upon different reading strategies, or interpretive schema, than they would use in their reading of conventional written text."[46] These particular books, the subject of *Perfect Copies*, are, with their combination of individualistic handmade look and remote and machine-made feel, playing with those material immaterialities in fascinating ways. The comic book is particularly positioned to become an animistic medium for readers through the precise triangulations of sight, touch, and subject matter produced—and reproduced—therein.

Questions of reproduction imagined within the plots of these texts often fall to those of biological reproduction and specifically to ideas of the family structure. In *My Favorite Thing Is Monsters* by Emil Ferris, Karen Reyes builds a family structure for herself that does not disavow the biological family that she is born into, but that strengthens her position in the world through a queered progression that includes the actual people around her and her desire to copy her artistic and architectural antecedents. For *The Black Project*, the material realities of Gareth Brookes's reproduced comics strain against his protagonist Richard's sexually frustrated Frankenstein-like attempts to reproduce women to be potential girlfriends. This anxiety of reproduction resonates in the sexual encounters that are enacted and enhanced by the tools of technological reproduction in Brookes's shorter embroidered works. Conor Stechschulte's plots are reinforced by the complications of printing processes in his works, which involve applying layers that register correctly in all the right places. The particularities of the mechanical reproduction of vision, and also sound, are used to surprising effect in the manipulation of perception that extend all the way to ideas of not only parentage but also pregnancy itself. In chapter 3, noise and interference might actually afford some reassurance that things are lining up as they are meant to

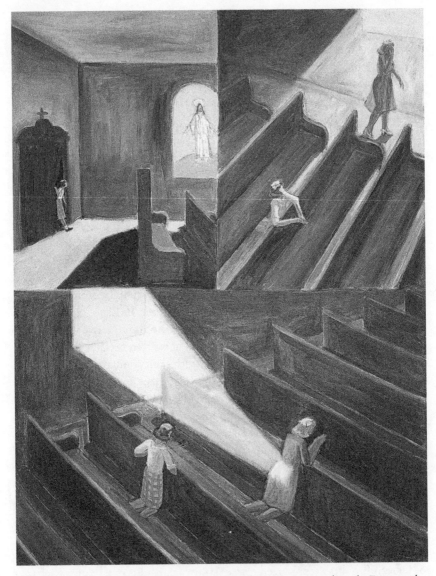

FIGURE I.2 "What's on my Head?" Jerry Moriarty, *Whatsa Paintoonist?* (Seattle: Fantagraphics, 2017), n.p. Copyright © Jerry Moriarty. (Courtesy of Fantagraphics Books.)

do. For the final chapters of the book, I turn to explorations of the brokenness of reified family structures and how there, too, mechanical reproduction plays a part in our understanding of human interactions. The notions of lining up, developed in the chapter on Stechschulte, are taken to their natural conclusion in the readings of Nick Drnaso's *Sabrina* and Brecht Evens's *Panther*. *Sabrina* and *Panther*, which each portrays the degraded family structure amid an even darker overarching story about a degraded society, bring to the foreground the

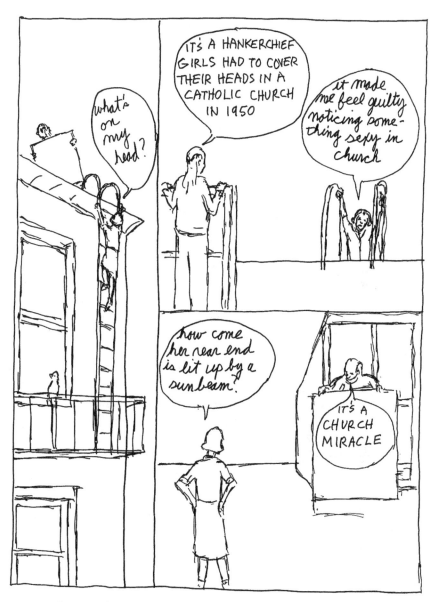

FIGURE I.2 (*Continued*)

devastating results that may accompany blindly and unquestioningly following along. In each, I explore the potentially devastating ways that applying family-framed structures creates blind spots and the opportunities to exploit those blind spots.

Comics studies has marked an emerging interest in the way that childhood, in subject or in readership, is imbricated in the form itself.[47] Likewise, books that highlight their themes of family continue to appear that highlight the materiality of the story form in which they are presented. In a book like Frank Santoro's *Pittsburgh*, for example, the narrative introduces the surface details of an "original" page as an additional component of the storytelling process. The wrinkled surface of the tracing paper on which the drawings are made is visible and present in the reproduced book, as are corrections, adhesive tape, alternations with simple outlines, and unapologetic traces of the cutting and pasting into pages that are usually construed as draft or construction stages (Figure I.1). Such "mistakes" that are typically blended and corrected out of the final product during the production phase are left there as physical reminders of the sticky unruliness of memory. In *Pittsburgh*, the deliberate inclusion of such marks on the page suggests a commentary on the way we should read the book itself. This artistic decision provides a key to reading Santoro's meditations on memory and the way that one's personal identity, especially with respect to childhood and family, is pieced together from fragments inherited, found, and stolen from those around us. Santoro took pains to point out that "there's no black . . . the only black is the words. It's markers, some colored pencils, sometimes some gouache paint. Markers tend to scan better. They're more true to the color you put on the page. With paints, the light of the scanner picks up and changes the color."[48] The artist's awareness of the story as inhering in the final reproduced text is emphasized by this attention not only to the materials used, but to how they will be translated by the scanner and printer into a printed book.

Jerry Moriarty's *Whatsa Paintoonist?* uses a formal structure that comments on the representation of memoir. His work, a combination of line drawings and paintings in which he tells his life story through a fictional narrator, can also be construed as "departures from generic conventions that extend, rather than deny, the parameters of auto/biography—be it by choosing a mode of writing that more accurately reflects the condition of the modern subject . . . or a form that activates additional levels of auto/biographical communication."[49] Moriarty, the titular "paintoonist" of his book, uses a series of narrative paintings in juxtaposition with inked images and speech bubbles, to present a "portrait of the artist." This painted memoir proposes a kind of life writing/drawing unconcerned with "real life." Moriarty, whose "Jack" comics had told vignettes drawn from his father's life in the 1940s and 1950s and were collected in 2008 by Buenaventura Press, uses the same fine art forms and visual playfulness for this memoir. In *Whatsa Paintoonist?* he draws and paints a conversation between a septuagenarian male artist and a twelve-year-old girl named Sally, who both represent Jerry Moriarty the author-painter "paintoonist" of the text. As the two characters discuss his formation as an artist, and his memories of his childhood, the pages alternate between ink and paper drawings and acrylic or oil paintings (Figure I.2). The characters in the drawings are given speech bubbles in which they comment on the paintings in the pages of the book, and in doing so they also muddle linear notions of temporality and singular notions of narrative subject.

The narrative sometimes presents the commentary prior to the pictured event, and sometimes after, denying a linear progression in the narrative that undermines the traditional form of the life narrative. Moriarty's book allows for a mutually implicating structure of narrative and media ecology, in which the material effects of the book mimic and fortify its construction through a network of family stories, playfully inviting the reader to identify with "Sally" as a crucial participant in the aesthetic experience of Moriarty's storytelling. Pentimento, the artistic term that designates the marks of earlier work that an artist nevertheless leaves visible, is at work on the material and textual levels in this book as well, showing smudges and covered-over marks on the page. This reminds the reader, alongside the narrative of *Whatsa Paintoonist?*, that the transmission of life stories need not be only transactions between presenter and observer, but can instead be objects of duration, assemblage, and mutual performance.

Santoro's and Moriarty's are only two examples of many texts published in recent years that conjoin questions about familial structures with the particular material characteristics of the reproduced word-image book. *Perfect Copies* suggests that reading and thinking about books like these, and contemplating how they take on the means of production as a tool to theorize themselves, enacts an approach to reading that we would do well to apply to all of our reading and interpretation practices. Applying the frameworks developed by philosophers, art historians, and literary critics to the study of surface as both a material and thematic mode of analysis, *Perfect Copies* reads instances where comics texts comment on and define themselves in frameworks that test the boundaries of how we define childhood and family. In doing so, this work challenges and broadens existing conceptions of the graphic narrative and offers a framework for understanding the relevance and impact of new media and word-text hybrids in the age of reproduction, in all its forms, while further exploring what surface reading could mean in this particular context.

1

The People Upstairs

Space, Memory, and the
Queered Family in *My Favorite
Thing Is Monsters*

As *Perfect Copies* is a book about staying close to the idea of an eternally possible future, and how we might weather its uncertainties, it feels apposite to begin with *My Favorite Thing Is Monsters* and its open passage toward that future. This is a graphic narrative that is, at the time of my writing, still in progress. When its first volume arrived on the scene, it appeared as if out of nowhere, like the monsters that are its subjects. The graphic novel by Emil Ferris, even at the close of its 2016 first volume, is already monstrously sized, measuring 8.1 by 10.5 inches and encompassing 416 pages. This monstrousness is conveyed by the heavy materiality of the book as a physical object, but also by its heavy subjects. The book is set in 1960s Chicago, in a stylistically hybrid—perhaps monstrous—form that combines the kind of grave melancholy of "serious" graphic novel with campy pulp floppies and television reruns of old horror movies. Specifically, the book layers together such disparate forms as the Holocaust memoir, with Art Spiegelman's *Maus* as exemplar; studied analyses of family psychodramas and their inheritance, of the kind explored in Alison Bechdel's *Fun Home*; and the near-delirious and melodramatically Freudian excesses of horror television and film with exaggerated plot twists and dramatic images, such as the 1935 feature film *The Bride of Frankenstein*.[1] Ferris's book presents a storyworld where genres and forms exist in a mode of continuous intermedial exchange within the pages, eschewing any assumption of dissonance, pointing instead to how these combinations describe the ways that the narrator takes in and consolidates everything as ontologically equal units of meaning. In the process, Ferris induces the reader to do the same.

My Favorite Thing Is Monsters is presented as the journal of its ten-year-old heroine and narrator, Karen Reyes. Karen's appetite for absorbing the information around her—high and low, private and public, factual and fictional—accounts for this meeting of seemingly incompatible categories in a dynamic and compelling narrative, all the more compelling because it ends with a cliff-hanger. The book mimics the look of a spiral-bound notebook, with the book spine resembling that of a notebook and individual pages projecting the verisimilitude of notebook paper, from visible spiral binding to the requisite holes on the page to the blue horizontal lines and pink vertical margins. *My Favorite Thing Is Monsters* professes to show the reader, in Karen's own hand, the things that she sees, hears, reads, remembers, and imagines in unmediated form through her handwriting, sketches, and doodles. The diary entries are thus presented as if they are part of an unedited found object; this situation puts the reader of these pages in a situation that is analogous to that of the fictional author of the journal. The style itself can be read as a kind of storytelling mechanism: "The eclecticism of her visual language reflects the perspective of a child experimenting with technique and subject matter, trying out different approaches much as she is trying on different identities and, in the process, trying to work through on paper the shifting line between liberating fantasy and crushing reality."[2]

Both Karen and the reader of *My Favorite Thing Is Monsters* are equally involved not only in the construction of the narrative but in a certain complicity of prying that is arguably present in any act of reading but that is heightened here by the fact that Karen's diary—itself a repository of things overheard and secretly observed—is not explicitly written for anyone's eyes but her own. Just as Karen's subjects are not always aware that their actions are witnessed and chronicled in her notebook, Karen is unaware that we are reading her book. Although it ends up collecting the doodles, musings, and ephemera that Karen encounters in her daily life, Karen's journal is originally created because she is trying to make sense of a specific event that occurs in the apartment above her: the sudden death of her neighbor Anka Silverberg. Anka lived in the apartment on the first floor of a walk-up building on Chicago's North Side, directly above two basement apartments: one where Karen lives with her mother Marvela and brother Deeze, and another occupied by a melancholy puppeteer named Seamus Chugg. The top floor of the building is occupied by the owners, the Gronans. While the death of Anka is presented as a suicide, there are suggestions from the beginning that she was a murder victim: the body, shot through the heart, not only has been moved from the living room into the bedroom, but has been neatly tucked into bed afterward. Anka's death and the identity of her killer are the most obvious of the book's mysteries, but Anka's mystery swiftly becomes tied deeply to other mysteries in the pages of the book. These mysteries include Karen's growing awareness of her sexuality; her questioning of the identity and whereabouts of her missing father; the workings of the cancer that slowly kills her mother; the behavior of a volatile and magnetic older brother who may have killed someone when he was eight years old; and the identity of her brother's supposed victim, Victor, who bears an uncanny resemblance to himself.

This chapter takes up the way that Ferris effortlessly braids together such disparate strands in an ethical gesture that becomes a potential model for reading her book specifically, but also other books in general. The intentional intermingling of references, media, and forms, and the insistent gestures to the flattening—but not impersonal—hands of the auteur in harmony with the flattening process of reproduction propose that a book can function as an animistic medium. Writing about the films of Apichatpong Weerasethakul, May Adadol Ingawanij notes a tendency in the director's work to eschew the privileging of sight. She notes that "in accordance with the paradigm of monocular perspective and its epistemological assumption of human centrality, this realism stimulates spectatorial perception through sound and tactility."[3] Though the reproduction of sound in the comic is reduced to marks on the page, the comic reading experience offers other potentialities: unlike the film viewing experience—which consists of the projection of light and sound—the printed page engages tactility in the reader's experience of the text. As with other examples in *Perfect Copies*, the printed comics page engages tactility cunningly, by juxtaposing the haptic experience of the page with the unfulfilled promises made by the visual. These texts frequently assert the possibility of touch through a variety of visual cues, and then they contrarily demonstrate the chasm between what we see and what we feel, a gesture that accentuates the ultimate unknowability of experience. It is this intentional shift of readerly perception as a mode of being in the world that we are after here. Indeed, the narrating characters in this book manipulate the very resistance of the reproduced page to offer surprising and intriguing versions of how we deal with that unknowability.

In *My Favorite Thing Is Monsters*, Ferris uses the reproduced page in a way that reminds us of how accustomed we are to reading such surface cues and intentionalities. Are we too comfortable when we elide the original work with its reproduced version, pointing to the comics page as an unmediated auratic substitute indistinguishable from the page of originally manufactured art? Szép, for example, argues that comics "can be regarded as performance" in which meaning is embodied by both artist (through mark-making using a variety of media) and by the reader (who holds the printed comic in hand). These two very different forms of embodied interaction are facilitated, Szép suggests, by the line: "Even though the final comic is printed and mass-produced, the reader feels the drawer's bodily trace in the drawings: As Jared Gardner explains, comics is the only reproduced medium where the original line, the trace of the drawer's hand, is not replaced by typography ('Storylines' 56). The Benjaminian *aura* of works of art needs to be reinterpreted in the case of comics: Even printed works establish an embodied connection with the moment and embodied performance of creation enabled by the drawn line."[4] To the extent that the discussed lines are represented by the majority of the medium, in which there might be little to visually distinguish the drawn line on the original page from its printed version in the mass-reproduced intended final product, one can acknowledge such claims of embodied connections and performance. Perhaps. But what does one do with the imprecations of pages like these? The pages I discuss in this book foreground mark making as an engagement with the surface of the page, creating meaning through literal layered applications, in the form of pasted in details, layers of color in the form of paint, ink, and risograph printing, and even embroidery. In such cases of what could be characterized as a confrontational presentation of medium specificity, how should the spectator interpret the chasm between what they see and the inferences they make, upon seeing it, about the processes of its production? This chapter examines how Ferris incorporates the delicate scratches of a Bic ballpoint pen and the hungrily absorbed felt-tip Flair pen with less-than-flat objects—such as pasted-in sheets, paper clips that affix other objects to the page, and the physical characteristics of the pages themselves—and then reproduces all these objects digitally, so that the notion of an "original page" is itself part of a contractual act of imagination.

Two versions of copying are deliberately engaged and intertwined here: there is the mechanical reproduction of the printing process that delivers these copies of *My Favorite Thing Is Monsters*, and there is the copying hand of the fictional narrator Karen in the book, whose hand, for all its unique originality, also performs its own version of the scrub of specific time and space that adhered to its original. With her copies of paintings from museums, drawings of the tattoos on her brother's body, transcriptions of voice recordings stolen from Anka's husband Sam, and drawings of the faces of the people she sees, Karen imbues her reproductions with her own style and perspective. Reproductions are thus engaged at the material and the spiritual levels. From the mechanical reproduction of the comic book to the drawing hand's reproduction of the artist's observations and human sexual reproduction, notions of the copy ramify and are mutually supporting, revealing striking insights about the nature of truly meaningful connections that Ferris strives to broker through the person of her hybrid narrator. By juxtaposing the contradiction between seeing and feeling and by emphasizing how seeing is itself the product of a writerly process of "filling in," Ferris is not simply commenting on comics form but suggesting ways to see (and feel) oneself into a more productive and inclusive future.

Near the end of the first volume of *My Favorite Thing Is Monsters*, Karen and her brother Deeze face their reflections in a dirty plate-glass door. Deeze stands behind Karen, grasping her tightly by the shoulders, and forcing her to look at herself. Karen appears to the reader as she has appeared since the book's first pages, when she first transforms into a werewolf: hirsute, with big, pointed ears, her underbite emphasizing two elongated fangs that protrude from her lower jaw. In these two pages, which depict this moment five times, the two are seen in their reflected state. With very few variations—mostly registered in the direction of Karen's gaze—Ferris draws the two consistently, and their distinguishing facial characteristics are unchanged. On the next page, however, for the first and only time in this volume, Karen looks different. A more conventionally human face appears in the reflection, the impenetrable surface of the glass door still there, emphasized by diagonal lines at the picture plane that cross both their faces. "Look at her!" Deeze says, "she might be a girl who needs her mouth washed out with a big bar of soap but she is a GIRL! . . . a girl!" (Figure 1.1). Karen's immediate response directly references his emphasis on the face and what the reflection shows her: "You're the two-faced jerk!" This confrontation with the mirror, in which her brother forces her to see herself as others see her, causes Karen to reveal what seems invisible to even those closest to her. On the bottom of the facing page, on the recto side, three panels again show Karen in the same position, from the neck up, forehead covered with a wide-brimmed hat. She appears again in her typical "Wolf Man" persona and stutters "I like . . . um . . . um . . . I . . . uh . . . / . . . I um like . . . I like . . . uh . . . / . . . girls."[5]

Karen's coming out to her brother is tied specifically to vision: to how he sees her and how she wants him to see her. She emphasizes that Deeze "stood for a long time staring at [her] with this look on his face like he'd just really seen [her] for the first time." At the bottom of the same page, the visible and the audible are emphasized in close-up views of Deeze's mouth, on the left, and, on the right, his eyes, one of which has its iris replaced by the hole of Karen's three-hole spiral-bound notebook. Just as quickly as Karen has come out to her brother, he pushes her back into the closet, citing the precarity of their mother's health, and his fear of how the neighborhood boys will react. These three pages efficiently weave the larger mysteries of the book's plot together with the mysteries of human relationships, especially those between family members. They crystallize a central question of the book: is it possible to get closer to understanding things if we look closely enough? *My Favorite Thing Is Monsters* takes full advantage of the word and image hybrid of the comic book form, repeatedly drawing the reader's attention to the sometimes unexamined ways that knowledge is communicated at the surface level.

Seeing is central to Ferris's work, and the eye is a central visual motif throughout *My Favorite Thing Is Monsters*. Eyes are the most obvious reminders of twins that function as a single unit. When we alternatively cover one eye, and then the other, we become aware of the very different perspectives that each eye sees, and of how our brain works to combine those two images into a single coherent image. This aspect of stereoscopic vision serves as a metaphor throughout the book: even each eye in a person's body experiences the world in a unique way. The lightning-quick ways that the brain manages those perspectives, blurring them into a single view, carries a charge of meaning in the context of a

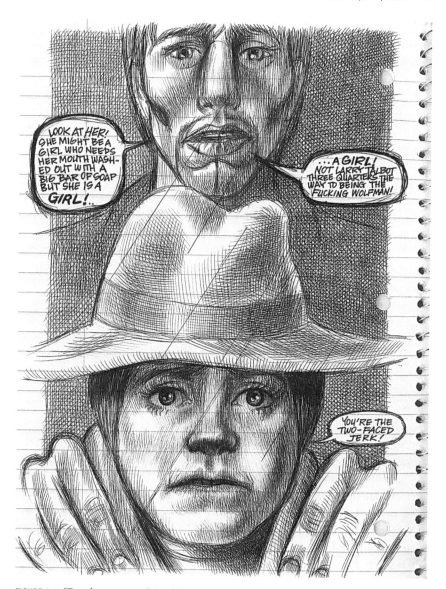

FIGURE 1.1 "But she is a GIRL!" Emil Ferris, *My Favorite Thing Is Monsters*, vol. 1 (Seattle: Fantagraphics, 2016), n.p. Copyright © Emil Ferris. (Courtesy of Fantagraphics Books (www.fantagraphics.com).)

story about making meaning out of what one witnesses. The miracle of stereoscopic vision is partnered with the faults of monoscopic thinking. While it is natural that we see things as fixed and coherent, and that this is a function of our physiological design, Ferris's book questions whether going about in the world with the assumption that one sees the same realities that others do is quite the right way to go about living. Further, the book shows us characters whose understanding of their world and experiences are limited by their positions in the world, their experiences, the people they meet, the books they read, the television they watch, the way they appear to others, their ethnicity, their gender, their beauty, and their ugliness. But by drawing our attention to eyesight itself, Ferris also shows us that the limitations of vision can be made prominent by even the few inches that separate one eye from the other. Seeing in stereo is not necessarily a bodily function that we are aware of at all times; but in a book that places special emphasis on doubles, with mysterious repetitions of images (Marvela and tattoo of Marvela) and of persons (Deeze and Victor) and several other even more enigmatic pairings, it becomes an evocative figure for the world of this profound book (Figure 1.2). Observations like these converge with the art lessons that Karen gets from her brother Deeze and from studying the work of earlier masters in museums, with lessons on perspective, shapes, and patterns. Through these pages the reader is asked, alongside Karen, to contemplate whether one half of a pair must always be sacrificed for the other to attain its complete fullness.

Eyes thus gaze naturally from the page, out at the reader from the many faces depicted on these pages, on humans, animals, and monsters alike. But they also make uncanny appearances elsewhere. The shape of the eye naturally shows up most often in iconography in these pages where an eye is intentionally depicted; but they also show up in unexpected places. Sometimes the appearances are incidental, as when Karen appears to doodle eyes in the margins or in blank spaces on the page. Eyes also manifest as a sort of partial pareidolia. Instead of a whole face, just the elliptical shape with a circle in its center appears: such as on the top of a woman's hat, for example. While the shape of the eye proliferates throughout the book, eyes themselves are repositories of meaning for Karen. Karen's mother Marvela's eye contains a fleck of green that Karen imagines as her ultimate safe space: when she feels troubled or frightened, she stares at this green place in her mother's eye and imagines herself simply sailing away toward the forest of pine trees that the fleck of color represents: "Her grey eyes are like a combination of Dublin fog and the smoke from peace pipes . . . in her left eye there is one patch of deep green . . . that I call Green Island . . . I wade through the grayness until I reach the green island in Mama's eye. It's covered with shrubs and trees and it smells like earth. It's like my mother made a place on Green Island for everything I am (even the secret things) and I lay down in a soft bed of moss and fall asleep underneath the really tall pine tree."[6] Karen describes Green Island in the earliest pages of the book, and the first volume ends with her return to the pine forest where she tears up her monster alter ego. This neat symmetry between beginning and end of the volume follows a dream sequence in which Karen brutally murders the monsters who have been her imaginary companions. Dracula, Frankenstein, the Mummy, the Wolf Man, even the Invisible Man are dispatched one after the other. This scene offers a commentary on what "normal" might look like: abjuring the natural comfort that Karen had managed, keeping

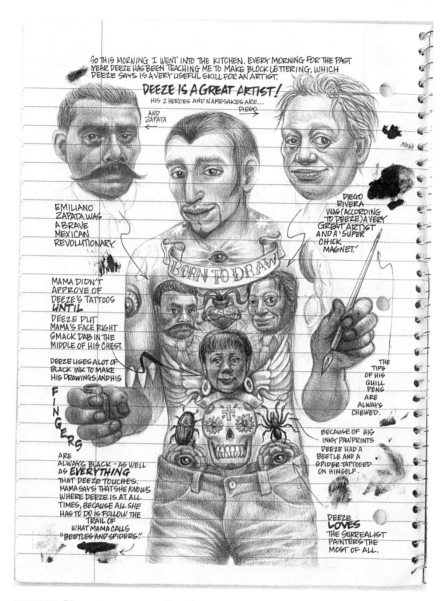

FIGURE 1.2 "Deeze is a great artist." Emil Ferris, *My Favorite Thing Is Monsters*, vol. 1 (Seattle: Fantagraphics, 2016), n.p. Copyright © Emil Ferris. (Courtesy of Fantagraphics Books (www.fantagraphics.com).)

two or more perspectives in suspended circulation, in favor of one where ambiguity is rejected and destroyed.

As the dream continues, Karen is invited by Anka to look into Anka's "View Mistress," a play on the children's toy, the stereoscopic "ViewMaster." In this conception, Anka has a red box over the bullet hole over her heart. Karen then heads toward Green Island, and suddenly finds herself in the museum, running at first on top of, and then from inside one painting after another. She finally finds Green Island and remarks, "I laid down and looked into the night sky. When I squinted the stars seemed like the tangled strands of pearls in Mama's jumbled jewelry box. I could not help thinking about the secrets I know now, but also about the mysteries and about the things that I've lost."[7] And it is here on Green Island, with a proliferation of eyes on his face and body, that another person appears for the very first time. This person is announced first by the sound of their footsteps. An extreme close-up of Karen's surprised eyes is accompanied by her speech bubble: "Deeze?" and the panel is followed by a close-up of the top third of another person's face, sketched in black ink, with a third eye, sketched just above his right eyebrow, next to his ear. The facing recto page shows a man seen from the shoulders up who looks like Deeze, with three more blue eyes on his neck and shoulders. This six-eyed version of her brother replies, making the last statement of volume 1 the soap-operatic cliffhanger: "No, I'm your brother, Victor" (Figure 1.3).

The limitations of monoscopic sight are emphasized when Deeze introduces Karen to Japanese *daruma* dolls. As Karen arrives home shortly after Mr. Gronan accuses her of being a "peeping Tom" and threatens to "introduce your 'peepers' to my buddy Mr. Screwdriver," she finds Deeze holding one of these dolls. As he explains, "These little guys are called darumas. I got them from Mrs. T at the import shop on Belmont. The way they work is you make a wish and draw in one eye, when the wish comes true, you draw the other eye. They're from Japan . . . they're based on this . . . freaking dedicated holy man who sat and prayed so long and hard that his arms and legs withered up and just fell the f-ck off."[8] Karen draws the head in a panel at the bottom of the page, and, on the opposite page, shows two darumas, overlapping their empty eyes in a sort of Venn diagram that mimics the "vesica piscis" that Deeze has used to teach her about identifying classical shapes in art. Until the owner's wish is fulfilled, the daruma must gaze out at the world with the use of only one eye.

The character of the mysterious next-door neighbor, Mr. Chugg, who has likely seen more than he lets on, is a character whose vision is literally monoscopic. He has only one functioning eye and wears a false glass eye in his left eye socket. In one of her drawings of Chugg, Karen muses, "If a person could see through a glass eye would the world look more breakable?"[9] Chugg works as a ventriloquist, plying his trade with a ventriloquist's dummy, named C. J., which itself is equipped with two perfectly formed but unseeing eyes. What Chugg might mean for the overall plot has yet to be revealed. Karen is convinced of Chugg's involvement after listening through a shared wall and noting that she "could hear him talking to his dummies, which is pretty normal for him, but the weird thing is that they were talking back." What she hears are the voices telling Mr. Chugg to keep his mouth shut. Later, Karen is convinced that something terrible has befallen Chugg when she sees that someone has moved his belongings out with the garbage. She knows that he would not leave his extra false eyes, photographs, and camera behind intentionally. So far, the book will not reveal what Chugg, with his single vision, a single vision like the singular eye of his camera lens, knows.

For all the discussion of what the eye sees, and the proliferation of eyes within these pages, the most significant representation of eyes may well be the very first image the reader takes in of *My Favorite Thing Is Monsters*. This is an image that precedes even the first page. On the cover of the book, the reader's gaze is arrested by the face of a woman who appears to stare out of the cover directly at the reader. Her face is blue, highlighted with pink, light and shadow cast by the bright full moon over her and the building behind her. The woman's lips are parted as if in concern, fear, or surprise; and her eyes, though gazing toward us, also seem slightly unfocused, as if obscured by a gauze of confusion. The reader will learn very soon that this is the face of Anka Silverberg; but for now the mystery of this woman's identity is secondary to a larger one. On this cover the reader is suddenly reminded of another function of the eye. Not only does Anka use these eyes to look outward, but the careful reader notices that the eyes also function as mirrors. Both of Anka's eyes reflect a small, rounded face with a pair of dark eyes, a small nose, and a firmly set mouth that may show traces of an underbite. The very first image that the reader encounters in this book dense with images attempts to show the reader something that exists outside of the picture plane. If, as the reader discovers, the process of reading this book forces the reader to identify with the author of the journal, Karen, what does it mean to be in the position, when one looks at the cover, of whomever it is that has caused Anka to react with such an expression? From the very beginning, the book shuttles between a distrust of what one sees as the full picture and an equally insistent conviction that the only way to get anywhere close to the truth is to look as closely as possible to every detail on the surface at hand, as made clear by the references to influential works of art that shape Karen's understanding of her world. As someone who has picked up the book for the first time, the reader is already confronted with a false reflection in the eyes of this stranger, for they are the ones in the position of the person reflected in Anka's eyes, but they see a different face reflected back.

By presenting *My Favorite Thing Is Monsters* as a found object, a record of the direct and unmediated musings in the protagonist's own hand, Ferris makes suggestive comparisons between the acts of reading, looking, and spying in pursuit of a solution. These are all literal and figurative acts of "connecting the dots." The book repeatedly references dots in relation to completed actions of understanding or wish fulfillment, from the pointillist paintings of Seurat to the completion of the daruma's eyes. A large part of Karen's artistic education involves learning not simply how to connect things but how to notice them in the first place. The medium of *My Favorite Thing Is Monsters* facilitates a direct record of Karen's learning process, which thus also becomes the reader's learning process, so that the copy is raised in esteem as a crucial player in knowledge

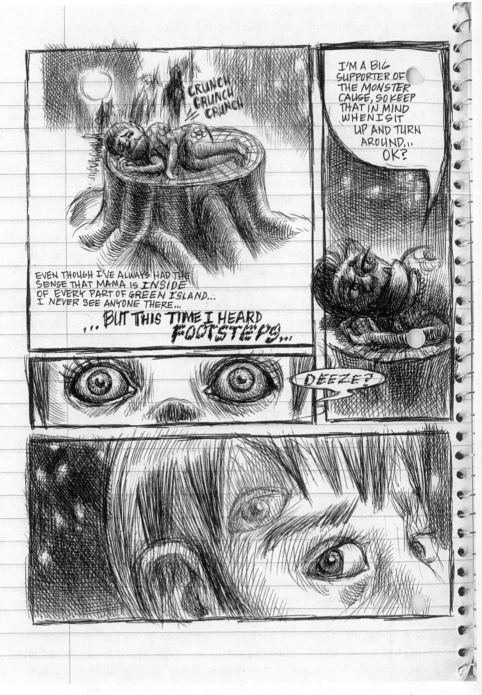

FIGURE 1.3 "No, I'm your brother, Victor." Emil Ferris, *My Favorite Thing Is Monsters*, vol. 1 (Seattle: Fantagraphics, 2016), n.p. Copyright © Emil Ferris. (Courtesy of Fantagraphics Books (www.fantagraphics.com).)

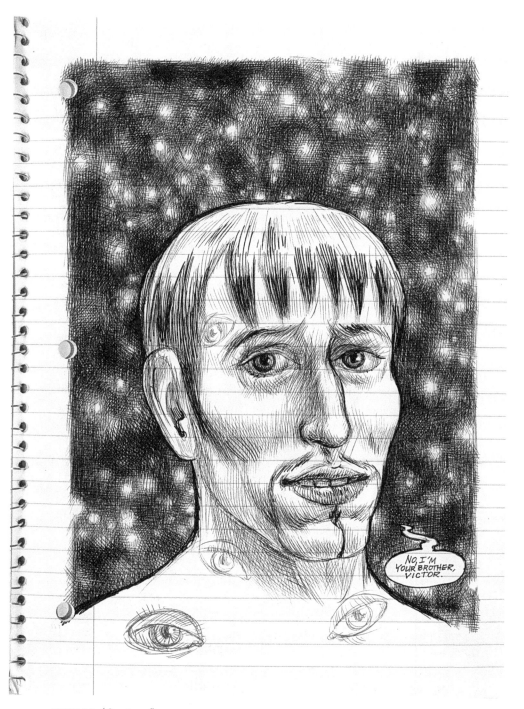

FIGURE 1.3 (*Continued*)

making. It is in Karen's copies of famous paintings, or copies of her sibling's face, and copies of sounds overheard on audiotapes or in the chambers of her memory, that significant visual and verbal details are emphasized. The visual narrative in *My Favorite Thing Is Monsters* allows contemporaneity between images separated by both time and space, as with Karen's copies of paintings in museums, the tattoos on Deeze's body, and the letters, words, and shapes that Karen records in her portraits of friends and family. The reader can see these clues in the text along with Karen, closely linking the reader's progress with the protagonist's. In learning how to develop visual literacy with Karen, Ferris's reader might develop a more sophisticated relationship to history. In her analysis of Richard McGuire's *Here*, a rumination on the passages of time that occur in one small corner of the world, Laura Moncion writes that "the visual literacy images demand can and often does complicate conceptions of linear historicist time and thus opens up alternate ways of viewing history: the adjustment of form necessarily adjusts content."[10]

Just as the cultural and everyday objects that Karen encounters become shaped by her own style and perspective in these pages, *My Favorite Thing Is Monsters* presents the copy as a mechanism of rewriting and inscribing one's own family as a choice rather than as an inheritance. Ferris presents inherited narratives spatially, whether through concrete structures like staircases in the apartment buildings of Chicago's North Side, or more figurative structures in the form of verbal and visual allusions and quotations. She then complicates the vertical line implied and imposed by those structures, introducing the ways that memories resist singularity as well as strictly vertical motions. Reproduction figures in the book as a method to extend life and representation within its diegetic world, but it is also referenced in the materiality of the book. The journal is Karen's own life story, a negotiation between the direct experience of her eyes and ears on to the paper through her hand. The reader is thus lulled into feeling that the images and text captured on the page are real and lived experience, but just as quickly becomes tripped up when reminded that the narrator's real and lived experiences are frequently formed by what they have been told by others, or are even potentially acts of the imagination.

Ferris's book is a reembodiment of the life stories of the people upstairs, patched together through materials that are not the effects of Karen's own direct experience. The comic book itself facilitates this patching together, suspending multiple perspectives and perceptions in what Groensteen calls the "braid" or *tréssage*.[11] *My Favorite Thing Is Monsters* raises these questions from beyond its pages to the world of its reader: what is Ferris's project, after all, if not a conscious engagement with inherited narratives, from Spiegelman's *Maus*, to horror movies and magazines, to paintings encountered as originals on museum walls and as copies in postcards, photographs, and catalogue reproductions? Ferris presents her book as a tribute to her own people upstairs, whose extant work does not diminish her own but rather provides it with layers of resilience. Individual memory and subjectivity depend on a vast variety of sources for their construction, and our understanding and acceptance of such diffuse constructions make us capable of positive, productive effect. One of the most profound effects made by *My Favorite Thing Is Monsters* is its radical rethinking of reproduction, which reframes our view of what family inheritances and family structures can be, proposing a braided formulation of inheritance that accommodates and supports Karen's queerness.

The People Upstairs: Postmemorial Artifacts

Photographs, audio cassettes, and the varied media records of other people's lived experience contribute to Karen's own memory, constructing what Alison Landsberg calls prosthetic memory, the kind of memory that "emerges at the interface between a person and a historical narrative about the past, at an experiential site such as a movie theater or museum. In this moment of contact, an experience occurs through which the person pictures himself or herself into a larger history [and] does not simply apprehend a historical narrative but takes on a more personal, deeply felt memory of a past event through which he or she did not live." This effect is important, Landsberg argues, because it has the ability to "shape that person's subjectivity and politics."[12] This relationship to other people's pasts not only changes the subject's perspective, Landsberg writes a decade later, but may well be a "strategy for activating one's own personal stake in that knowledge, for making the past matter."[13] This parallels the argument that Marianne Hirsch has made in her investigations of postmemory. Hirsch regards the subject's attention to other people's memories as the work of reactivating and reembodying "distant political and cultural memorial structures by reinvesting them with resonant individual and familial forms of mediation and aesthetic expression." Hirsch argues that memory, unlike history, engages "less directly affected participants . . . even after all participants and even their familial descendants are gone . . . through an affective link to the past . . . mediated by technologies like literature, photography, and testimony."[14] Memory allows for a sense of direct connection to the past. In Hirsch's view, this is especially linked to testimony in the form of word and image. Focusing her argument specifically on the traumatic ruptures and breaks of the Holocaust on the memories of generations who did not themselves live through those experiences, Hirsch explores "affiliative structures of memory beyond the familial, and . . . [sees] this connective memory work as another form of affiliation across lines of difference."[15] Memory is not only handed down from parent to child but is passed on through "structures of mediation that would be broadly available, appropriable, and, indeed, compelling enough to encompass a larger collective in an organic web of transmission."[16]

The comics form is integral to the construction of meaning in a narrative that is premised on the success of looking closely and of developing a more discerning visual acuity. Reproduction is the central and most salient metaphor of *My Favorite Thing Is Monsters*, offering a postmemorial way to understand reproduction in families. Although it is customary to think teleologically about parent-child relationships as the unquestioned structure for transmitting family narrative, Ferris offers instead a radical conception of the way that her queer protagonist creates her family, a family that is similarly ruptured by trauma. Paralleled in the copies recorded in the journal and in the material form of the book itself—a text that, in spite of its sensuous materiality, is also a copy—she proposes that copies are productive of originality, capable of producing new versions of the past or a new origin narrative. In Karen's story, the reader finds a firm connection between her developing sense of self with reproductions of her biological family that intersect with family as defined spatially—and, ultimately, temporally—through the narratives of the tenants in her walk-up apartment building. This is a departure from the typical metaphor used to describe kinship filiations: the tree. The tree lends its vocabulary of growth, branching, roots, and, indeed, "nature" to conceptions of familial relations, a kind of biological imperative.

The idea of the "family tree" is directly contrasted with the metaphorical vocabulary of the building, especially an apartment building like the one occupied by the Gronan, Reyes, Chugg, and Silverberg apartments. The structure itself is fixed, it does not grow, it does not branch, its roots do not feed the units above, and there is nothing natural about it. The structure is a shell, accessible to new residents who may have no original obligations or attachments to each other, and who may develop them due to circumstances, inclination, and proximity. This conception of family as apartment building is more congenial to the postmemorial family system and to the systems of inheritance that are pervasive in an age when domestic and international migrations take place as a matter of course. These migrations do not disrupt structures as much as they offer alternatives. This is a family system of the "people upstairs," people who transmit narratives to the next generation, but whose filiations are more flexibly constructed through proximity and through narrative than through biological determinism.

The varieties of reproduction in the narrative itself recur in the protagonist's attempt to copy down the memories of her own lived experience as well as the memories she acquires at second- or even thirdhand. The fact that all these pieces of information are recorded in Karen's own hand—not as photographic reproductions of original primary documents—emphasizes how the memories of the subject and the prosthetic affiliative postmemories are effectively equalized in Karen's hand, the hand that mediates and writes from her own style and perspective as the journal keeper. Ideas of normativity are persistently modeled and enforced by those around her, and Karen's queerness is ignored and sometimes explicitly refused by the authority figures in her family line. Crucially, in the elision of memories and a new claim to authority that comes with authoring this journal, Karen revises and reshapes her own narrative. Sara Ahmed has noted the difficulties of shifting one's orientation, sexual or otherwise, in response to the straight line of inheritance that is traditionally imposed by biological and social narratives. Ahmed writes that "[for the] mixed-race queer the choice is not either to become white and straight or to disappear. This is a choice between two different kinds of death. The task is to trace the lines for a different genealogy, one that would embrace the failure to inherit the family line as the condition of possibility for another way of dwelling in the world. If orientations point us to the future, to what we are moving toward, then they also keep open the possibility of changing directions and of finding other paths, perhaps that do not clear a common ground, where we can respond with joy to what goes astray."[17] The pressure to accept this strictly linear and vertical line as the only line of family inheritance stresses the queer subject by pushing a narrative that precludes alternative paths. Ahmed calls this a "pressure that can speak the language of love, happiness, and care, which pushes us along specific paths. We do not know what we could become without these points of pressure, which insist that happiness will follow if we do this or we do that. And yet, these places where we are under pressure don't always mean we stay on line; at certain points we can refuse the inheritance—at points that are often lived as 'breaking points.'"[18]

By focusing on the collective memory of the literal and figurative people upstairs rather than exclusively on the sovereignty of the biological family, Ferris's book argues for the people upstairs as a powerful metaphor for new family systems, systems that stop to pay attention at precisely those spatial and temporal breaking points that Ahmed suggests represent challenges to the straight line. Houses, especially apartment houses, rather than trees, are the suitable model for the queered family unit, in which filiations are dictated not by "naturally" given branches but instead by human-constructed rooms that are affiliative, occupied by any, and all kinds of, people. What if, the book asks, instead of family trees, we think of family buildings, where the structure is fixed but the population is open? *My Favorite Thing Is Monsters* explores how such spaces could be constructed and nourished. Karen lives in a basement apartment with her mother and brother, with the Silverbergs and the Gronans stacked above them. The characters and their narratives may occupy the same plot of land; viewed from a flattened perspective, as with a map, they are all together at the same coordinates. We are reminded, through the many homes entered and observed in *My Favorite Thing Is Monsters*, how vertical divisions and walls, even hallways, separate people entirely from each other. Notions of vertical space, native both to trees and to apartment buildings, especially facilitate our understanding of how the latter iteration better inscribes others' memory and experience, creating new prosthetic memories for both Karen and the reader.

A critical framework of filiation built around the metaphor of the apartment building produces the possibility of radically different versions of family and inheritance, following the form of the braided, rather than straight, line. In her exploration of the possibilities of reproduction and reinterpretation that comes down to us from the people upstairs, *My Favorite Thing Is Monsters* rejects the unidirectional and teleologically fixed family narrative in favor of filiative tenancies.

Looking Closely, Looking Back, and Looking Up

The resistance to the straight line in Landsberg's and Hirsch's critical works on memory, and in Ahmed's on cultural and affect studies, becomes especially resonant in the material form of the comic book. Ferris's graphic narrative accommodates multiple temporalities on its page, even though it does not typically follow the grid format of sequential panels that read from above to below and left to right. Instead, Ferris reminds the reader of other ways that sequence is suggested in an image, pointing to implicit shapes that Deeze shows Karen in drawings and paintings: "How the lines of the things in paintings . . . create triangle compositions." He tells her to "get up close and look at the painting."[19] Deeze shows her the ubiquity of circles, namely "the vesica piscis" that recur in manmade shapes. Deeze tells her "that out of this shape, that is like an eye laying on its side, 'the whole world is born.' Every shape that is known comes from the vesica piscis"[20] (Figure 1.4). The almond shape, or sideways eye, created by the intersection of two circles with the same radius, becomes a kenning for metaphysical inquiries: the center of one shape sits on the periphery of the other, as Deeze shows Karen with a compass. Not only does this keen attention to shapes highlight the strategies of reading that are integral to these pages, but it introduces major themes embedded in the book, namely that of the twin, or copy, and the "pattern of creation" that structures their world. Reading and looking are thus heavily freighted with the expectation of interpretive work: the reader is trained, from the start of the book, to be alert to meaning in forms. Ferris's book might be misapprehended as suggesting that there are hidden elements and symbols that surround us, but the actual argument it proposes is that hiddenness is actually a symptom of careless looking: the elements and symbols are already present at the surface of the image, if only we know how to see them.

Varieties of narrative are kept simultaneously in place, in the same ways that the eye might travel around the comics page, limning the shape of a circle or of a triangle. In his reading of Richard McGuire's *Here*, Thierry Groensteen discusses the *bande dessinée*, or comic strip, and its traditional narrative associations with a strict linearity that follows a straight line, and "unfurls from its beginning all the way to its end, regularly, with neither obstacle nor interruption, like

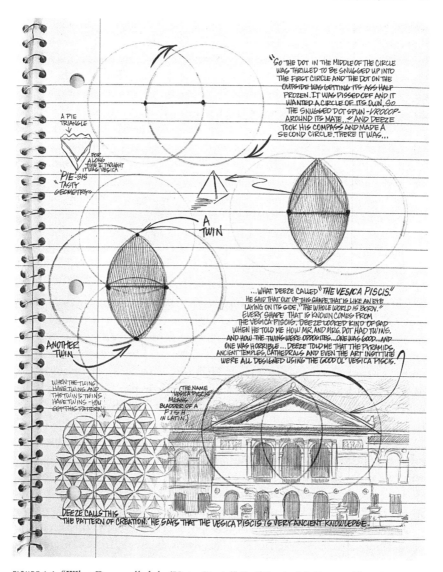

FIGURE 1.4 "What Deeze called the 'Vesica Piscis.'" Emil Ferris, *My Favorite Thing Is Monsters*, vol. 1 (Seattle: Fantagraphics, 2016), n.p. Copyright © Emil Ferris. (Courtesy of Fantagraphics Books (www.fantagraphics.com).)

a roll of film or the Bayeux tapestry" (*d'un récit qui se déroulerait depuis un début jusqu'à une fin, régulièrement, sans obstacle ni interruption, à la manière d'une bobine de pellicule (ou de la broderie de Bayeux)).*[21] Groensteen proposes alternate methods of reading, articulated by the form of the network, or *réseau*, that are better apprehended not through the sense of a continuous unfurling, but rather through the idea of braiding, or *tréssage*. This metaphor addresses how comics, "far from producing a continuity that mimics reality, offers the reader a story that is full of holes, which appear as gaps in the meaning. . . . It is the role of art in general to manufacture 'the surreal with the elliptic' [and] every comics reader knows that, from the instant where he is projected into the fiction . . . he forgets, up to a certain point, the fragmented character and discontinuity of the enunciation."[22] The thread of the narrative has a singularity and continuity that is guaranteed by the understanding that, once broken, the whole network would also fall apart. Even though we do not see the continuity, we trust that it is there. The reader, then, is trusted with the responsibility of following this thread, which dips above and below the open work netting of the *réseau*.

My Favorite Thing Is Monsters builds on the reading structure of the *réseau* in the comics form to conduct a series of variations on reproduction that redound to the central question of sexual reproduction, what Karen calls the "night machine," at the heart of her quest to understand herself by understanding how her biological family is constituted. She has no memory of her father, which estranges her from half of her own genetic and narrative memory. She identifies herself most with the Wolf Man, as played by Lon Chaney in the 1941 horror movie of the same name, that Karen loves.[23] The Wolf Man's own hybrid identity emerges not from genetic determinism but from an encounter that the protagonist Larry Talbot has with a wolf who bites him, thus imparting him with the curse of becoming a werewolf. He learns of his fate from a gypsy named Maleva, who reveals that the wolf that bit him was in fact a werewolf, and her own son. In the film, the Larry Talbot Wolf Man is killed by his own father, as he can no longer be fully human.

Likewise, *Frankenstein* is, according to Barbara Johnson, a story that offers another opportunity to think about problems of family and of parenting. She writes that *Frankenstein* is "the story of two antithetical modes of parenting that give rise to two increasingly parallel lives—the life of Victor Frankenstein, who is the beloved child of two doting parents, and the life of the monster he single-handedly creates but immediately spurns and abandons. The fact that in the end both characters reach an equal degree of alienation and self-torture and indeed become indistinguishable as they pursue each other across the frozen polar wastes indicates that the novel is, among other things, a study of the impossibility of finding an adequate model for what a parent should be."[24] Karen's growing observations of sexual reproduction, as witnessed firsthand or encountered in the stories she learns through Anka's recordings, accompany her growing awareness of her own sexuality and the questions she has about where she fits in.

The Wolf Man and similar narratives present an alternative form of reproduction. Werewolves, Frankenstein monsters, and vampires are all corporeally distinct new identities produced by nonsexual reproduction. These productive acts are related to human origins but incorporate unorthodox influences: a bite, an infection, a suturing together of disparate parts. Significantly, Ferris's transformation into a graphic novelist, was occasioned in 2002 on her fortieth birthday by a "bite that changed [her] life." Ferris was bitten by a mosquito and infected with West Nile virus, an infection that caused a severe debilitation and slow recovery but that also caused her to begin drawing again, to go to art school, and to ultimately write *My Favorite Thing Is Monsters*.[25] As Karen stands over her sleeping mother, after learning that she has cancer, she too wishes for a bite to change her life and vows, "I will find us a maker and get the bite and I'll bring it home and bite you and Deeze and we'll live forever together I promise." Monster life offers sanctuary to Karen, a promise of renewal, and regeneration. The book is equally interested in these alternative forms, meditating on reproduction in all its varieties, including the reproductions of likenesses, testimonies, and canonical and popular works of art copied by the characters in the book. The tools of technological reproduction contribute to this network of copies: photography and audio recording play central roles in preserving records of people and events that are no longer there. Ferris's book itself extends this inquiry, in its overt references to copied forms, by laying bare her own artistic and storytelling inheritance with direct quotations of her influences. Using those influences to create her original and future-looking narrative, Ferris shows a way toward a relationship with the past that is radical, celebratory, and pathbreaking.

Verticality and the Act of Looking Up

Karen's book offers a version of reproduction, in the form of the copy, that is informed by the copies that surround her, making literal the act of "looking up" by showing how much she looks up to her brother as role model. Deeze is both teacher and protector, and Karen writes that "it is because of Deeze that [her] favorite place is the Art Institute."[26] In a drawing that memorializes the first time he brings her to the museum, when he is twelve, and she is "so little that he had to lift [her] up so that [she] could see things," they are pictured at the bottom of a long stretch of stairs. Holding her hand, Deeze reassures her: "Don't be scared Kare, we're going to see some friends" (Figure 1.5). This pattern of looking upward, repeated in the image of being literally held up to see pictures and of going up the stairs so that they may "see some friends," is emblematic of the relationship between Karen and an inexorable pull from above. The staircase is evoked repeatedly in the book, suggesting a vertical line of transmission from the possessor of wisdom and experience that one looks up to, and that also sends knowledge downward to the child inheritor who receives it.

The book frequently presents Karen at the bottom of stairs, looking upward. Those at the top of the stairs possess privileged knowledge that Karen seeks, and from which she is typically excluded. Upstairs, in the apartments above, and in the landings between the floors of the building, is where people have sex, as

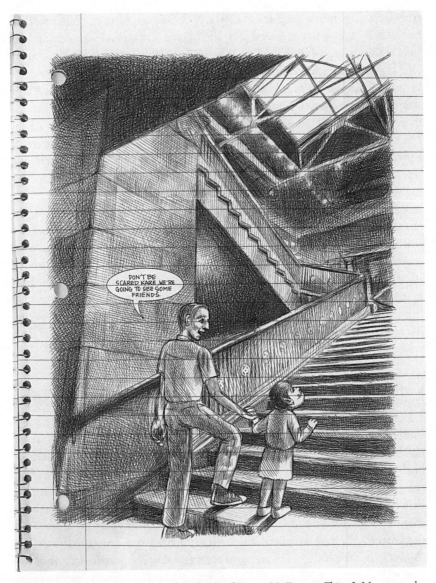

FIGURE 1.5 "We're going to see some friends." Emil Ferris, *My Favorite Thing Is Monsters*, vol. 1 (Seattle: Fantagraphics, 2016), n.p. Copyright © Emil Ferris. (Courtesy of Fantagraphics Books (www.fantagraphics.com).)

her brother does in the apartment landing with his "Broadway friends," and upstairs with Mrs. Gronan in her top-floor apartment. Upstairs is also where Karen's always hungry, wraithlike, friend Sandy, invisible to everyone else, lives alone in an abandoned apartment. Upstairs is where the surviving belongings of the murdered neighbor Anka Silverberg remain, in the form of the plants she kept on the landing, the cat with an ankh on its forehead, and the audiotapes kept by Mr. Silverberg of Anka telling her life story to a volunteer. The Chicago apartment buildings of Karen's childhood function as what Bachelard noted are guarantors of a "phenomenology of the imagination,"[27] in which the attic and roof are associated with the rational and the cellar with the irrational, or subconscious. He writes in particular about the way that stairways seem to work in only one direction in the imagination: "Then there are the stairways: one to three or four of them, all different. We always *go down* the one that leads to the cellar, and it is this going down that we remember, that characterizes its oneirism. But we go both up and down the stairway that leads to the bed-chamber. It is more commonly used; we are familiar with it . . . we always *go up* the attic stairs, which are steeper and more primitive. For they bear the mark of ascension to a more tranquil solitude."[28] Going down the stairs is linked to mysteries better left unknown as well, as when Karen discovers a locked door that leads to a subterranean level beneath their basement apartment. Her mother warns, "Promise me you'll never go down there or tell anyone about it!"[29] Karen's investigation of the subterranean is further emphasized by a hallucinogenic encounter in Chicago's Graceland Cemetery with the ghost of Pinkerton agent Kitty Warn, who tells her "that hidden room . . . is very likely not a room at all but an entrance—of which there are many to a great network of underground tunnels and rooms . . . a city beneath the city."[30] This city can be accessed, pointedly, through a mausoleum engraved with the name "Macguffin," the term coined by Alfred Hitchcock to signify a red herring.

The staircase highlights the realities of the progression of time, but the reconstruction of meaning in Karen's notebook shows how diffuse these pathways really are. Karen's version of reproduction marks out the potential for a newly constituted identity composed of Sara Ahmed's nonlinear breaking points. Reproduction of faces abound in the pages of her journal, and like a *mise en abyme*, they also appear on Deeze's body (Figure 1.2). His torso is inscribed with portraits of his namesakes Emilio Zapata and Diego Rivera, flanking their mother's face, which sits "smack dab in the middle of his chest."[31] Because the entire book takes the form of Karen's journal, where images, taken from life, and images, taken from representations, are all copied out in the same drawing hand, reproduction is the dominant and consistent framework through which the diegesis is created. Marvela the tattoo on Deeze's chest is indistinguishable from Marvela the mother who shares an apartment with Karen and Deeze. Likewise, Deeze's entire back is covered with tattoos based on drawings he's made "of ladies he's dated." Five disembodied faces peer out from under a giant bat, wings spread from shoulder to shoulder. This time, however, Karen's drawing not only shows the faces featured on Deeze's back, but shows how these women look after the affair, significantly worse for wear. The blurring between reality and representation created by Karen's copying hand nonetheless introduces an element of leveling that erases hierarchies of authority.

The reader is left unsure about the reliability of what Karen sees, but this allows for a converse effect: there is no alternative but to accept her perspective and experience completely. In Karen's case, the structure accommodates a sense of monstrosity that she associates with her growing understanding of her sexuality, one that she instinctively understands as the good kind of monstrosity: "I knew there were good monsters and bad ones ... the monsters who murdered Reverend King and the President were the worst monsters ... those are the kind of monsters who want no one to be free. ... No, the bad monsters want the world to look the way they want it to. They need people to be afraid ... they don't live in their lair and mostly mind their own biz. ... I guess that's the difference ... a good monster sometimes gives somebody a fright because they're weird looking and fangy ... a fact that is beyond their control ... but bad monsters are all about control ... they want the whole world to be scared so that bad monsters can call the shots."[32] The book that the reader holds in their hand thus becomes the good monster's guidebook to the world, what Maaheen Ahmed calls "a plaidoyer against the unfair monstrocization of others ... embrac[ing] the denigrated genre of horror and its frequent denizens, monsters, as well as the popular medium of comics and its fraught history."[33] In her embrace of influences that enfold and equalize comics, tattoos, beet marks, paintings on the walls of museums, and the edifices on the buildings that hold them, Ferris destabilizes those hierarchies. What matters, she argues, are the distinctions between bad and good in the context of displays of control and fear, and which apply to all categories of being.

Early Work: Touching the Past

Extradiegetically, Ferris frequently reminds the reader of her debt to her own people upstairs. Resonances activate a sense of proximity to other characters and works that are not registered or acknowledged by the characters in the book, but which are available to the reader of *My Favorite Thing Is Monsters*. While within the book characters have namesakes, as Deeze does, other characters in the book are associated extradiegetically with similar namesake characters as well. Karen's mother's name, Marvela, for example, evokes the figure of "Maleva the gypsy" from the films *The Wolf Man* (1941) and *Frankenstein Meets the Wolf Man* (1943). This parallelism takes on even greater visual resonance when Marvela starts to wrap her head in a scarf after she begins treatment for cancer. Karen's journal shows how much these late night horror films influence her experience of the world. Her protective classmate, Franklin, has scars on his face like Frankenstein's monster, and the comparison is emphasized by portraits of each on facing pages (Figure 1.6). Likewise, Karen understands her abandonment by her best friend and first love, Missy, as a kind of vampire-like burial: "Inside of Missy that part is in a coffin, in a crypt, staked, and hungry and all alone." These images recall the two girls' past shared love of Dracula and Alucard and, transitively, of each other, before Missy rejected Karen. On the very next page, following a page turn, Karen immediately makes a new friend, Sandy (Figure 1.5), who looks like a cross between Andy Warhol and the encrypted Missy drawn in the imagined X-ray of the previous page. Sandy, like the hungry and staked entombed Missy, is "always hungry" as well.[34]

The most striking and direct extradiegetical reference in *My Favorite Thing Is Monsters* is to Art Spiegelman and his monumental work, *Maus*, a book that Ferris describes as having "a profound and timeless beauty that emboldened [her] to make [her] own graphic novel."[35] *Maus* details Spiegelman's parents' experiences during the Holocaust, largely taking the form of his father Vladek's story as told to the author. Spiegelman's work is also a rumination on the toll that his parents' trauma has taken on him and his relationship to his art.[36] In *Maus*, writing and art are figured as a way of resurrecting not only Vladek's story but also the vanished story of his mother, Anja Zylberberg. As Anja and Anka are both diminutives of the name Anna (or Hanna), and Silverberg and Zylberberg are alternate spellings of the same name, Ferris's character Anka Silverberg is barely distinguishable in name from Spiegelman's mother. As clarified in *MetaMaus*, "Anja was born 'Andzia Zylberberg.' Her Hebrew name was Hannah, though in her assimilated household that wasn't something she was called regularly. She became Anna Spiegelman when she moved to America."[37] Later in the book, Ferris again highlights the ways that writing can obscure how sounds are received and understood, when Karen realizes that what she has earlier recorded as the word "shoots" was actually the name "Schutz." Art's mother, Anja, haunts the pages of *Maus*, especially in the pages of an earlier short comic from 1972, "Prisoner on the Hell Planet," in which the same characters who are drawn as mice in *Maus* are depicted as human figures. Spiegelman reproduces the entire comic in *Maus*, showing it in the mouse Art's hand and then, after the page turn, in a close-up of the hand and a near full-page spread that copies the first panel in "Prisoner": a drawn hand holds a reproduction of a photograph of the young Art and his mother. "Prisoner" is presented as a separate artifact, different in style from the rest of the book, and reproduced on the pages of *Maus* against a black background.[38] In "Prisoner," Art dissects his guilt about his mother's suicide and his rage about her figurative second death, which occurs when Vladek reveals to Art that he has destroyed all of Anja's meticulously kept diaries. In providing Karen an audiotape testimony to transcribe in a large section of her journal, Ferris resurrects the first-person testimonial that Vladek had denied Anja. Giving her own Holocaust survivor the name Anka Silverberg, Ferris inserts a network of associations and parallels from the earlier text. Spiegelman's reproduction

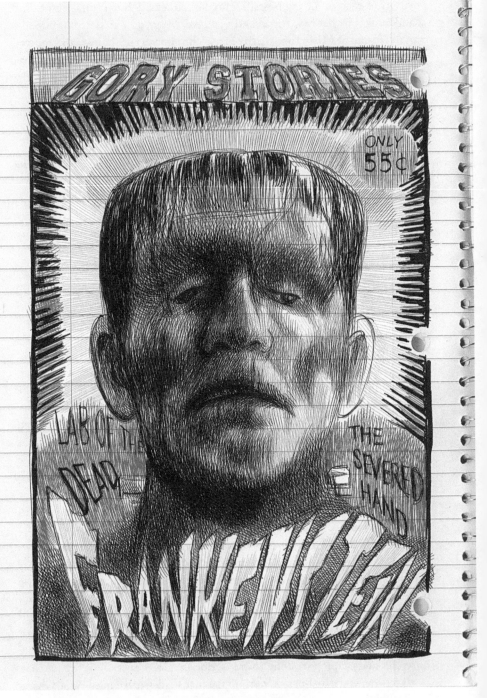

FIGURE 1.6 "Frankenstein." Emil Ferris, *My Favorite Thing Is Monsters*, vol. 1 (Seattle: Fantagraphics, 2016), n.p. Copyright © Emil Ferris. (Courtesy of Fantagraphics Books (www.fantagraphics.com).)

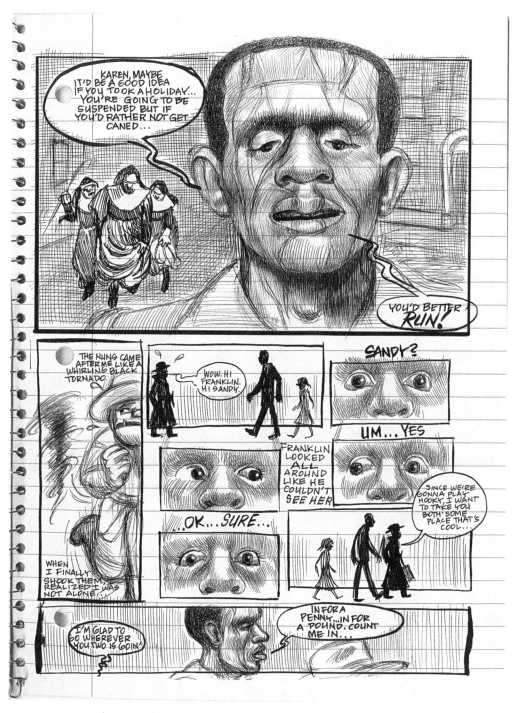

FIGURE 1.6 (*Continued*)

within his own text suggests a way to understand Karen's narrative, from the substitution of the animal-like faces for the human to the overwhelming sense of guilt that the child feels about disappointing the mother figure, and the "trope of maternal abandonment and the fantasy of maternal recognition."[39]

Karen's and Ferris's drawings remind the reader that while one can imagine the trauma that Anka experienced, it is after all only an act of imagination. The documents included in the book double down on that surface-depth divide,

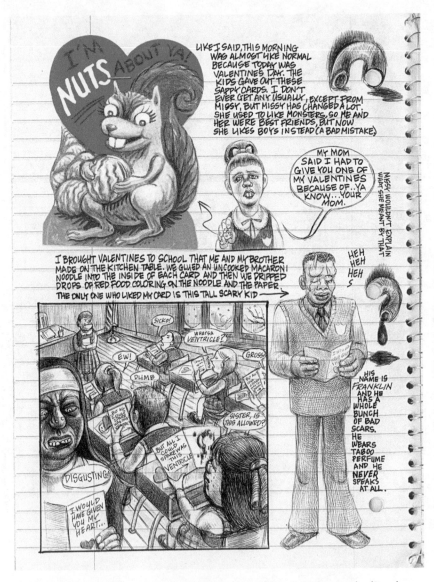

FIGURE 1.7 "I'm nuts about ya!" Emil Ferris, *My Favorite Thing Is Monsters*, vol. 1 (Seattle: Fantagraphics, 2016), n.p. Copyright © Emil Ferris. (Courtesy of Fantagraphics Books (www.fantagraphics.com).)

reminding the reader that these are prosthetic memories. Artifacts on the page entice the reader to distinguish foreground from background, pasted-in scraps as layers on top of a lined page, the metallic intrusions of spiral binding and paperclips as real objects holding together sheets of lined paper. Just as quickly, the material facts of the page remind the reader that this is simply an illusion, the result of technical reproduction. The book counterbalances the trompe l'oeil effects of pasted-in pages by referring to the way it has tricked the reader's eye. Paper clips on one side of a page are not seen on the other side when the page is turned over. The paper clip has no depth, its reflective quality is simply shaded in. The drawings on one page do not show traces of ink or pressure marks from ballpoint tips on the other side of the paper, even though the faint markings of the pink margin show through as if from the other side. The book encourages the reader to, like Karen, look closer. Looking closer, however, reminds the reader that this is a reproduced text, one whose layers are flattened and inaccessible, whose lines literally do not line up.

While there are many slips of paper that appear as if clipped in or pasted into the book, only one of them is not a drawing. It is a card that Missy gives to Karen for Valentine's day (Figure 1.7). Unlike the works of fine art that appear in the book as copies in Karen's hand, the valentine appears as if photographically reproduced. This object, unlike the one of a kind works that are copied, or the one of a kind drawings that are made by Karen or Deeze, is a mass-produced greeting card, free of sentiment or personal association, one of many of its kind, much like the comic books and magazine covers that Karen religiously copies into her notebook. The holiday that this card commemorates is itself a commercial enterprise, reinforcing heteronormative sexual pairings as mass-produced souvenir. What does this preoccupation with reproduction reveal about the family romance, the constructed family that is so crucial to the self-identification and self-formation of the successive generation? Like the monsters that Karen categorizes, there are good forms of reproduction and there are bad ones. The child narrator at the center of the narrative embodies and also offers a way through the disruptions and breaking points of a permanently decentered line. In Karen's pages we are given a new conception of the family as an inextricable mass of images and words circulating in popular culture, individual testimonial, the world viewed through her own body with all its unreliability and incomplete understanding. This perspective offers the promise of a justice that exceeds the juridical, one that reclaims reproduction as a special power even when, perhaps especially when, it does not follow a straight path, and does not only move forward. For all of its musings on reading as a kind of spying, on its critiques of the poisonous dangers of the male gaze and its expectation that the female body will naturally receive it, *My Favorite Thing Is Monsters* serves as a pointed reminder that while it is the eye that perceives and reads the clue, it is the hand that makes the final assenting act of drawing it all together by connecting the dots.

2

Reach Out and Touch Someone

The Haptic Dreams of Gareth Brookes

In its most commonly used form, touch is "the sense by means of which physical contact between an external object or substance and the surface of the body is perceived." But "touch" is also the feeling or sensation produced by an object when touched. It is a sense, but it also is the sensation that it manufactures. It is the aftereffect of that action, too, a mark made by touching; and, also, a part of the body used for touching. And while compound forms with the word touch can have a positive meaning, as when a person has "a touch," say with babies or animals, or with playing an instrument, it also bears negative meaning. A slang use of "touch" conveys the meaning of an act of deceiving someone out of their money, as in "putting the touch on" someone. To be "touched" is to be mentally or psychologically unsound, to be someone who is not quite right in the head.

Touch once used to indicate the testing, or assaying, of a metal for its purity. The examination process consisted of "touching"—or rubbing—the metal against a touchstone, and then analyzing the trace it left behind. The entire process of rubbing and analysis was referred to as "touching" the metal. And then again, the word "touch" was also used to name the quality of that metal as discovered through testing. Having been touched to define its touch, the name for the "touch" possessed by the metal was referred to as its "touch." Its touch—as in the quality that defined it—would then be marked or inscribed onto the metal itself. That mark too was called a "touch." One of the early uses of "touch," from the twelfth century, specifies sexual intercourse with another person, especially a woman. A later use from the early fourteenth century uses "touch" in the sense of making physical contact in order to harm or injure. We can be touched by the sun, we can be touched by wine, we can even be touched by time. Very frequently, being touched means being stirred with emotions, especially of gratitude and compassion. One is touched when registering a gesture of kindness from another person, for example, even though the gesture need not incorporate any physical touching at all. So, one can touch another, without touching them at all.

Chapter 2 is about visual tricks, but it is also about the connections between the sense of physical touch, which we call *haptic* perception, and the emotional and social meanings of touch that affect the haptic. It explores this connection through the work of Gareth Brookes, whose diverse output provokes a serious engagement and appraisal of the tensions between the literal and the figurative. Brookes's first long-form graphic novel, *The Black Project*, was published in 2013. The book, like *My Favorite Thing Is Monsters*, is a first-person narrative told from the point of view of a lonely child who keeps trying, and failing, to make a connection to others. The age of the child, a boy named Richard, is never made clear, and much of the sympathies of the reader may be abetted or challenged by their assumptions made about his age and relative innocence or deviance. The reader's ambivalence is triggered by the events that unfold in the book, in the precipitating action of the plot, when the narrator decides to create a girl-friend for himself out of odds and ends that he finds around the house and, later, from farther afield. Having been taught to sew by his grandmother, he goes about the house stealing women's undergarments and produce and creates an, if not anatomically *correct*, at least anatomically *specific*, simulacrum of a woman who can be his girlfriend.

A Thousand Coloured Castles, published in 2017, tells the story of an older woman named Myriam who lives a quiet life with her husband, but whose quiet existence becomes untethered when she begins to have fantastical visions. Crenel-lated towers leak out of her kitchen faucet. Vines steal out from behind mundane objects and coil around everything. Brightly clothed figures appear in quick and startlingly identical succession. Her grasp on what is and is not real is undermined by her grumpy and insular husband and her distracted daughter, who are all too ready to dismiss her experience. It eventually transpires that she has been suffer-ing from a disease of macular degeneration that has caused her to see hallucina-tions, but this interference in vision does not prevent her from properly identifying legitimately aberrant behavior by a next-door neighbor. The grounding of the nar-rative within a medical condition, and the subsequent implications of this diag-nosis, has put *A Thousand Coloured Castles* on medical humanities reading lists and led to a reissue in Penn State University Press's Medical Humanities series. While Brookes's book provides an empirical explanation for the fantastical visions, it is equally invested in examining the encumbrances of sight and the possibilities of visions that exceed scientific explanation. Brookes's most recent publication, the 2021 *The Dancing Plague*, tells the story of a historical dancing plague in medieval Strasbourg. The occupants of a village become struck by an irrepressible urge to dance and dance themselves to bloodied feet and even to death in some cases. The book is told from the perspective of a woman named Mary who is haunted by visions that are alternately read as saintly or as demonic, depending on whom she encounters. For this book, Brookes uses a wood burning tool to singe his story on to muslin cloth and augments the brown tones of these panels with brightly colored embroideries of demons and angels.

Each book uses materials and techniques that play up the themes in the story lines themselves. The carefully crafted pages put on full display the limits of their materials. For example, *A Thousand Coloured Castles,* created with wax scratch art, employs a process that recalls an early childhood classroom activity. An initial image is created with colored crayons, then completely covered over with black crayon. The black wax is then scratched off in sections, to reveal the image underneath it. In the context of the decaying vision of its protagonist, Myriam, and the truth behind what she has in fact seen, the choice of scratch art invests the reader in reading meaning from several aspects of the art's facture. The uncovering of the mystery at the center of the book mimics the scraping away of the obscuring surface layer, and the grainy blurred images of each page mimic the uncertainty of Myriam's vision. There are all kinds of metaphors that we may read into ideas of surface, and what they uncover, and how they reveal things beneath them. The fact that *A Thousand Coloured Castles* is a printed reproduction of the crayon scratch art is likewise crucial to our reading, and this surface aspect of the printed page is effectively used to make meaning.

It is not that only some books have page surfaces, naturally. It is the case that all physical printed books are material objects, held in the hand, that make physical contact with the reader. In some cases of the printed text, especially texts that have specific formatting structures such as poetry, they emphasize the specificity of their construction, so that placement or arrangement is crucial to the meaning making in a way that resonates with the composition of the comic.[1] Graphic narratives like the ones discussed in this chapter certainly fulfill and emphasize compositional specificity, but in their engagement with the surface of the page itself, they do something more. A reproduced work that insists on showing the marks of its construction stresses a material vitality that must be produced by the reader. Presenting the visual traces of their facture and simultaneously withholding the tactile confirmation of surface that the eye insists on, the works in this chapter identify how inaccessible that vitality is to us readers except through an act of the imagination. It is a process of perception that is mimicked in the interpersonal connections experienced by the subjects of these books. Since physical evidence is impossible, we must rely on what we see. And if what we see directly contradicts what we feel, what might that say about how and why we perceive, and how and why we believe?

Things Great and Small

In 2015, Brookes published a short story called "No Strings" for the "BFF" volume of the Latvian comics anthology *Kuš!*.[2] The story is eight pages long, although in the context of the story it might be more accurately described as a four-page story. This is because the short story is best understood by counting the number of sheets of paper, rather than the number of sides of paper. Such mental decisions are not frequently made when thinking about reading or interpreting a short story. While a page turn may be used, as a line break is similarly used, to construct a meaningful transition, this even more stringent emphasis on the page is noteworthy. Instead of referring to "No Strings" as an eight-page story, the discussion in this chapter refers to it as composed on four pages with two sides each because the sides in this printed comic are intentionally linked in such a way as to suggest inseparability. This is because each page is a reproduction of an embroidered page, so that the recto and verso of a piece of embroidered fabric are photo reproduced to coincide with the original article of fabric produced by Brookes. As with the reproduced pages in *My Favorite Thing Is Monsters*, there are obvious impediments. The weave of the fabric, porous, flexible, and "open" in the original, is smoothly impermeable when reproduced on the printed page. The raised nubs and loose ends of thread on the page repel the expectant touch of the reader's fingers.

"No Strings" takes the form of a conversation that occurs before, during, and after sex, and the banality of the words exchanged never waver in tone. On the recto side of the first page, there is only one legible word.[3] The undressing woman, in the foreground on the right side, is not seen from behind, in the traditional sense of the phrase, but is in fact presented from the other side, or what is traditionally called the "back" of the embroidery. The loose ends of thread and the obscured image are emphasized by a series of connected black marks at top and bottom that invite the reader to turn the page in order to see what the reverse reveals. The back side of an embroidery, with all its messy loose ends and effortful connections, is usually hidden from view; in the cases of embroidery where both sides of the work will be visible, care is usually taken by the maker to present a back side that is as clean as its front. Not so with "No Strings," where there is no possibility of avoiding the back side of figures or words. The obstinacy of this fact is central to the understanding of "No Strings," functioning as a commentary not only on the relationship between the two people on the page, but also on the relationship between the reader, the artist, and the page that brokers that relationship. Because the work is constructed with embroidery, Brookes purposely exploits the added potential of meaning making in the materiality of the embroidered work. The result has some interesting formal implications, for example in the construction of sequence by the reader.

On encountering the first, or recto, page, the reader reasonably assumes that the expletive uttered by the undressing man is a response—of appreciation or of

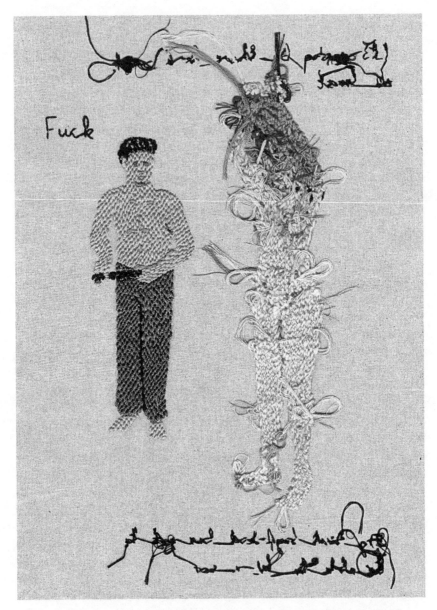

FIGURE 2.1 "F-ck." Gareth Brookes, "No Strings," *Kuš!* (2015): 127. Copyright © Gareth Brookes. (Courtesy Gareth Brookes.)

awe—to the sight before him. But upon turning the page, the verso of the page, which reveals the other side of the embroidery, the reader encounters legible dialogue that, coming at the top of the page, suggests that it should be read first to give context to the man's response (Figure 2.1). Now the woman appears, along with the words that she speaks, embroidered on what would be called the "right side" (of the fabric), but also on the "back side" (of the page). This requires a con-scious act on the part of the reader to hold these multiple instances in suspen-sion in order to make sense of a presentation that complicates the typical reading order in multiple ways. Sequentially speaking, if read vertically from top to bot-tom, the man's "F-ck" is in response to the woman's statement that an unknown "It" is going to be an unknown "there" for a week. It is only later that the reader can intuit that the "it" is a car at the mechanics. Yet, as with the belated under-standing of the man's exclamation, the reader's understanding of the situation is delayed by the action of turning the page and reaching the other, or back, side of the same image and text. It might make sequential sense to have the undress-ing woman's perspective as the first page of the story, but the sense of disorien-tation caused by illegibility and tangled lines is crucial to the experience of this story.

This action should be read as a deliberate mechanism, one that points to the mysteries of encountering surfaces and never quite knowing what might be beyond them. In the case of Brookes's story, the way that this unfolds is by hav-ing us realize that we are looking at the front and back of a piece of fabric, and that depending on which perspective you take, either side can be the front or back, the "right" or the "wrong." It incidentally reminds the reader how one takes for granted, when reading, the two sides of an item such as a sheet of paper or a piece of fabric as two completely separate and independent entities.[4] The over-riding idea is that although they may be having sex with each other, they are, figuratively and literally speaking, not on the same page. Notable as well is Brookes's anchoring of the loose ends of the threads underneath the stitches of the other figure, so that the figures are entangled even when that fact is not appar-ent on one side. This is most noticeable in the last of the four pages, after the couple has had sex, and the woman offers the man some Marmite on toast. "I'm fine," he says, and the last look is of the two characters completely separated from each other with, literally, no strings attached (Figure 2.2).[5] But we have our mem-ory of the previous page, in which threads cross chaotically back and forth, insinuating themselves between the two bodies.

Here one must clarify what we all already know but that, for the sake of effi-ciency when talking about a reproduction of a piece of art, we tend to take for granted: that what we are looking at when looking at the printed pages, and at the reproductions of those printed pages in this chapter, are not in fact pieces of embroidered fabric, but reproductions of a piece of embroidered fabric. In the case of the reproduction seen here in these pages, they are photographic scans printed from digitally manipulated scans of a single piece of embroidered fab-ric. The dimensions of the original piece of fabric are already obscured by Brookes's initial digital scan, which can be enlarged or shrunken to scale, depend-ing on the decisions made by the artist and the printer. It is also impossible to see, from observation of the printed page, that in fact different portions of the embroideries on the page have been constructed separately. The figures have been

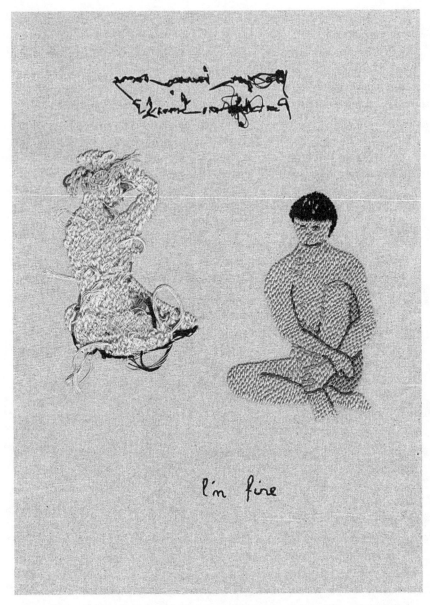

FIGURE 2.2 "I'm fine." Gareth Brookes, "No Strings," *Kuš!* (2015): 134. Copyright © Gareth Brookes. (Courtesy Gareth Brookes.)

constructed on one piece of fabric, but the dialogue has been embroidered separately on another piece of fabric, and the two layers have been combined as a separate stage of production for this final printed version. Brookes's deliberate exposure of the traces of his making hand explicitly gestures out toward the reader, offering the possibility of creating a complicity of reading that reaches across chasms of disconnection created by both space and time. These works thus assert the "virtual actual" connections, the strings that are neither severed nor hidden, that are there even when not always seen.

These layers—material, spiritual, imaginary—may point to what some might identify as the alienating condition of living in an age of reproduction, in which identical simulacra not only separate us from the original but obviate our sense of ever having had an original. Works like "No Strings" complicate such arguments, urging us to consider the forces of our memories and of our imaginary capacities. How is it that we make sense of things at all—whether they are little things such as recalling what exactly those words were saying on the other side of the page we just saw, or the larger things, like believing that there is a person on the other side, wherever that other side may be. That even when one of us cannot see those entangling threads, another person, even perhaps the person sitting directly next to us, may be hopelessly tangled in them. By presenting his carefully handmade work through the smooth reproduced page, by using the hand to equal force in painstakingly matching positions on a page via Photoshop so that they will reproduce images that are visually as close as possible to the original piece, Brookes redirects our attention to the careful scrutiny of all that we are able to scrutinize: the surface of the page.

When Brookes does this, his work shows us that no matter how much we think we have uncovered—about someone else, about something that draws our attention—there is still always more that cannot be reached. That unreachability need not be read as a refusal but rather as a natural state of being that still allows for affective reciprocity. This is particularly true in works like "No Strings." Brookes represents a node in a movement among certain contemporary artists who draw attention to the technologies of mechanized printing native to comics by drawing attention to them in the construction of meaning. They apply those technologies toward using the surface of the text to pose questions about how they and, in turn, we, might choose to see the world.

A 2003 graduate of a fine arts program in printmaking at the RCA in London, Brookes challenges the limits of categorization with his work, experimenting with embroidery, pressed flowers, fire, and different printing techniques. Here, as with the other examples in this book, the end goal is to produce multiple reproduced copies of sequential image-text narrative; this is a practice distinct from the traditional conceptions of the art book. This chapter examines embroidered comics by Gareth Brookes that engage seriously and variously with the material surface in the production of their narratives. These are visual reminders of the physical processes embedded in the reproduced surface, embedded in such a way as to induce an accord in the mind of the reader. This accord manifests a sense of understanding that not only matches but perhaps can even surpass the engagement with an original "auratic" object. The animistic medium of the reading process is set in motion by necessitating the active participation of the receiver in imagining the "how" of the object because of its appearance. The reader who holds a book like "No Strings" in their hands develops certain expectations based on how the book appears. This is the element of surprise in reading that Stanley Fish describes as being embedded in our encounters with certain texts where our uncertainty directs our relationship with its meaning. In *Surprised by Sin*, Fish articulates that what Milton does is to

> grant the reader the convenience of concreteness (indeed fill his mind with it) and then tell him that what he sees is not what is there ("there" is never located). The result is almost a feat of prestidigitation: for the rhetorical negation of the scene so painstakingly constructed does not erase it; we are relieved of the necessity of believing the image true, but permitted to retain the solidity it offers our straining imaginations. Paradoxically, our awareness of the inadequacy of what is described and what we can apprehend provides, if only negatively, a sense of what cannot be described and what we cannot apprehend. Thus Milton is able to suggest a reality beyond this one by forcing us to feel, dramatically, its unavailability.[6]

This feeling of unavailability that is experienced in the purely textual experience of reading *Paradise Lost* is activated in works like "No Strings," where the image also suggests the convenience of concreteness but nonetheless withholds actual concreteness. Fish suggests that the troubled relationship between the reader and the text, the doubt incurred at this impasse, is central to our comprehension, the focus of our reading.[7] When expectations are thwarted and present alternate routes, the text not only makes the reader ask "how?" but also, in turn, suggests that they ask "why?"

A Doubling Back: On Surface Reading

Derrida describes the history of philosophy as a "photology," as it so often depends on metaphors of darkness (self-concealment) and light (self-revelation) as the foundations for arguments.[8] Metaphysics is construed there through a figurative discourse on light, suggesting that surface, which can be suggested by light, is the material partner that makes light and its absence visible. Surface is defined scientifically as the topmost or outermost layer of an object, as with the skin of a fruit. It can also be understood as the limits of an object, where the object reaches its boundary and meets another surface: the surface of the water drop is where the water interfaces with the air around it. In some cases, the removal of the surface layer exposes something completely different that lies beneath, and again we turn to metaphors to explain this phenomenon. Fruits, bearing bright innards and surprisingly enrobed seeds, become tangible references for abstract ideas. In the case of fruits and their rinds or peels, a new, different, surface is exposed. In other cases, the removal of the surface layer exposes more of the same beneath, and simply marks a reduction of surface, as with the drop of water. These distinctions are at times unquestioningly ignored in the theoretical discourse that employs surface as metaphor. In other hands, the distinctions between definitions of surface are scrutinized in great detail to make finer points within a certain analytic framework: surface is a thing, the boundary between things, perhaps even that interstitial space between those things.[9]

Surface theory, as applied to literary theory in particular, both benefits and suffers from this muddiness of definition, and the transitions between literal and figurative. "Surface" appears many times in theoretical literature, but the term is used in various ways that are not always consistently comprehensible.[10] Surface is invoked to account for distinctions from depth, interiority, substance, and structure.[11] The many forms in which surface is used as a generalized term also include discussions of screens, skins, fabrics, shells, exoskeletons, walls, and interstices.[12] In writings on architecture, for example, the distinctions between structure and surface are construed visually for three-dimensional objects in space, as with the visible mantle of a building that is contrasted with a tectonic structure beneath.[13] Can we transplant this use of the word "surface" figuratively to describe two-dimensional objects, or philosophical concepts? Although the term is applied figuratively to literary texts, we are very rarely discussing the actual surface of the text but rather a metaphorical use of the word, where the call to "look beneath the surface" is frequently made to argue for how things "really" are in spite of how they "seem."

Surfaces and the senses of sight and touch most affected by them are not activated in our encounters with literary texts in the same way that they are when we encounter a building or an object. Instead, the surface of a text is experienced figuratively and differently, as the surface of a film must also be experienced and described differently. Thinking about surface, figuratively as well as literally, pointedly suggests that we think about limits. Derrida writes,

> How to touch upon the untouchable? Distributed among an indefinite number of forms and figures, this question is precisely the obsession haunting a thinking of touch—or thinking as the *haunting* of touch. We can only touch on a surface, which is to say the skin or thin peel of a limit. . . . But by definition, limit, *limit itself,* seems deprived of a body. Limit is not to be touched and does not touch itself: it does not let itself be touched, and steals away at a touch, which either never attains it or trespasses on it forever.[14]

I have argued elsewhere that the interest in surface theory as applied in literary criticism—and, in my case, including reading methods for image-text comics texts—may be thought of as "recent interest" only in the sense that there is a renewed interest in describing our approaches to reading. I would argue that we have always been interested, in fact always have been engaged with scrutinizing, surface and the limits that surfaces portend. The vocabulary of our critical apparatus falls frequently to the employment of surface metaphors, as occasions to discuss such complementary terms as "depth," "texture," and "layer." Yet the proliferation of studies of the surface in the past two decades, in novel and multiple ways, can also be read as a response to the ways in which surfaces as we have understood them have changed and continue to change in response to innovations in technological and digital reproduction in the past several decades. The surfaces of the cinematic screen and the television screen present cases where surface ornament takes the form of projection onto screens and projections from behind screens, thus drawing attention to questions of unity between surface and its ornament with the additional element of an engagement with temporality. Proliferating computer screens have hastened the relationship with humans and screen surfaces, culminating with the 2007 release of the touch-screen iPhone, a pocket-sized portal of surface and light, which presents an even more vigorous and marked change in how we conceive of and interact with surfaces.[15]

Merleau-Ponty famously used an example of the body in relation to itself to express the central ideas of his phenomenology of perception. The condition of a person whose two hands touch each other inspires a consideration of touch and the limits of surface: "When I press my two hands together, it is not a matter of two sensations felt together as one perceives two objects placed side by side, but an ambiguous set-up in which both hands can alternate the rôles of 'touching' and being 'touched.'"[16] We live in the age of the inanimate object that, nonetheless, can seem to touch us back, mimicking this touching and being touched. The touchscreen device, which is portable and invisibly connected and is a portal to infinite responsive communication platforms challenges the ways that we interact with the surface. With its responsive and transforming displays, the smartphone, which adds innovations in haptic technology and is small enough and ubiquitous enough to constitute a piece of body furniture, if not yet body, responds to direct touch. It also announces itself unexpectedly. It vibrates, emits light, and makes noise without our activation. It thus behaves in ways that Bill Brown described as "the story of objects asserting themselves as things."[17] One does experience the device touching us back: it is almost part of one's own body, almost sentient. The complicated ways that touch occupies our bodies, and our minds, pervade the comics discussed in this chapter. It is explicitly at the juncture between being "touched" with sight, where the sensation of touch is reproduced by vision, and the actual experience of touching that Gareth Brookes operates.

Stitch in Time

Brookes uses an unusual combination of embroidery and text, sometimes in concert with other media such as ink drawing and linocut print. These are sometimes arranged in ways that suggest the narrative panels of stained glass and medieval illuminated manuscripts, highlighting the connections between the handmade and the active reading practices created here. The stitch as method presents a medium-specific and materials-based commentary on the relationship between surface presentation and hidden "other sides." For example, although the standard embroidery "running stitch" may look the same on front or back, images and text are reversed when viewed from the back side. Likewise, a single thread may be pulled, or "carried," across the back side of the fabric so that a color appears separately on the front side of the fabric in various discontinuous seeming places. The active enactment of a stitch suggests a certain degree of violence—a puncturing and piercing—toward the surface that typically goes unnoted as well: the "touching back" of the surface is rendered both silent and invisible. Yet, for the stitches to appear as they do, the fabric must be penetrated, and its back side, typically hidden from view in photographic reproductions and in displays of original artifact, can be read for a great deal of meaning by the knowledgeable viewer. The front side thus also can imply, to the knowledgeable viewer, the hidden work that does not simply bear the traces of the front side but that quite literally holds the patterns and figures together as they appear on the front side.

Rozsika Parker, in her foreword to the reprint of her 1984 book *The Subversive Stitch*, remarks on Louise Bourgeois's turn to textile work in her later years, quoting Bourgeois to suggest a potential reading of stitched art:

> "When I was growing up, all the women in my house were using needles. I have always had a fascination with the needle, the magic power of the needle. The needle is used to repair damage. It's a claim to forgiveness. It is never aggressive, it's not a pin." Her work, to my mind, associates stitching not only with reparation but also with aggression and destruction. A theme that recurs in *The Subversive Stitch* is the dual face of embroidery. Historically, through the centuries, it has provided both a weapon of resistance for women and functioned as a source of constraint. It has promoted submission to the norms of feminine obedience and offered both psychological and practical means to independence.[18]

The needle, in ways subtly different from the pen or the paintbrush, brings with it these many connotations and, indeed, rather than suggesting either/or distinctions, the stitch itself shows in its very being the fact of simultaneity and continuity, an either/and. It is a disrupting puncture that exists in order to mend. It is a messy back that allows a thread to move continuously, but without showing that path on its front. The stitcher's manipulation of a single thread across the barrier of the fabric surface is thus what Parker, following Bourgeois, calls an evocation of both trespass of barrier and repair of such trespass. In the case of mending in particular, the need of an embroiderer to cultivate knowledge and experience of different kinds of stitches is also apparent: such stitches are contrived to resemble the weave of a textile as closely as possible so that the mending is indistinguishable from the original. Consequently, a viewer familiar with these stitches and practice is more capable of appreciating and understanding the work as it appears as finished product.

The presentation of text-heavy needlework is an unusual medium for contemporary comics, though it is commonplace in other forms of textile art. Needlework shows up frequently in literature, most notably in domestic contexts concerning female characters; but it rarely shows up *as* literature. In both Eastern and Western traditions, embroidered pieces frequently do present narrative information visually. These are sometimes elaborated with embroidered text as pattern or even with full sentences. Still, embroidery is typically not treated as reading material or object of art as much as it is appraised as ornamentation for dress or other forms of decoration.[19] While more and more examples of comics may be found that use media such as paint and pastels, as well as photography and collage, as drawing tools, embroidery is very rarely seen in the printed comic. Hanneriina Moisseinen is a rare exception who uses a variety of media, including embroidery at times, to construct her comics stories.[20] Needlework shows up rarely in the comics form, so that when it does it represents an opportunity for the viewer to attend to the labor of doing with needle and thread what could be more efficiently executed with pen and paper. Such works go even further, committed as they are toward producing a reproduced printed copy as final consumable product. They thus demand from the reader some kind of reconciliation between method and object: a consideration of the works' theory of existence.

The embroidered comic in Brookes's hands is differentiated, quite literally, by the mark of his hands. The printed pages show the traces of the artist's hand, still legible on the reproduced printed page. The fabric is creased where it has been crushed in the scanner bed, and circular indentations can be seen where the fabric was deformed under the pressure of the round embroidery hoop. In comics like "No Strings," the reader is confronted with the backs of image and text on each side of the page. In the longer-form work *The Black Project*, panels are elaborately framed with embroidery that resembles cutwork. While the reverse of the image within the frame is not represented on the overleaf, the reverse of the embroidered frame is shown. Details like this, much like the incomplete paper clips that lose their verisimilitude with the page turn in Ferris's work, call to mind what is missing. When only part of an image is represented from the other side on the actual overleaf of a page, the reader's attention is drawn to what is not represented, and thus to a consideration of the reality of the printed object as reproduction. The pages are reproduced so precisely that the reader can see the weave of the fabric, its warp and weft, and the way that the thread ends have been tucked into the back of the embroidery. They can see the way that external pressure has caused the fabric to wrinkle, to fold on itself in surrender to a hand or a scanning bed. It is so real that we can almost feel it. And yet, the flat and smooth surface of the page simultaneously refuses and repels the longing touch of the reader's own hand.

Reach Out and Touch Someone

The long-form works created by Brookes, different as they are from each other, have protagonists who share a position of relative lack of power in their respective societies. While the later *A Thousand Coloured Castles* and *The Dancing Plague* focus on women whose voices and visions are marginalized, Brookes's first graphic novel, *The Black Project*, makes a case for the haplessness of adolescent boyhood. Richard, in *The Black Project*, is a boy of indeterminate age whose desire for a girlfriend is limited by many factors, primary among which is that he lives in semi-isolation in the suburbs with a limited social network and an even more limited grasp of how to expand it. *The Black Project* begins in a scintillating manner. The first page opens with the sentence "She was the first one I had any real feelings for." It continues on the other side: "I took my time with her. It wasn't really like that before. There had been others but that was just messing about."[21] These are accompanied by embroidered telephone wires and a residential streetscape. This is a disquieting opening, and the ominous sensations inspired by these sentences are not dispelled as it continues. Within the lace-like borders that frame the text, the narrator continues to discuss his plans for "Laura" and how he "lay awake planning everything out and deciding what [he] needed to do so that [he] could make her."[22]

The reader may begin to wonder if this book might be detailing a planned kidnapping by a serial killer, against the backdrop of an ironically naïve embroidered frame. On the reverse side of the page, however, it is finally revealed that something less dangerous, but perhaps equally unsettling, is happening here. The narrative detailing the "plans for Laura" is quite literally a plan for construction: out of tights, socks, rags, a pillow. Breasts are fashioned out of a bra stolen from his mother, stuffed with grapefruits (Figure 2.3). The narrative acquires its humor from a blend of pity and admiration inspired by Richard's ingenuity in the face of limited means: "The head was the hardest part to make look realistic. Laura's head was made from the planet Neptune that I made out of papier-mâché for a school project about the planets. I tried to paint a girl's face on it but in the end I pasted a picture of a girl's face from a magazine onto it instead. I cut a hole for the mouth so I could stick my tongue inside like they kiss in films."[23] The narrative builds in this way, like a technical instruction manual at times. Sections furnish diagrams and the kind of excruciating details that are not necessarily recognizable in their specificity, but that nonetheless transmit a sense of incipient sexual curiosity mixed with childish innocence. The images of "Laura" with her pillow torso and taped-on magazine face do much to generate the reader's

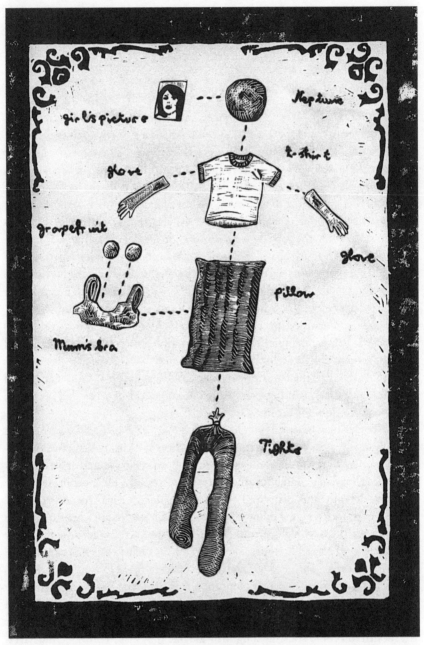

FIGURE 2.3 "Laura." Gareth Brookes, *The Black Project* (Brighton: Myriad Editions, 2013), n.p. Copyright © Gareth Brookes. (Courtesy of Myriad Editions.)

sympathies, so much so that when Laura is nearly discovered by Richard's friend Daniel and has to be dismantled, it cements a desire in the reader to see Richard fulfill his quest to create a girlfriend.

The Black Project continues in this fashion, developing as a sort of *Frankenstein*, a sort of bildungsroman, in which the protagonist grows and changes, both emotionally but even, arguably, as an artisan. Of course, alongside his own growth, there is the literal building of the successive girlfriends. With each trial, Richard becomes more resourceful about tools and materials, and learns more skills. By the time he makes his second attempt, to create "Charlotte," the face is upgraded from a magazine cutout to a plaster cast based on his own face, and a lower body carved out of polystyrene. Likewise, Richard's construction of Charlotte occasions a trip to the library, where he researches a book on female reproductive organs. Once again, Charlotte is discovered, this time by his father; and because Richard lies that he built her for a school bonfire contest, she is surrendered to the bonfire when he wins the prize. Although the girlfriend dolls are created to satisfy Richard's sexual curiosity, it becomes apparent that they fulfill something else, a curative for his essential loneliness. When he builds a third girlfriend, named Melissa, he uses a Halloween prop skull that he modifies to say: "We are best friends" and "fish fingers are the best food ever but normal fish is disgusting."[24] He modifies basket-weaving techniques to create limbs and shares intimate details about himself in his conversations with Melissa's head as he constructs the rest of her body. Melissa and the details that Richard shares with her about his life are depicted using linocut printing. Another trip to the library broadens Richard's knowledge from anatomy to the specifics of sexual activity. When he returns to the shed where Melissa is kept, he discovers that much of her lower body has been taken apart by mice. This is followed by his mother's announcement that his grandmother has passed away. Because of this new development, he is now able to salvage some of his grandmother's belongings, including a bag of sewing notions and materials.

Once again, Richard is introduced to a new skill. This time Richard and his mother spend time together, and she teaches him embroidery stitches, and the panels are lovingly portrayed in linotype and embroidery surrounds (Figure 2.4). The craft projects gain greater ambition as Richard devises a plan to create "Jessica" as well as a proper hiding place for her under his bed. The face is now upgraded to fabric and embroidery stitches, and Richard's innovations in construction are, though still equal parts ridiculous and disturbing, also admirable. Once again, he is nearly discovered by his mother and contrives to hide Jessica in the woods, where she is discovered and vandalized. Following this, his mother speaks to the school about him and tells him that unless he begins to make friends with children his own age, he will have to visit the school psychologist. She brings him to his old friend Daniel's house, where he spies a perfect head

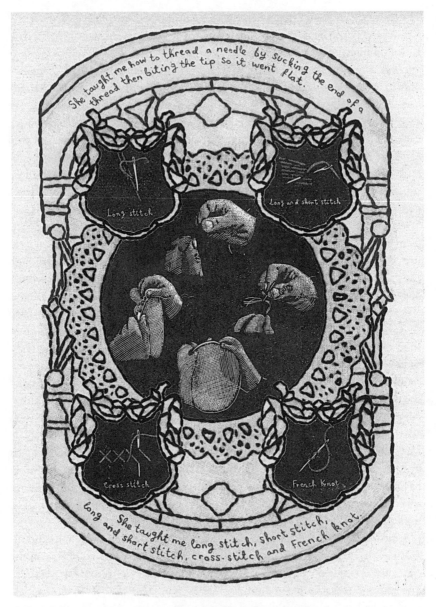

FIGURE 2.4 "She taught me long stitch." Gareth Brookes, *The Black Project* (Brighton: Myriad Editions, 2013), n.p. Copyright © Gareth Brookes. (Courtesy of Myriad Editions.)

in Daniel's sister's room. Richard steals the head, and this act precipitates a series of events: a fight between the mothers, a chase by Daniel and Daniel's friends, and a fight in which both Richard and Daniel fall into a river and spend time afterward convalescing in the hospital. Through these experiences, Richard makes human friends and reenters the normative social order.

In the afterword to *The Black Project* Brookes shares that when he was writing the book he "thought a lot about the time between being a child and becoming what [he would] describe as an established teenager—the first stirrings of a desire you can't articulate and have no way of externalizing." Later he clarifies that the indeterminacy of Richard's age is purposefully so: "When you're in your mid teens, you want to be caught doing things like smoking or vandalizing things, but sex still remains a closely guarded shameful thing. The question of how old Richard is isn't something I've made clear in the book but from a societal point of view it's key to how we judge Richard. Anything to do with sexuality and childhood is a massive taboo, whereas teenage sexuality is a matter for innuendo and mirth: one year either way could change the character of Richard's behavior from slightly odd to downright abhorrent."[25] This aspect of Richard's character is particularly beguiling for our understanding of the book, as it highlights the ways that Richard's world is constructed from the limited means available in pre-internet times: library books, television programs on the BBC, skills learned from grandparents, teachers, and parents, a bicycle. It also formally models how the reader finds a way through the text with similarly limited means, and how the interaction with the text is also marred by constraints of information and fueled by acts of imagination that could go in unpredictable ways.

Richard's world is even more constricted than Karen Reyes's Chicago in *My Favorite Thing Is Monsters*. The pages of Karen's book also reflect her rich imagination and artistic skills, but she has the advantage of access to museums and, importantly, many more actual people with whom she interacts. Richard's neighborhood is based on the place where Brookes grew up, the West Byfleet area, which Brookes feels "represents the Thatcherite ideal of private property, of everyone owning their own house and being autonomous. It's an ideal place to have a secret life. As long as you keep your front garden neat no one would suspect a thing!"[26] This strategy of reflecting the emotional drama through the built environment is apparent in Brookes's other work. *A Thousand Coloured Castles* also uses the unkempt garden of the next-door neighbor to draw attention to the child who has been imprisoned in the house, showing the possibilities and limitations of the single-family dwelling. As much as these books dwell on the limitations of physical dwellings, bodies and houses alike, they offer a view of the kind of mental, emotional, and spiritual building that allows a person to broker new accords with others. In this model of growth and development we see something of the growth and development of the surface reader as well, who is limited by what the text allows and whose abilities to appreciate what is in fact there require that they cultivate a knowledge based on being more attentive.

The book's use of innovative formatting and compositions that require active participation from a reader guided through specific movements across the page takes on a choreographic quality at certain moments. Brookes's

innovations employ familiar—to comics but also stained glass and illustrated manuscripts—panel forms in unusual formulations to conduce the
recognition of one's active generation of meaning in the animistic medium
of reading. Richard's trip to the library foregrounds reading as a pathway to
knowledge that is sometimes guided or thwarted by questions of access and
of hermeneutic sophistication: knowing what to ask for and how to ask for
it. Fittingly, the four panels on the page that anchor the library visit direct
a reading process that is legible, but also protracted through a specific
sequence of movements across the page. Framed with embroidered outlines
and ornamentation within those outlines near the center of the page, the
panels are embellished with Brookes's handwriting font and five images of
the same woman executed with linocut printing. The top of the page is
inscribed "So I went to the library. The lady who worked there was called
Carol." The text continues at the top of the first quadrant on the left side of
the page: "I asked her for a book about sexual reproduction." Richard's subsequent exchanges with Carol disarmingly portray the kind-hearted librar-
ian's discomfort and concomitant sense of duty in response to Richard's
desire for knowledge. The repetitions of her attempts to redirect him, and
his insistence of purpose, take on a ritualistic quality reminiscent of the
denials and persistence depicted in folkloric and religious texts. In the four
quadrants on the page, Carol is portrayed in a saintlike posture, on her
knees and turned to face outward from the picture plane (Figure 2.5). In
each image, she presents a different book to Richard in her hands. At the
very center of the page, she appears in a small, embroidered circle in standard miniature portrait form, from the shoulders up, and with a plain
background.

Looking out from the page, the kneeling Carol is surrounded by the
words she speaks, which, in the first three quadrants, curve around her
image, encircling her. Richard's obstinate insistence to have "a book about
sexual reproduction" pen her in. This effect is created with the cartouches at
the tops and bottoms of each panel and in the surrounding diagonal panels
that form a diamond around her portrait at the very center of the page.
Viewed alone, they convey a singular and unchanging message. "A book
about sexual reproduction" is repeated five times on the page in these cartouches, playfully reinforcing the single-mindedness of the young boy. In
the last panel on the bottom right of the page, Carol is shown unsmilingly
holding a book in both hands, and the oval frame around her is empty of
text. Instead, the diagonal frame at the top left of the panel simply reads,
"She said, 'Oh dear.'" The cartouche at the bottom of the panel continues,
"and gave me a book about sexual reproduction." The reader's progress shifts
from circular movements around Carol to the decisive responses from Richard in the central diamond. This is followed by Carol's eventual capitulation.
The parallel structures between the cartouches at the top and bottom of the

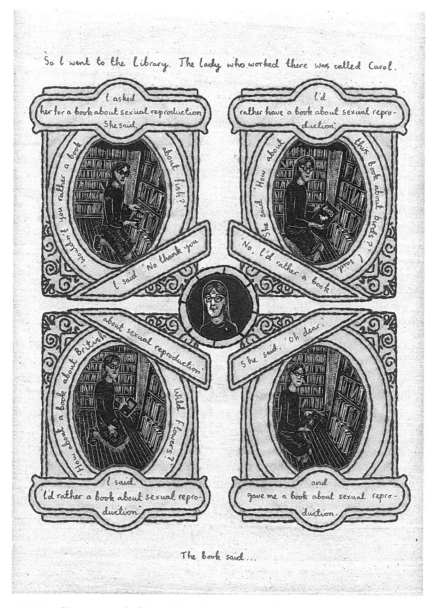

FIGURE 2.5 "So I went to the library." Gareth Brookes, *The Black Project* (Brighton: Myriad Editions, 2013), n.p. Copyright © Gareth Brookes. (Courtesy of Myriad Editions.)

page ("I asked her for a book about sexual reproduction / I'd rather have a book about sexual reproduction" and "I said 'I'd rather a book about sexual reproduction' / and gave me a book about sexual reproduction") underscore the way that comprehension requires a very specific movement through and across the text.

In this way, the protagonist completes his trials, and the facing page reveals the result of Richard's quest. A full page is dedicated to Richard's discovery, framed with linocut print outlining with white ornamentation a piece of fabric decorated with black embroidered stitches that themselves frame an oval linocut print. The print is a copy of a scientific diagram of an erect penis, with its anatomy carefully labeled. The text surrounding the embroidered fabric explains "a man needed to have his penis standing on end so he could put it inside a woman's vagina."[27] The humor of this page is accomplished by the buildup of its facing page and the assiduous decoration of the page, to be sure, but also at work is the juxtaposition of the mechanics of sexual activity with the dry and, literally, detached manner in which the information is communicated through the pages of the long-desired "book about sexual reproduction." This very distance between what appears on the page and what that content can become, once activated by the reader, is the very point of pages like these.

Another similarly structured pair of pages occurs closer to the middle of the book. Richard has been crying because he has discovered the remains of his Jessica girlfriend, who has been torn apart by vandals who discovered her in the woods where he had hidden her. When his mother asks him why he is crying, he tells her that it is because he misses his grandmother. In a similar style to those panels featuring Carol in the library, Richard's mum is the subject of a series of six panels on the page. Again, Brookes juxtaposes a continuous sequence of movements in a mundane activity in the inset images, using linocut print, of Richard's mother eating a dinner of shepherd's pie. The banality of the depicted scene is contrasted with surrounds that mimic more exalted forms, such as the treasure bindings of codices, that hold jewels in each of their corners. Instead, all of the panels of mum eating are surrounded by embroidered frames that contain Richard's summary of what his mother tells him: "She had had a talk with Peter the Caretaker and found out I didn't have any friends. She said a boy of my age needed lots of friends and why didn't I go and call for Daniel and ask him to play football with me . . . I said I didn't like Daniel because he's stupid. Then my mum said I had to make friends otherwise the school was going to send me to an educational psychologist."[28] Richard's recording of his mother's words and his own internal responses to her advice surround the images in the semicircular shapes around each linoprint. The words are read from left to right, and then from top to bottom within each panel, and the panels are read in the same direction from left to right and top to bottom as well.

The facing page is devoted to a full image, this time framed by the backside of an embroidered frame, with its loose ends on full messy display, reflecting the image and its accompanying caption: "I threw my shepherds pie at my mum."[29] The indentations of the embroidery frame can be seen as round creases at the edges of the page, surrounding the image and its caption. The overleaf does not show the other side of any of these artifacts, suggesting that the reader's attention is meant to be focused solely on these traces of work, an unusual distinction from the typical representation of "finished" work. Richard's reaction and its relation to the pie are embedded in the surround of the panels on the left side of the spread. In each of the corners a single letter is placed; from left to right and top to bottom on the page it reads, "Shepherds pie is disgusting!"[30] The reader is engaged by this arrangement to piece together this information from the collection of letters that countenances neither spacing nor punctuation, save for the exclamation mark at the end. The next two pages show Richard's visit to Daniel's home, where he and Daniel eat toast with alphabet spaghetti. This time Brookes shows the manipulation of found letters within the text itself, when Daniel spells out "You're gay" to Richard on his plate.[31] The potential of language as found object and the way that readerships are guided by the specific hand of the maker are repeatedly and potently transmitted in the pages of this book. This occurs directly in the arrangement of the letters of the alphabet on the page, and perhaps it is that attention to placement and the movement of the eye that contributes to our appreciation of the actual material ways in which those more traditional forms of meaning making are given to us as readers.

Although Brookes's other long-form graphic novels *A Thousand Coloured Castles* and *The Dancing Plague* are quite different from each other in setting, time period, and the media selected to create them, they are similarly concerned with the epistemic injustice of being someone who sees—and subsequently feels—something, only to be ignored and denied by the people around them. The two books are not concerned with questions of sexual reproduction, but they do highlight the contrast between materials and reproduction. Both books are process- and surface-oriented constructions that are presented as reproduced copies of books. *A Thousand Coloured Castles* uses the wax crayon removal process, or "scratch art," such that the layers that remain and the layers that were integral to the construction of the text are crucial aspects of both text and story, yet are inaccessible once converted by digital scanning and print into the final printed book.[32] Similarly, *The Dancing Plague* also uses embroidery to show Mary's striking visions: Christ's blood washes over everything, demons appear to dance among the afflicted, and angels descend to address her.[33] Alongside the embroideries, which may be thought of as additions to the text, the images of the narrative are drawn with a wood-burning tool, and Brookes also occasionally burns the fabric through, severing the weave. Whereas embroidery, even with its hidden backs, can be theoretically unraveled and redone, the burning of the textile communicates a finality, a terminus of action that cannot be undone, revised, or reversed. In that case, too, the reproduction of this work conveys another kind of terminus, a flattening from which even the author can reveal no more.

Message Received

Through an assessment of works like those produced by Gareth Brookes, we are invited to think about what we seek and what we accept in our efforts to be close to another person. When I say that I touch "you," is it rational to assume that I am, in fact, touching a someone only if they can be construed to feel themselves being touched? When we are moved by a piece of art, or words of a work of literature, or something that we hear, and we say that we are touched, is that the same thing? This chapter closes with a short story by Brookes, told through the encounter of the reader with a reproduced embroidered page. It deals specifically with questions of touch and sight, complicating what we now think it means to touch and respond to surfaces. The relationship between the surface of the page and the surface of the touchscreen phone, especially when it is a drawing of the surface of a phone on a comics page, is something that fixes our attention on the painstaking work of creating a comics page in contrast to the instantaneous responsiveness of the touchscreen device. Perhaps this accounts for the many funny and also deeply jarring and profound comics that actually feature screens, apps, and text exchanges.[34]

With the 2019 *Threadbare*, Brookes employs embroidery to tell a deeply entangled story about cell phones and text messages. The premise of the story is that Brookes is on a train listening in on a conversation between two older women that is so tantalizing that he begins to transcribe it on his phone. The conversation that he records is presented in the pages of this book in the form of a text message exchange. The first woman's speech appears as a text in green and the second woman's speech in gray. Their respective sentences are justified to the right or left of the page in the same way that text messages appear on the screen of smartphones. There are, of course, material differences. Here the text messages are depicted in embroidery stitches, emphasizing the difference between the speed at which each is produced. Interspersed between the speech bubbles are floating embroidered figures of a nude man and woman who are shown taking photographs to send nude selfies to each other. Their intimacy is alternately represented as intimate physical encounters and by even closer connection to their handheld devices.

The cover of *Threadbare* resembles the pages encountered in the earlier story "No Strings," where the page turn reveals the "other side" of the embroidery on the verso of the page. But whereas "No Strings" could arguably be seen as a four-page comic that required the consideration of both sides as part of the same "page," *Threadbare* does not maintain such an illusion. The recto and verso of pages exist independently of each other, at least from the perspective of the presentation of the original fabric that is now reproduced for the paper book. The logic of "image" versus "text" in the comic is already challenged by the fact that letters and figures are all constructed with stitchwork. The back of the lettering does not appear anywhere, in part because at least some of it has been produced by Brookes using a font created to mimic the look of embroidered letters: there isn't an actual back side because these are only digital artifacts made to look like stitched ones.

Confusion is further engendered by the unpredictable ways in which the front and back sides of a single piece of embroidery are represented in the pages of a book. The cover shows the front and back of the embroidered figure of a naked woman holding her smartphone. When she appears several pages later wearing a T-shirt and pants and hunched over to look at a phone on the table at knee level, the verso of the page does not show the reverse side of the embroidered image. A page later, two facing pages show both sides of an image, instead of aiming to simulate a single page where the embroidery shows on both sides as it would with the original fabric piece. In this page, the woman is seen reproducing—photographing—herself with the device that she uses to send a photograph to someone, and on which she presumably receives responses as well. The loose ends of the black thread used for her hair and for the smartphone, from both the right and wrong sides of this fabric, meet and seemingly cross each other near the center of the page, even though this is physically impossible to produce with the original.

Unlike "No Strings," in which the depicted man and woman are entangled by threads that go from one of their bodies to the other, the loose ends of threads are seen here wound between each individual body and its respective smartphone (Figure 2.6). This, in combination with the loneliness of the words, enhances the solitariness of the figures and their awareness of this solitude. The reader is made sharply aware of the artificial nature of the presentation by the intrusion of both photoshop and the print layout. That sense of artificiality overflows into our perception of these people's solitude as well. This point is made particularly well by the perceptual problems created by, for example, page turns through the image of a snapshot or scan of the page. The best that can be done is, like Brookes does himself, to juxtapose side-by-side images that rely on the reader to imagine things "as they should be." That the "should be" invoked by this phenomenon is actually impossible to realize is worth our serious consideration here.

When a two-page spread is used to show two figures in relation to each other, it is possible to present them with the images on the front and back of each page if there are no shared threads pulled between the two of them. However, when the connections between the figures on a two-page spread are explicit, as in the case of threads that run between the two figures, the illusion of holding an embroidered piece is made impossible by the realities of the paginated book. Whereas the reproduction can suggest continuity between front and back for each side, the continuity of the backs of the spread in the book is blocked by the way that the fronts intervene unless the book consists of only a single bifold page.

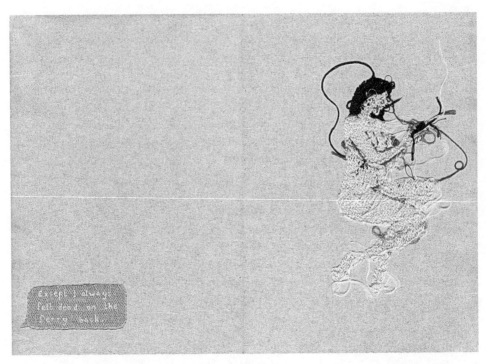

FIGURE 2.6 "I always felt dead." Gareth Brookes, *Threadbare* (self-published, 2019). Copyright © Gareth Brookes. (Courtesy Gareth Brookes.)

Multiple bifolds, when collated together, create interruptions in sequence that muddle the artificial construction of reality. Intentional or not, this alerts the reader to the predicaments of representation that are of course already inherent in *Threadbare*. These predicaments are highlighted from the artist's device of booklet as appendage of twitter messages to the use of text message format to record surreptitiously captured conversation and the use of the embroidery stitch as the chosen mode for presenting the entirety of these different forms of representation.

Threadbare, like "No Strings," ends with the same two words: "I'm fine"[35] (Figure 2.7). Just as in the earlier story, which began this chapter, where the last words were uttered in response to an ordinary question about marmite on toast, this time it is in response to whether one of the speakers needs any help getting her bags off the train. The images in the pages of *Threadbare* are disorienting, not only because they show, simultaneously, the front and the back of the embroidery, but because they are not illustrations of the conversation as transcribed on these pages. Questions of simultaneity, of being "on the same page," are suggested variously, sometimes by titles but more often by the content of the narratives. The reader mostly encounters parallel or complementary narratives.

FIGURE 2.7 "I'm fine." Gareth Brookes, *Threadbare* (self-published, 2019), n.p. Copyright © Gareth Brookes. (Courtesy Gareth Brookes.)

The effect on us as comics readers is to respond with some degree of interpretive sense of the modes of communication at play in the story. There is a great deal of attention paid to touching and its many definitions over the course of *Threadbare*. There are the figures who touch themselves and their phones more frequently than they physically touch each other. There are the two unseen women, turned into text message speech bubbles, whose memories retain actions and emotions that are now temporally remote. There is the artist who overheard these conversations and transcribed them by touching the screen keyboard on his smartphone. And there is the fabric on which he later applied this story, which experienced the puncture of the needle and bore the passage of the thread from front to back and back to front. There is the way that the fabric of that embroidery was pressed up against the glass bed of a scanner, and the way the pages and letters were manipulated on a computer screen so that they would appear to line up, or appear to be embroidered, or appear on one side of a sheet of paper instead of another.

We come up against these issues at the surface of the page, feeling its smoothness where we ought to feel the bumps of the stitching. These characters come up against these issues at the surface of their phones, as well, feeling its smooth-ness where they ought to feel each other. They touch themselves, it is true, and the surrogacy of gestures reminds us of Merleau-Ponty with his two palms pressed together. What are we praying for when we reach outward like this? Is there a difference between touching another, touching an object, and touching our-selves? Is everything really going to be fine?

3

Phantom Threads

Seeing in the Dark and Conor Stechschulte

Can an error be intentional? To some degree, the works discussed so far in this book recuperate that possibility. The two preceding chapters identified the discord between the visible and the haptic afforded by the reproduced page as a formal device, becoming a central metaphor for the stories they tell. Ferris's book suggests that the frustrations and incapacities of mechanical reproduction may dilate our awareness of alternate pathways regarding biological reproduction and kinship. The embroidered textile narratives by Gareth Brookes highlight the insufficiencies of photo reproduction: his use of such prominently textured and dimensional media with the intended result of multiple printed copied books is impossible to ignore. Such juxtapositions demonstrate how frequently we rely on limited, and often contradictory, information to form our opinions about what reality "must be." In both Ferris and Brookes, the confrontations between what we see, what we feel, and what we must acknowledge to be "really there" are highlighted through this formal device. Confronting these divides is an essential part of narrative building as much as it rouses the reader to question their assumptions about viewing and consuming the comic. The disruptive force in these earlier works is engendered by the conflict between what is seen and what can be felt, where the insistence on visually apprehended dimensionality is thwarted by the smooth-surface feel of the page itself. This chapter argues that this kind of conflict prepares the reader to engage with the kinds of philosophical questions pursued in those pages.

In this chapter, the discussion turns to the work of an artist who deliberately uses the articles of disruption, documenting those disruptions as a key aspect of his storytelling text. At times drawing the reader's attention to the disjoint in the expectations of the printed reproduction, these works also highlight the disruptions enacted by various technological apparatuses that affect the characters in these comics. In both content and form, these works linger on moments when objects do not function as they should, thus making their "thingness" vividly apparent. Conor Stechschulte deliberately foregrounds "noise" and distortion created by tools of technological reproduction as plot elements in his comics. His works represent a keen interest in not only moments when tools fail to function as they should but also moments when tools are purposely used to interfere with their usual expected functions. The comics deliberately incorporate interference and noise into their facture, with the purposeful and aesthetic display of noise and other artifacts of interruption and distraction that reveal the madeness of an object and confronting us with elements of the process used to make it. Stechschulte commits works for the reproduced page that reflect a deliberate material strategy in their physical production. These involve various printing processes including screen print, offset printing, and risograph printing, and this process-oriented practice extends throughout an ecology of texts that independently engage and comment on each other.

The *Generous Bosom* series, which is the central subject of this chapter, is complemented by the small independently self-published booklet *Generous Impression*, as part of Stechschulte's own imprint, Crepuscular Archives. The booklet shares reproductions of the front and back sides of Stechschulte's tracing papers, used to make copies of line drawings. By shading the backs of these drawings and then retracing the image from the front, he creates a carbon copy "impression" of the images. As with Brookes's reproductions of embroidery in *Threadbare*, the printing of the fronts and backs of individual drawings requires modifications of layout when put together for presentation in a booklet, introducing new narrative sequences in interaction with the original artifacts. The backs of drawings are not necessarily presented on the backs of their corresponding page in the reproduced book. Instead, fronts and backs sometimes face each other, like mirror images where one image is more heavily marked than the other. When Stechschulte depicts two heads facing each other belonging to the characters Glen and Art, the front and back of the image are shown in two consecutive two-page spreads. By folding the remaining pages of the booklet so that they are all gathered behind a single page, the reader can generate a visual simulacrum of the "original" as it were, so that reversing the flattened booklet as if it is a single sheet of paper simulates a two-sided object. This necessitates an act of will and an ignorance of the pages that come between. The alternations of "right" and "wrong" sides and the purposeful foregrounding of sequence in a process book such as *Generous Impression* form a profound intervention in the reading process that may well be the point of these stories.

There is a tendency in certain forms of what are called serious or literary comics, comics like Conor Stechschulte's, for example, where the artist draws attention to the disruptions brought on by the communicative form itself to mobilize the incapacities of the form so that it contributes to its meaning. This disruption occurs most markedly in the tensions that emerge in the union of the expressive and unique hand of the artist with the technologies of mechanical reproduction, what I have described as attending to imperfect fits.[1] This disruption has also been called "autoclastic" by Christopher Pizzino, who defines the autoclastic moment as "a kind of self-breaking, as if it is designed to work against itself . . . as if self-destruction is its ultimate function as a signifier."[2] The metaphors of disruption and fragmentation in simultaneous accord with cohesion and unity meet sometimes in interesting ways in the comics form. The disruptive and imperfect fit, emphasized as it is in certain graphic narratives, can be used as a provocation to the reader, a formal device not only to think about the comics medium but to confront epistemological questions about personal identity and coherence.

This applies especially to the metatextual commentary that exists in the ambit between Stechschulte's texts, where the reproduction of gesture, image, and situation creates a sense of repetition even as it generates more questions about meaning in its execution. In *Generous Impression*, the last page and both sides of the back cover of the booklet present the back matter of the book as a metacommentary on its production. "This book is composed of tracings used in the making of the book 'Generous Bosom' forthcoming from Breakdown Press in November 2014" is printed on the inside back cover, along with the copyright information and smudges. Its facing page, or the last page of *Generous Impression*, shows what looks like the back side of the text on the inside cover or, perhaps, the back side of the page that had been used to trace the words that are on the back cover. The recto side of that page, however, does not show the imprints of the same text. The bottom of this page does not contain the words "Crepuscular archives 2014" and "crepusculararchives.tumblr.com," although those do appear, in reverse, on the back cover of the booklet. The remainder of the back cover appears as the reverse of the front cover title, author line, and cover image (Figure 3.1).[3] The reader of *Generous Impression* attempts to trace the process of the maker as well as to consider the sequence in which he created the final images in *Generous Bosom*.[4] Engaging in this simple act of imagination is ample reminder of the processes of elision committed in the production process as well as how it is reproduced by the reader in the reading process. It is obvious from this example that the sequence of reading these pages is quite different from the sequence in which they are made, and that, under the typical conditions, we give no thought at all to that difference. These texts reveal something of what might be lost when we rely on reproduction to generate a sense of "being there."

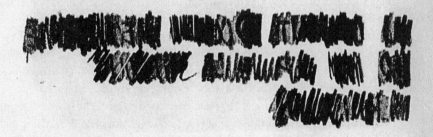

FIGURE 3.1 Inside back cover. Conor Stechschulte, "Generous Impression" (Crepuscular Archives, 2014). Copyright © Conor Stechschulte. (Courtesy Conor Stechschulte.)

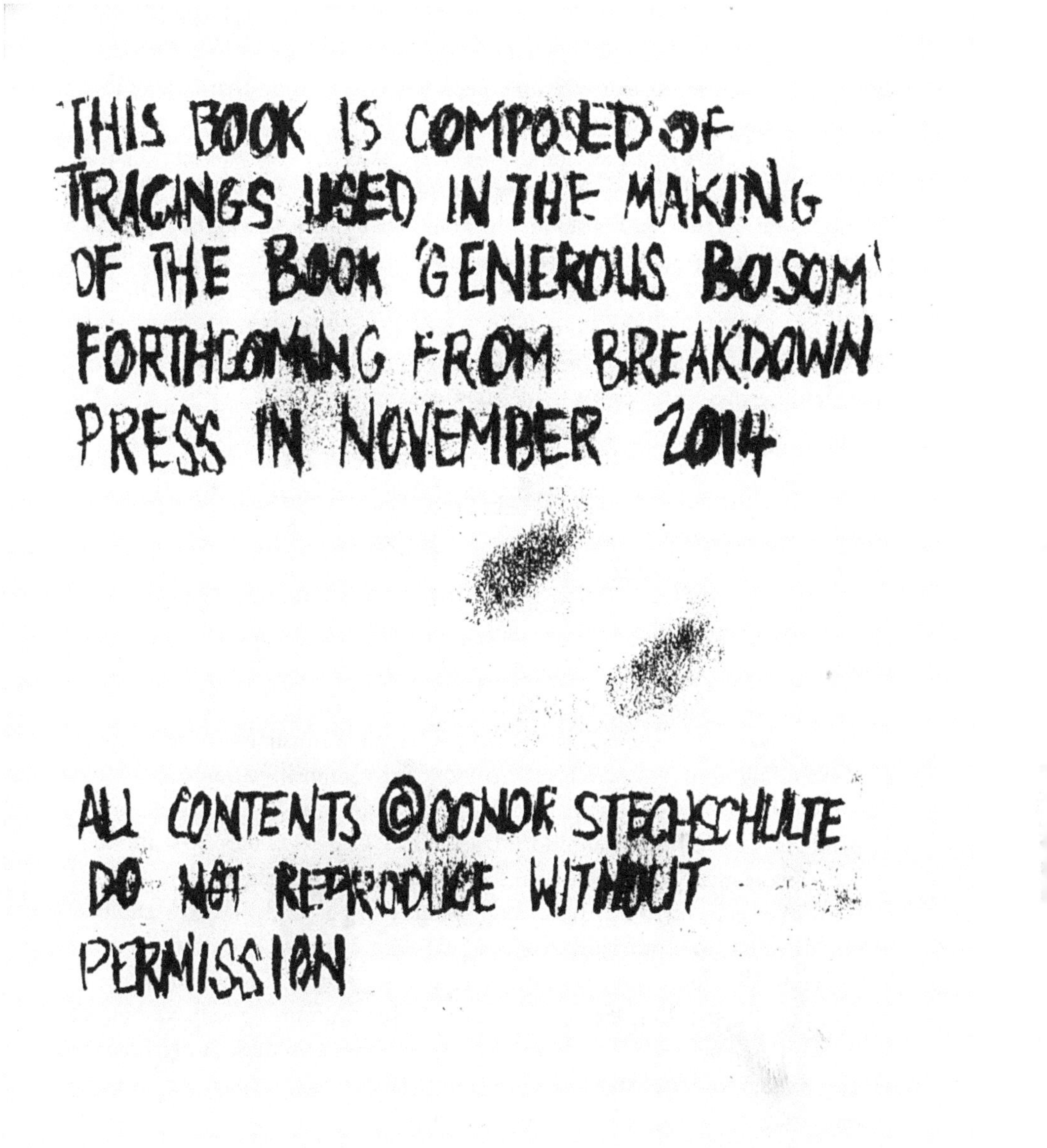

THIS BOOK IS COMPOSED OF
TRACINGS USED IN THE MAKING
OF THE BOOK 'GENEROUS BOSOM'
FORTHCOMING FROM BREAKDOWN
PRESS IN NOVEMBER 2014

CREPUSCULAR ARCHIVES 2014
crepuscularanchives.tumblr.com

FIGURE 3.1 *(Continued)*

In the book *Christmas in Prison*, "Drawn by Conor Stechschulte November 2015–2016," a detailed table of contents shows how and by whom the pages and cover were printed. This table of contents is a declaration that the content of the stories is inextricably bound to the methods used to present them on the page and a reminder that individuals were responsible for assembling the final product. *Christmas in Prison* deploys screen, offset, and risograph printing variably in, as he suggests in his acknowledgments, an "inchoate approach." No matter how inchoate the narratives presented in Stechschulte's comics, they beguilingly draw the reader through a complex series of actions toward discovery. This complex series is accomplished through an interpretive process that commands an interaction between reader, text, and author. This chapter analyzes how that interpretive process is modeled by the text.

Registration, the process used by a printer to ensure that separate layers of color are applied at precisely the same place, is read in this chapter as a presiding metaphor for the human relations that occupy Stechschulte's narrative projects. With the color printing process, each layer of color is applied separately, and overlapped with precision so that colors are mixed to create specific shades or do not overlap at all to maintain the colors separately. Registration errors, when layers overlap imprecisely, result in blurriness or imperfect fits where white space or overlapping colors and images show. Systems of registration generally function by lining up physical coordinates on paper and inked surface, whether using tiny holes or the commonly seen registration marks that resemble crosshairs: a circle with a cross extending from its center. Such methods offer a compelling framework for a narrative concerned with epistemological questions about how one's perception of the world may correlate to the world as it actually is. Colors are purposely allowed to occasionally misalign in these works, and their autonomy suggests the discord between each character's experience and memory of an incident. Stechschulte's characters suffer from problems of ontological alignment, and they discover that the only reliable solution is to develop a system of cross-checking that aligns their respective understanding of events. Near the end of the fourth and final volume of *Generous Bosom*, three characters have escaped from a mysterious psychological experiment undertaken at a facility. On the last pages of the book, as they emerge, they check with each other that they see the same thing. This is a kind of interpersonal registration mechanism, establishing how their perspectives align, both literally and figuratively. This resolution of uncertainty about what has or has not occurred is akin to the vocabulary of the printer registration, and it is akin to the experience of encountering and reading the text by the reader.

That Thumbs Thing

As much as this is a chapter about alignment and registration, it is also a chapter about those artifacts that draw one's attention to our human impulse toward coherence. The phantom threads that float in suspension between the damaged and often conflicting ecologies of the characters in these books demonstrate how they may cohere and bond with each other, creating a firm and unified web where there were only disparate fibers before. This formal conceit is recognized best at the moments when the traces show their stray filaments. Marks of the process by which a work has been made often occur incidentally on the surface, as visual reminders; at other times, they are incorporated into the final work, as part of the piece. In the works studied in *Perfect Copies*, such marks and objects are also sometimes deliberately placed into these texts. Originally unwanted and unanticipated, "noise" becomes its own aesthetic device. Such objects, with their capacity to arrest, disrupt, and redirect the attentions of the viewer, attain their power from the processes that bring them into being. They are usually read as the debris of a failure of attention and care.

The creased surface, the smudge, and other kinds of visual noise possess capabilities of meaning making that are wielded in these artworks. They are assertions of the uniquely human capacity for failure that is too often fastidiously erased in the final stages of the production process, where the interference of human error is carefully wiped away. Carolyn Kane has argued that such artifacts that escape erasure are particularly affecting because they speak to a general malaise of the twenty-first century brought on by an ambient sense of failure extending throughout our political, economic, social, and emotional landscapes. She writes compellingly of "the way in which twenty-first century acts of visual discord symbolize broader economic, psychic, and environmental failures, generating a registry of unrequited longing in the age of information."[5] These "acts of visual discord," as she puts it in *High-Tech Trash*, allow her to explore the discursive ways that practitioners in fine arts take up the rhetoric surrounding failure in the tech world to comment on "a necessary and often unconscious mode of structuring existence in a digital age which valorizes information, transparency, and speed against a political and historical background chockfull of noise, static, and breakdown."[6] Noise, static, and breakdown, the phenomena of interference, are the materials that draw these tentative and damaged subjectivities together.

In their assertion of their own fractured and dislocated presence, the markers of noise become stand-ins for possibilities that usually escape our interpretive practices: the blemishes that remind us of the surfaces we behold, and how they do and do not function. Michel Foucault argued,

> At life's most basic level, the play of code and decoding leaves room for chance, which, before being disease, deficit or monstrosity, is something like perturbation in the information system, something like a "mistake." In the extreme, life is what is capable of error. And it is perhaps this given or rather this fundamental eventuality which must be called to account concerning the fact that the question of anomaly crosses all of biology, through and through. We must also call it to account for mutations and the evolutionary processes they induce. We

must also call it to account for this singular mutation, this "hereditary error" which makes life result, with man, in a living being who is never completely at home, a living being dedicated to "error" and destined, in the end, to "error." And if we admit that the concept is the answer that life itself gives to this chance, it must be that error is at the root of what makes human thought and its history.[7]

Foucault's argument ultimately redounds to a claim that error is not simply an irritating part of human life, although it certainly is that, too. Error, or perhaps more accurately the capacity of error that comes just short of "disease, deficit or monstrosity," is what defines, creates, and constitutes human lives. This framework identifies the notion of dedication to the constant commission of error as critical to what makes us human. Rather than try to avoid error, or to hide it in part of a narrative of triumph over failure, then, we might find some value in staying with the errors. Foucault's recalibration of how error can be understood suggests the salutary effects of choosing to attend to the mistake as the very thing that affirms our hold on the actual. This is especially relevant to the works of art in the twenty-first century and even more so to the comics encountered here. These comics show how errors and mistakes are embedded in their making and also, therefore, how errors in our consumption and interpretation of these works are equally productive for meaning making.

Over a decade ago, both Alison Bechdel's 2006 *Fun Home* and Dash Shaw's 2008 *Bottomless Belly Button* brought distinctive and highly specific stylistic approaches to their examinations of family dynamics in the graphic novel form. *Fun Home* scrutinized Bechdel's childhood and especially her relationship with her charismatic and inscrutable father, an English teacher who tirelessly "spun garbage into gold" while restoring their gothic revival home with meticulous period detail and sometimes arranging his family members as props in this tableau.[8] The narrative is scattered with details that display the various elided structures that gave meaning to Alison's life as a child, and serve as the scaffolding of her formation as an adult. In *Fun Home* this takes the form of architectural details, the titles of the books and magazines scattered around the characters, and the photographs that are both artifacts of the past and narrativizing clues that give purchase to her present-day understanding of her world then and now. Photographs are especially figured as providing a kind of trace that is meaningful in the context of the drawn page: a noise that strikes the viewer because of its ability to capture imperfection in the unpreparedness of subject and surrounding. Unlike the cartoony style of the rest of the mise-en-scène that extends to book covers, television screens, and most of the photographs depicted in the book, certain significant photographs are drawn in a heavily hatched style, distinguishing them from the rest of the drawing style. Unlike Spiegelman's traces of photorealistic reproductions of photographs in *Maus*, Bechdel reproduces the photographs with her own hand. These distinctive drawings of photographs serve to accompany chapter title pages and occur at times within the pages to mark the narrator's key moments of discovery.

One such moment notably occupies an entire spread near the center of the book, where Alison discovers a photograph taken by her father in 1969 of the family's "yardwork assistant/babysitter, Roy."[9] In a series of text boxes scattered over the image, drawn with black pen and ink and surrounded with blue wash, she notes the trace-like quality of the image: "A trace of this seems caught in the photo . . . just as a trace of Roy has been caught on the light-sensitive paper."[10] The emphasis on the low quality of the photograph occasions an interesting artistic choice in presenting this distinction. In this comic, where Bechdel has been typically drawing with a spare cartoony style, the low quality of the photograph is paradoxically emphasized with a complex web of hatched marks that would elsewhere be described as detailed. Instead, here the hatched drawing is described by Bechdel as "low-contrast and out of focus." At the same time, Bechdel emphasizes that the distortion of the photograph as she sees it contributes to the truth-telling traces it offers and indeed to its beauty: "The blurriness of the photo gives it an ethereal, painterly quality. Roy is gilded with morning seaside light. His hair is an aureole."[11] Bechdel the viewer sees Roy as her father must have seen him at the time: as an object of beauty and desire. Through this encounter with the photograph, Bechdel notes the way that her father had attempted to censor the image by removing the date from the photograph. The comic itself comments on the different registers on the page, which is emphasized by the presence of the thumb of the left hand holding the photograph. The contrast between the hand holding the photograph and Roy's hand in the photograph is marked: Alison's thumb is so sparingly drawn that the lines needed to draw it are countable.

The thumb in the comic may be construed as an artifact of deliberate noise here, reminding the reader of the authorial presence just beyond the page, and reminding the reader of the resolute madeness of the work. It also draws attention to the relativity of reality and truth-telling manufactured by the drawn text: the acuity by which the reader sees things as more capable of revealing truth or reality is, after all, a negotiation between the reader's attention and what the text directs the reader to understand in the context of the text's full ecology. The thumb also appears with the family photograph in Dash Shaw's weighty *Bottomless Belly Button*, a story about the Loony family, in which three adult children return to their childhood seaside home following their parents' announcement of their intention to divorce after forty years of marriage. Shaw's graphic novel applies a similarly forensic lens to scraps of evidence, hints, and clues in the landscape of the family home and also to the family photo album that eldest son Dennis takes off the bookshelf. As he looks through the pages, the reader is reminded that Dennis is looking at these pages from the intrusion of thumbs on the pages, places where the reader's own thumbs might rest. These thumbs, with their scale orienting the reader to the relative size of the photographs, are rendered with the same degree of detail as the images in the photo album, and

Shaw draws the other traces that are visual artifacts of material presence: sticky tape, slits in the album paper for photo corners, and, finally, an "actual" key taped to the page. The thumbs rendered on these pages suggest the additional and unacknowledged presence of other lives who interact with the text.

The noisy thumb is brought to a literal head in the middle section of Stechschulte's willfully inchoate and fragmented *Christmas in Prison*. The book is composed of a series of narratives that may or may not be related. The divisions are marked in the table of contents by a detailed explanation of how sets of pages were printed, and by whom, but none of these units have titles. Pages from distinct items in the table of contents tend to leave their marks on each other; still, wet ink is allowed—or perhaps made—to mark the page it faces, so that it is impossible to distinguish intentional artifact from inadvertent one. Indeed, the entire book works to interrogate whether it is even possible to articulate separate categories of noise in the sense of interruption from noise as intended meaning making. In a section that appears several pages prior to the section discussed below, a single risographed page shows an orange thumb at the bottom right end of the page. There is no accompanying text, and the thumb is not directly related to the preceding pages, except by color. The table of contents suggests that the risographed thumb was preceded by three offset printed pages. The first shows a seven-panel spread, in green and orange, of a head in profile drawn on the beach and being washed away by the tide. The next two pages show the head in profile in a position that suggests that the green ink from the first page has leaked through the verso of the first page and onto the following page as well. This sequence of the creation of an ephemeral mark on sand, followed by that of a permanent mark in ink that is so intensely concentrated that it has bled through to leave its mark on the subsequent otherwise blank pages, is brought to its conclusion by the seemingly errant thumb on the fourth page of the sequence, as if photographed unawares by the indiscriminate capture of the scanner to be reproduced in perpetuity.

The disruptive quality of the thumb results from the ubiquity of placement for both the reader of the text and the maker. Our thumbs play a necessary role in holding the pages of a book apart, whether for photostatic or other scanning procedures during the printing process, or in the reading process when holding a book open. Yet we are trained to see through this bodily presence in its interaction with the surface, ignoring the process as merely incidental to the processes of reading that we select as the primary processes. If we are to follow Foucault's lead, we might aim to stop seeing through objects to which we typically attach words like "error." Two pages after the image of the orange thumb, Stechschulte shows a body of calm water from which, as the pages progress, a woman's head emerges from the water and begins to speak. Both her head and the speech are printed in green, and she tells a story about a man whose occupation is to survey the surroundings from a watchtower that is part of a series of relay watchtowers. Eventually, he travels to verify that there really is someone at the next watchtower, which he finds empty. She continues, "He searched and called out but all was quiet and still. Perhaps seeking some reassurance, he looked eastward toward his familiar post. He saw a light there where he had left none burning. Taking up his spyglass, he looked again at his lighted cabin. A human shape stood silhouetted against its glowing interior. Had his comrade from this western tower shared the same suspicions he had? Had they undertaken a similar journey? Had they traded places?"[12] When he returns to his own watchtower, he finds that he does not encounter this counterpart, nor has his home shown any signs that it has been occupied. As she reaches this point in the story, the page turn reveals two thumbs entering the picture plane from the far margins of each page to obscure the panel from left and right. The thumbs also introduce a new color, red, to the page. She finishes, "He looked to the western cabin but the setting sun made it so he could not see if anyone dwelt within. Exhausted from his two days of travel he fell into a deep sleep. He dreamt of a fire approaching his tower from the west."

At the page turn, the woman's head sinks back under water, while the thumbs turn slightly away from the page, revealing little bumps on the surface of each thumb pad. The thumbs, as the next page turn reveals, have faces: the little bumps were each the tips of a nose. As the last traces of green are absorbed back into the ripples of blue water, the thumb on the left now takes over speaking, addressing an unknown "you" with a speech bubble printed in the same red tones: "This just reminded me—I had a dream with you in it last night. We were trying to have a picnic and we were looking for a spot to put our blanket down"[13] (Figure 3.2). The thumb on the right does not speak but merely looks on. On the next page, the thumb on the left side is again seen only from the back, and the speech bubble still points toward it: "But there'd just been a fire in this field—this like, prairie where we were. It was all soot and ashes." On the page to the right, the thumb still looks on across the water; both the blue ink and red ink are significantly faded compared to the page on the left, and the speech continues, increasingly faded, over the next three pages: "And we didn't want to get the blanket dirty. The fire was why I remembered . . . and it was raining . . . in the dream."[14]

On the overleaf, the story seems to end with the thumb intoning "Are you there?" and a new thread, taken up on its facing page in thick green ink, has been allowed to bleed onto the last page, creating a sense of continuity within the narrative in spite of the shift in print process between offset and screen. The following series of pages involve a head in profile addressing another unknown "you" on questions of perception and memory. This time, pages are alternately executed in green and black ink, and allowed to impress their afterimages on their reciprocal pages. This effect creates a series of visual echoes on the pages that also reflect the reversal of orientation and text depending on whether the image is the "original" printing or its reverse afterimage that has occurred by accident or error. This is complicated by the subject matter of the head's musings, which are

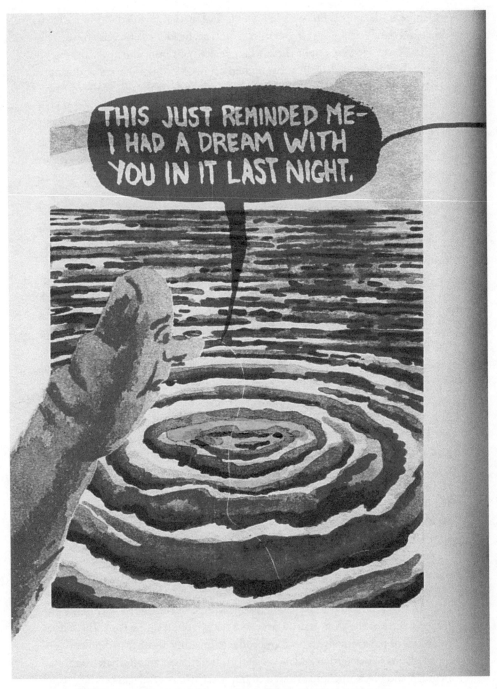

FIGURE 3.2 "This just reminded me." Conor Stechschulte, *Christmas in Prison* (Crepuscular Archives, 2016). Copyright © Conor Stechschulte. (Courtesy Conor Stechschulte.)

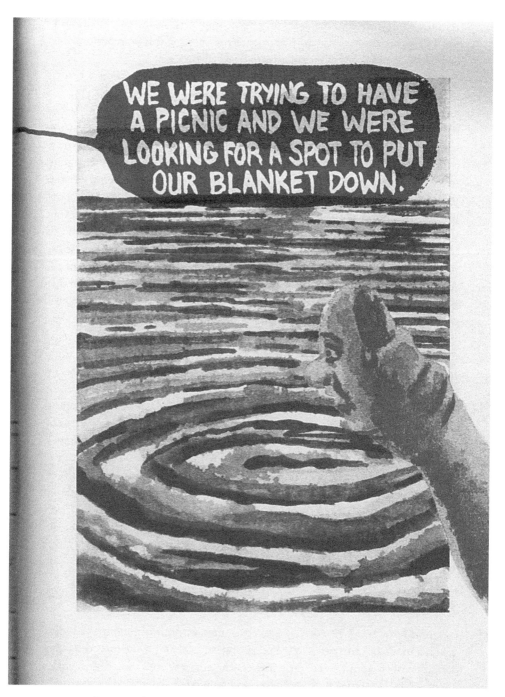

FIGURE 3.2 (*Continued*)

committed in a circular fashion, often returning to the same combinations of words and repeating them to interrogate the subject of how repetitions are embedded in processes of return, dream, and memory.

Early in the narrative the speaking head remarks, "I can see you're getting older. Breaking down. You don't feel as happy as often. Or not as often but less happy when you're happy, am I right? Do you often look in the mirror? When you do, are you looking for something there?" He continues, "You begin to wonder if perhaps the more you ask yourself if you were happy, the more you're convinced that you were. Do you try to see yourself as others do, to acquaint yourself with what they'd see? Do you make allowances for the reversal of your image? Do you consider the lighting conditions?" Several pages later, the head repeats these same words: "Do you make allowances for the reversal of your image? Do you consider the lighting conditions?" The incantatory nature of this series of sentences is enhanced by the fact that the subjects being discussed—perception, iterations, and memory—are reinforced in the materiality of the page. The words seem familiar because they have been read once before, and they have been glimpsed maybe more than once, echoed as they are in reverse on the opposite page. The memory of these words already haunts the surface of the page, printed in ghostly and fading reverse on opposing pages, faded and illegible, yet distinctly not invisible. Because of the way that the amount of ink, the alignment, and the pressure of the pull are variable every time, these particular printing techniques create final works of art that are never identical to each other. As such, the error of the imprint is incorporated into the artwork: an aesthetic of the smudge that affirms our desires to have our humanity confirmed by any means and especially by the kinds of imperfections that remind us of our imperfect humanity. In my own personal copy of the book, the second to last page of this section shows the registration mark, the mark that the printer used to verify that the color layer iterations lined up, in its upper corner on both sides of the page. That this mark exists on the same surface as colors that have fugitively sprung, seeped, and adhered with various degrees of freshness from opposite sides feels something like life, with its careful planning, its surprises, and its mistakes large and small.

Watery Recesses

The motif of water is persistent in Stechschulte's work. It functions as a hiding place, a mode of transportation, a reflecting surface, and, with even the representation of its sound, a semantic trigger. The 2011 *The Amateurs* begins with a premise that combines all these effects, and more, that are created by water. The endpapers of the floppy book are patterned to resemble the surface of water. The first page presents a handwritten account of events as a framing device for the narrative that follows. It takes the form of a letter from Dr. Morris Lime-kiln, with its year redacted, describing the discovery of a half-rotten head by the riverbank. The observer notes that the lapping of water against the neck of this object results in a series of sounds that occur in a pattern from its mouth, and the doctor and other witnesses determine to transcribe it. The document transcribes all of these observed phrases, including what cannot be made out: "We made an effort not to [indecipherable] unsociable [indecipherable] . . . necessary and unavoidable murdering. Woulda made a better bellmaker than I did a butcher. Pa told us to throw whatever wasn't useful; whatever went bad into the water, let it . . . let it. . . . Running noses, [indecipherable] in your stomach, downstairs." The narrative is framed by a series of unrelated words, the notation "[indecipherable]" where the transcriber cannot determine what is being said, and indeed most of the transcription resembles the transcription of nonsense language. Limekiln writes, "Upon close investigation I was able to recognize that these sounds were in fact language. The thing was reciting disconnected phrases in what we discovered to be a set and repeating pattern." Yet the "discovery" of meaning, when faced with the subsequent transcription, suggests that its enactment is as much an act of will from the listeners, recalling the deciphering of spirit writing popular among the nineteenth-century spiritualists, and oracle readings of all kinds. This document is accompanied with a rendering of the head by "a draftsman who works for the Cafton Picayune" who "record[s] an illustration."

The Amateurs opens with a ten-panel comic that presents the same perspectival view of the river that is rendered on the cover. The cover shows two figures in silhouette who watch two women washing clothes on the other side of the river: a red stain blooms ominously in the blue waters. Unlike the image on the cover, the initial image of the comic shows only the rocks and trees and the mild movement of the waters. At the bottom of the page, the reader is introduced to the two characters by name: Jim, whose face is visible on the page, comes up to Winston, who faces outward but whose features are obscured by shadows. At the turn of the page, Winston is shown standing to face Jim and his round and hairless head and features resemble those of the severed head that was first seen in the doctor's letter from two pages before. The two men discuss an illness that they both suffered the previous night with fevers, sweats, and numbness. As the narrative continues, the two appear to have also suffered from amnesia of some kind. As they explore the space that they enter, they seem befuddled by the emptiness of the case and shelves. Winston remarks, "I got a strange feeling . . . I feel like I can't remember what we do here. I mean, I know we're butchers an'all, but beyond that, I can't seem to remember," to which Jim confides, "I can't remember nothing either!"[15] Their frantic conversation is interrupted by the arrival of two regular customers, who ask for "the usual," which neither of the men can remember.

The men stumble through a series of actions that plunge them even deeper into disarray. After taking the women's orders, they realize that they do not have a meat supply and, after surveying the back of the property, which appears to directly abut the river, they discover a pen with two pigs and a cow in the field in the distance (Figure 3.3). Determining that they will have to

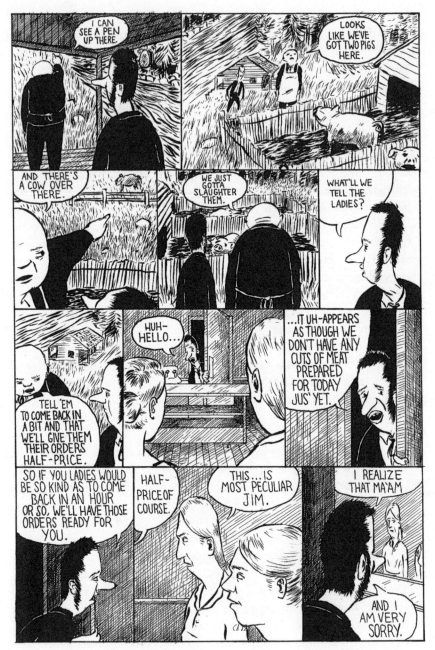

FIGURE 3.3 "We just gotta slaughter them." Conor Stechschulte, *The Amateurs* (Seattle: Fantagraphics, 2014). Copyright © Conor Stechschulte. (Courtesy Conor Stechschulte.)

slaughter these animals and butcher them, they report back to the customers and ask them to come back for their orders. The preceding pages have been printed in black-and-white, but the two-page spread after this section is represented in blue, marked with lines of varying thickness that range from thin continuous lines and broken and expressive thick brushstrokes. This spread both presents itself as visual noise and, with its intrusion in a mysterious narrative, the return of the color blue from cover and endpapers. The brushstrokes that resemble the grasses behind the butcher shop obtain a perlocutionary effect on the reader as well. Is this a static interval in the story? Is it a space that, like the spaces between panels, is meant to be read as the passage of time or action? Such questions are temporarily inspired by the insertion of these pages, but the action barrels along as the two men endeavor to slaughter a cow.

Winston's methods prove incredibly unsuccessful, and amid the violence and gore of this botched performance, Stechschulte manages to maintain a balance of slapstick comedy alongside the horror in the situation. The women return to find Winston with his face battered and teeth missing, resembling even more the head discovered at the beginning of the book. Sending the women away again, Winston endeavors to kill a pig, which also escapes his attempts. This sequence is again followed by two pages of smudged blue, this time the marks are even more abstracted, although the haphazard shapes shaded in blue feel suggestive. The story resumes with Winston returning to the house and discovering Jim preparing to slaughter the pig. The narrative continues with a kinetic force that trembles on the page: even Winston's desperate urging "C'mmon!" to the meat grinder as he struggles to produce a pound of ground chuck for the waiting customers is drawn with the irregular outlines of a hand that has repeatedly traced the outlines of each letter.[16]

The two women escape from the men and the store and, arriving at the riverbank, take off their stained dresses to wash them in the river. These are images that the reader recognizes from the cover of the book, and, on one side of the river, the women perch on rocks as their dresses dry on the tree branches behind them. Again, the pages are followed by another two-page spread of vigorous and overlapping blue, the color nearly annihilating the pages with glimpses of the white of the paper breaking through from underneath these thick brushstrokes. The men are seen again, sitting in the debris of their shop, the carnage of their recent activities now static in regularly shaped and arranged panels. The men undress as well and get into the river as Jim says to Winston, "You think they'll come back." The next spread contains the familiar blue marks on the page, but this time they are overlain with smudges and spatters of red. The horror washes downstream as the two women stand in the river and Shelly remarks, "Is the water red?"[17] The final panel of the page shows a series of limbs flowing toward the women as Martha clambers out of the river, and the next spread returns the reader to the relatively calm and regular patterned representation of water from the endpapers. This alternation between the abstract blue pages and the narrative black-and-white pages has by now acquired the perlocutionary function of preparedness for alarm: every blue interlude has been followed by increasingly chaotic and violent pages. Yet this regular blue pattern is also suggestive of a return to calm in contrast to the noise of the other blue spreads.

The irony of the denouement of *The Amateurs* is that, for all its formal regularity, it promises to be as chilling, for whereas the amnesia of Jim and Winston was both antic and gory, the story ends on what appears to be a willful amnesia on the part of one of its witnesses. Martha and Shelly are reunited at a dinner party, and the small talk between them takes a turn when Shelly brings up "that place." In response to Martha's confused response, "If you're talking about those hidden rumors that were flying around, I don't know, nor do I care to know about it," Shelly is surprised. She says, "We were there! We were there that day! Don't you remember?" Martha continues to deny any knowledge of this exchange.[18] The prolonged and miserable attempts by Jim and Winston to present the women with meat were arguably fueled by a desire to recall the social roles that they were aware belonged to them. As for the two women, on the other hand, they do not share a similar amnesiac mode: one woman has an acute memory of the events and places, whereas the other may share that knowledge privately but denies it publicly.

This conflict takes place at the site where noise prevails, where the denial is not only of sense but of even the desire to make sense. The elisions of action and the refusal of meaning making are best represented by the words preserved in the prefatorial transcription. Although the transcriber frequently reverts to writing "[indecipherable]" where words cannot be made out, the transcript contains the repeated phrase "escunte ock undersane,"[19] which resembles language cognates and incites a desire to make sense out of them since they have not been marked as indecipherable. As Jacqueline Flescher wrote half a century ago about *Alice in Wonderland*, "Language offers endless possibilities of upsetting the order of behavior, because it can establish a coherent system in a variety of ways. Provided that the backbone of such a system stand out clearly, it can act as a regulator for the most disorderly examples of behavior. The pattern of nonsense in this case is no longer one of simple reversal. It is a clash of opposing forces."[20] This reciprocal relationship between the pressure that nonsense language puts on form to allow the reader to make sense of the text acquires what Lecercle has identified as a "strong perlocutionary effect."

The perlocutionary act describes the way a text can act upon its reader, demanding an active relationship with the text in order to assemble meaning from what is presented through a process of interpretation. Lecercle argues that nonsense texts are able to summon this response because of "a powerful affect, the need to understand what not only passes understanding but also forbids understanding by withdrawing sense. The deep-seated need for meaning, which nonsense texts deliberately frustrate in order to whet it, will be accounted for in terms of the nontransparency of language, of the incapacity of natural languages reasonably to fulfil their allotted task of expression and communication. Nonsense both supports the myth of an informative and communicative language and deeply subverts it—exposes it as a myth in the pejorative sense."[21] Lecercle discusses the flourishing of nonsense literature in the Victorian period as a response to the constrictions of schooling that prescribed formal education structures. In *The Amateurs*, both textual noise and visual noise combine equally to convey a near urgency in search of a sense-making reader, "upsetting the order" as a perlocutionary gesture to the reader to make things right, to make sense out of what seems like nonsense. The result, then, is a reader who is left to ponder over the promise of "escunte ock undersane." Is it an ancient language? Is it a phonetic rendering of the otherwise sensible words of a now toothless head that cannot understand? Likewise, how to make sense of those interceding pages of blue marks that come at more frequent intervals as the reader turns the pages of the book: the marks do at times resemble the water and the brush that flanks the riverbanks. Then again, the reader is reminded that what they have so efficiently ascribed as "the water" and "the brush" are also mere renderings in ink and brush or pen stroke, apprehended and made legible through a series of cross-checks and confirmations tacitly made between artist, text, and reader. Such confirmations and accommodations are almost invisible until the opacity becomes too difficult to ignore.

Our Technologies of Reproduction

The first panel of Stechschulte's *Generous Bosom* volume 4 takes up the full width of the top half of the page, largely composed of a series of vertical lines, thick and expressively textured, which are printed in monochrome in the same turquoise ink that composes the figures and shapes that they obscure (Figure 3.4). Closer scrutiny of this panel reveals that behind these vertical stripes is a barely visible scene composed of thinner clear lines. A rectangle occupies much of the center of the panel, with a toweled figure at its center, seen from the waist up. The face is blocked by the thick vertical stripes, but the figure's hands are visible, raised at each side of her head. In the second panel that fills the bottom half of the page, half of that scene is revealed. The textured vertical stripes, it turns out, were hair, and the rectangle that they obscured was a mirror in which a young woman is cutting her fringe, or bangs. The clarity of the lines in the background, in comparison to the smudged and textured shapes in the foreground, enhances the sense of perspective and depth here, and the reader shares the point of view of the woman, scissors in her right hand, who faces her reflection in the mirror.[22] This is one instance of many that draws the reader's attention to a moment of interference, or noise, its resolution, and the realization that the noise itself is crucial to comprehension of the visual narrative. It also figures the body as complicit in generating both noise and its comprehension.

Questions about the coherence of identity and its confirmation by the affirmation of shared experience map onto the kinds of mind-body problems directly expressed in the four-volume *Generous Bosom*, which has been republished,

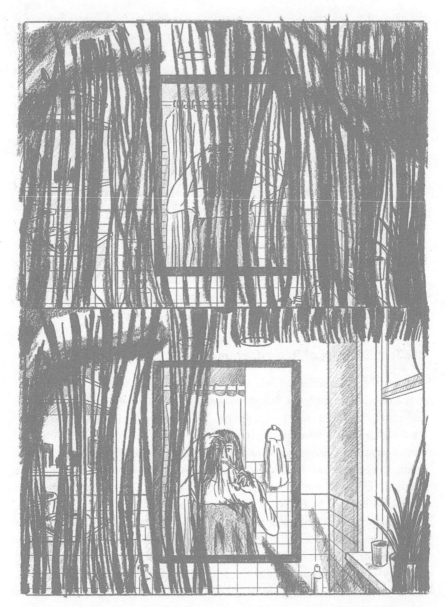

FIGURE 3.4 Bathroom. Conor Stechschulte, *Generous Bosom*, vol. 4 (London: Breakdown Press, 2021). Copyright © Conor Stechschulte. (Courtesy Conor Stechschulte.)

following its 2021 adaptation to film, as *Ultrasound* by Fantagraphics.[23] The risograph is notoriously unpredictable and introduces variations between copies so that no two copies are exactly alike. *Generous Bosom* is risograph printed like some of the comics already discussed in the sections above, which requires the application of color in individual layers, with a screen generated for each color run. Due to the particularities of this process, colors often appear slightly misaligned, and the nature of the color is susceptible to change with each page and printing, contributing to the singularity of each printed version. This process takes on more significance in the context of the complicated plot developed over the course of this series, which has been serialized by Breakdown Press since 2014 and finally came to its close seven years later in 2021. The first page of *Generous Bosom* introduces the reader to Glen, who, driving in a remote area on a rainy night, encounters car trouble that is, unbeknownst to him, the result of a premeditated trap. He seeks shelter in the house of a stranger named Art, and as the night unfolds, Art invites Glen to have sex with his wife Cyndi. This entire narrative is described visually and textually in the narrative as it occurs, in blue; but the narrative is nested within another framing narrative, printed in red, as a narration of these events by Glen to his friend in a bar.

The opening sets the tone for the rest of the series, showing how color is crucial to the storytelling process, and how events may be filtered through the unique perspective and experience of individual characters, whose truths are unreliable. The intermingling of blue and red on the page clearly delimits the separate narratives, while showing how easily they can run together. Most interestingly, the formal structures expose the ways that these characters deceive each other through their narratives, have completely different recollections of events, or operate within a fog of self-deception. This is relayed from the very beginning in the story that Glen ends up sharing with his friend in the bar. From the start the two men disagree about their memory of the weather, as Glen describes a terrible rainstorm while his friend distinctly remembers a clear sky. The fourth page introduces a blue color layer to the print. At the bottom of the page, the view is seen as if through a windshield, from the perspective of a driver on a highway. Rain pours down in vertical lines from the top of the page, and the ink is faded and sparse at the top while heavy and dark at the bottom of the page.[24] The next page is printed completely in blue, signaling to the reader that Glen's perspective is dominant, although questions remain about how this action is situated in Glen's telling. We are shown that he appears to have driven over a board embedded with nails that he cannot possibly have seen as he was driving. In the blue pages that follow, Art asks Glen to have sex with his wife. Glen approaches the bedroom door at the bottom of the page and enters the room. The page turn abruptly introduces a two-page spread in purple and green ink, showing teenage girls whose non-generous bosoms are beginning to develop. One of them is named Cyndi, who appears younger and with shorter hair.

Glen's story resumes, and he details a conversation with Cyndi in which they both express their desire to fulfill Art's request. When they begin to undress, the representation of the page takes on a different quality, suggesting that the images are drawn on a semiopaque paper that is partially reproduced in the scanning process of the original drawing. The material interference of the paper is adduced especially when wrinkles appear on the reproduced page in contrast to the wrinkles drawn on Glen's pants.[25] The extended sex scene fails after a series of mishaps. At this point, the faces of Glen and his friend reappear in red, and when Glen is asked by his friend if she was "happy with [his] performance," Glen replies, "Oh, uh, yeah, I think so . . . she woke me up later on and we did it again."[26] In the story as it is told in blue ink, after their failed first attempt, Cyndi actually rejects Glen's request to try again. This stark difference in what Glen remembers and what Glen shares is nonetheless plausible; the reader recognizes that perhaps Glen would not want to let down his machismo-fueled frat buddy conversation. Stechschulte appears to have more complicated aims, however, as subsequent volumes suggest. As for the first volume, it ends in red, the color of Glen's present tense, as Glen returns home. It is on the last page that Stechschulte reveals that the entanglement is not over: Art is following Glen.

As the story evolves, the two versions of Glen's story shift away from the binary of storytelling and real event. The version Glen remembers and the one retold for his friend turn out to both be false. We discover, along with Glen, that Art is a hypnotist; and, as the plot unspools, readers continuously revise their understanding of Glen's and the other characters' situations. It becomes clear that the traditional metrics for reliability are severely compromised. Characters are frequently shown confronting their reflections in mirrors, where the contrast between self and image is marked. In one stark example, where the disjunction of reality and perception is most evident, a visibly pregnant character changes clothes in front of a mirror, and her reflection in the mirror has a flat stomach. The gazes of the people around her suggest that they see the green version of herself, whereas she sees the blue version in the mirror and does not understand why those around her look judgmentally at her[27] (Figure 3.5). This puzzling disjunction highlights how the central anxieties of being in the world are not always in fact aroused by a conflict between how things are and how they appear to be. Neither does it suggest that the only significant problem is one of distinguishing between original and copy.

Stechschulte's comics are not interested in showing how we are incapable of discerning distinctions between two things or two states. Rather, these works emphasize that we are highly capable of noticing differences, and are in fact primed to do so. The more difficult matter is that we absolutely cannot be certain, once we have identified two distinct entities, which one is credible: how do we know which is the so-called true state, and which the false? Most frequently in *Generous Bosom*, as in life, the problem of deception lies in other people, but that problem can be resolved only by reports or testimony from the very same thing: other people. Our reading of *Generous Bosom* is based on emphasizing the processes through which we puzzle through whether truth can be determined, whether such efforts are worthwhile, and what we are to do if the answer to both of those questions is no.

In the case of Stechschulte's works, the artifacts of reproduction themselves— whether physical or otherwise—are crucial. These artifacts have been grouped

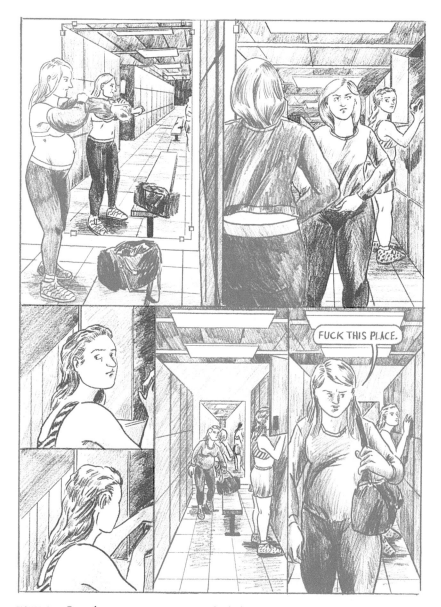

FIGURE 3.5 Gym changing room. Conor Stechschulte, *Generous Bosom*, vol. 3 (London: Breakdown Press, 2017). Copyright © Conor Stechschulte. (Courtesy Conor Stechschulte.)

together in this chapter under the general term "noise" used in the sense of interference. In the case of *Generous Bosom*, however, "noise" describes the very specific examples of sonic interference within the diegetic world: a mysterious machine that distorts sound waves into specific frequencies appears to trigger hypnotic states in patients. Noise also functions in Stechschulte's medium-specific uses of onomatopoeia to communicate sounds that are not spoken by the characters. Additionally, it functions, as discussed in the previous sections, extratextually in the actual visual presentation of the print process, with the unplanned striations and textures that emerge as visual noise on the printed pages. We are again reminded of Bill Brown's distinction between an object and a thing: we are used to seeing (and perhaps also hearing and feeling) through objects. We do this because there are "codes by which our interpretive attention makes them meaningful, because there is a discourse of objectivity that allows us to use them as facts."[28] Objects assert themselves as things at the very moment that they stop working for us, so that thingness is a word that describes and defines the relationship between ourselves and the object. Thingness, in these cases, is marked by the doubt we develop about that relationship. The thingness brought about in *Generous Bosom* is summoned by the obstacle to the reader's desire to make meaning from the text, as in seeing past the visual noise of the hair on that first page of volume 4.

What does it mean to make a comic about noise? I have argued in this chapter that noise is a necessary artifact, one that is frequently also "seen through" in the sense of the discourse of objectivity that allows us to use them as facts. By emphasizing noise visually and with onomatopoeia, Stechschulte reminds the reader of the many instances in which noise both visual and aural is read "through." Walter Benjamin's arguments about art in an age of technological reproduction identified photographs and films as examples of how reproduction based on process is designed separately and expressly for the consumed end product. This is separate from, and unlike the processes of making, a so-called original work, which is bound by its time- and place-specific aura.[29] Instead, the process-oriented reproduction highlights those aspects made possible by its technologies: innovating new accessibility to the eye and bringing the work to wider distributive networks.

The second volume of *Generous Bosom* begins with four panels printed in teal, each the width of the page, showing a rooftop and the tops of trees surrounding it, as this is the volume that most fully develops the effect that noise can have on people and their perceptions. There are no words on the page, but many letters that present an onomatopoeic sound are represented by variations on "kshshhhkshk" across the tops of the panel.[30] The reader may surmise that the sounds are the soughing of the wind in the trees, but the onomatopoeic renderings on the overleaf use the "ssshhk" sound to represent the cutting of hair as well. The next four pages are printed in layers of green and purple suggesting, by the established logic of the comic, a separate temporal and spatial story plane. The first two involve the character named Shannon, who was introduced on a single page in volume 1 stuffing her bra with toilet paper in front of a mirror.[31] The second two show a teenaged Cyndi, and neither of these sections make any attempt to contextualize themselves in the initial pages of the book. Instead, the story resumes in its teal printing to show the interior of Glen's apartment and the "shkshk" sounds enter the apartment along with some light through the closed blinds of a window. These sounds are interrupted by more onomatopoeia: the thumping of Art banging on Glen's door. Art proceeds to show Glen a videotape and to the accompaniment of "ssshhhh" suggestive of the running water of a shower, tells Glen that Cyndi is pregnant.

When Glen and Cyndi eventually meet to discuss the situation, the conversation in the speech bubbles suddenly begins to break apart with visual interference that conveys the inaudible as well. Fifty pages into the second volume of *Generous Bosom*, the reader learns that all of Glen's and Cyndi's movements, activities, and conversations are under surveillance. The conversation appears to be recorded in a van.[32] Stranger still, the reader is reintroduced to a conversation that occurred on pages 46 and 47, but now these sentences are being spoken on pages 64 and 65 within what appears to be a lab facility in a cavernous building. On the final pages of this volume, Glen waits in an observation room to have this conversation with Shannon. While the mysteries seem to have multiplied— Glen is in a wheelchair and Cyndi no longer pregnant—the third volume reveals that Glen and Cyndi have been subjects in a mind-control experiment initiated by Art at an earlier stage and that now incorporates their continued observation in this facility. The reader learns that there never was a car breakdown in a rainstorm, and that Glen's seduction began as part of a regular shakedown of audience members through hypnotism. By the time we reach the fourth volume, however, we discover that the small operation has been absorbed by a larger private corporation seeking to develop the technological processes originally invented by Art to be marketed to government defense contractors. We learn that Art has independently continued his work, with far fewer resources, in order to take advantage of teenage girls and, more recently, to solve the domestic problems of individuals, including a politician running for senate whose mistress is inconveniently pregnant.

Noise plays a significant role in the intricate plot throughout the series: in the third volume Glen is asked repeatedly to identify what he hears, and sounds are represented by a series of diagonal lines, circles, and inverted Vs.[33] When Glen suddenly announces that he recalls an image of Cyndi not pregnant, the lab director urgently tells his technicians to "mark that frequency."[34] Noise in *Generous Bosom* is not simply used to mark an interruption but is figured as a tool that can alter the perceptions of these characters. The reproduction of sound through the various boxes that the hypnotist Arthur has placed in the homes of his subjects is being used to alter their memories and perceptions. As Shannon tries to explain in the fourth volume, Cyndi and Glen are "test subjects in a number of experiments into the use of audio frequencies for hypnosis."[35] When Cyndi finally distinguishes reality from simulated perception with Shannon's help, it is through her memory of a sound that Shannon had recorded and "given" to her. The tools of technological reproduction are uncannily linked to the control of biological reproduction in Stechschulte's text. Through the consideration of whether basic corporeal markers of growth, generation, and reproduction may be manipulated through tricks of the mind, the comic asks readers to consider whether our beliefs in technological reproduction can form and shape our beliefs about biological reproduction as well.

People Are Black Boxes

The fact that Arthur conveys the news of Cyndi's pregnancy to Glen with the use of an outmoded form of video recording technology is particularly potent. Arthur arrives at Glen's home with a VHS tape in hand and the two men go to a thrift store to buy a VCR, then attach it to Glen's television to view this evidence.[36] This scenario is organized around anachronism, which is another preoccupation with time and sequence that permeates the series. The intensity at which technological innovation and invention becomes outmoded is highlighted by the frequent references to such modes of communication: the VHS, the various iterations of mobile phones, CDs, and digital sound files are all transmitters of time as well as markers of time. The ubiquity of technology's intrusions in lives is muddled, and notions of will and accountability are likewise complicated by the length of time these so-called human subjects have been controlled. At the end of the series, when Shannon objects to "priming" Glen to comply with their experiments, she is told, "These subjects have been primed for months—years in the case of the female." This rationalization is enough for the scientists to agree to adjust to a sound frequency that puts Glen into an unconscious state. The experimenters have become entangled by their experiment: whereas they once argued that the subjects were able to devise their own narratives to explain any situation, they are now confronted with recalcitrant subjects who can identify and question the noise. They resort to inducing the subjects to receptivity, and Glen is told to "be eager to participate in today's session. You know that the more you cooperate, the better your chances for recovery are."[37]

Shannon is increasingly frustrated and suspicious of the ethical position of her employers. She had initially signed on to the project because of her belief that it was intended to treat victims of PTSD. She independently explores the facility, letting herself down to the lowest level of sub-basements in the facility where she is confronted with a padlocked door. *Generous Bosom* could not be more different from *My Favorite Thing Is Monsters*, and yet here too the female character who has fast become the most heroic also confronts a subterranean locked door. Ferris's graphic narrative is an exploration of a queer girl growing up in 1960s Chicago and the way that the ghosts of the past continue to shape her developing future. Stechschulte's narrative explores a contemporary landscape of scientists who use sound waves to induce hypnotic states in subjects. Those subjects participate in their own self-deception by generating ingenious narratives to explain away even the most aberrant events and situations. Both texts site their explorations within the context of a more universal transformation: sexual maturation and its imminent hazards.

The rapidity of technology is thus juxtaposed against those that cannot be rushed or simulated. In the case of *Generous Bosom*, the way that things can change with the simple flip of a switch or the removal of a plug from an electrical outlet is contrasted to the bodily mechanisms that dictate their own schedules and can neither be hurried nor slowed down. People are, like Art's mysterious machine, no different from black boxes. We may gather conclusions based on what is observable from their output and input, but the inner workings are just guesses: stochastic meaning making over time. "Reliable" markers of time are so often suggested in *Generous Bosom*. The most pressing question of this series is how we can judge the truth of any given situation, so eager as we are to understand our surface observations for indicators of what resides within.

Why are we so ready to do this when we must already know that we have access only to exteriors? Are some markers more reliable than others? Here we are given the option to consider a few: hair growth, for example, which is a measure of time that can only be manipulated in one direction. We may cut hair off, as many characters do to mark a shift in their identity; but we cannot hurry its incremental growth. Does this concept of measuring bodies by biological metrics take its most perverse form in the idea of the growing fetus? As the plot develops, the reader recognizes that there is a *problem*, on a definite timeline, that has been created by the pregnancy of a politician's mistress. Art is attempting to address this problem through a complicated series of hypnotisms generated, it seems, to reallocate the unwanted pregnancy to a fabricated story involving Cyndi. He has created a sort of mental surrogacy via Cyndi's phantom pregnancy, and an adoption engineered in a fake office with an unsuspecting real couple. He leaves the narrativizing conclusions to the participants themselves: they will fill in the blanks according to their own desires and interpretive modes.

Nearly a century after Benjamin's essay, we live in an age when crypto art and NFTs are sold at auction for millions of dollars, demonstrating the value of something not only non-fungible, but non-tangible, that is indistinguishable to the naked eye from its duplicates. As with other objects and transactions that we have learned to "see through" to the extent that we rarely question their systems of valuation, these recent renditions of version control, provenance, and originality lay bare some basic facts about value at a time when tracing an origin is no longer subject to interpretation nor vulnerable to hoaxes: lines of code obviate that potential and make contemporary understandings of connoisseurship irrelevant. They also make the physical object irrelevant. Trust is moderated and verified by unfalsifiable computer code, such that value, especially in relation to the idea of a unique original, is laid bare as the product of a mutual accord between parties. Yet, simultaneously, what is the "thing" that is afforded value? The very idea of original art takes form as an agreement between parties enforced by mutual acknowledgment, so that art is based neither on ritual nor on politics, as Benjamin wrote, but on affect, where the accord between parties is its own aesthetic category.

Reproduction is central to the problems that constitute Stechschulte's mysterious plots, exposing the messy constructions of human identity and how people resort to all kinds of apparatuses to facilitate their understanding of shared reality. Thus the interest in noise, which transmits information by bearing intentional or accidental marks, artifacts, and distortions. The artifacts of the processes of reproduction, usually carefully corrected out of reproductions, to generate as close a likeness to the original as possible, are instead emphasized in these comics. *Generous Bosom* is about a man significantly named Art, whose vocation involves the manipulation of mechanical reproduction to create new storyworlds. In the case of the book, noise itself is manipulated, as Art plays sounds through a mysterious box that induce hypnotic states. Later, he uses an outdated VHS tape to show Glen that Cyndi has become pregnant from an unsuccessful one-night stand. Noise in comics cannot be transmitted aurally but relies on language and visual presentation. Stechschulte's use of onomatopoeia describes noise powerful enough to change the listener, and the perceiver's view of who the person is. The noise is without meaning, yet it is crucial to the construction of meaning and truth in the worlds of the characters. This, and other mediated forms, reveal the hazards of the way we unquestioningly manage to see through blurs in photoreproductions, audio background noise, pixilation, frozen screens, and other varieties of noise. We may even rely on that noise to assure ourselves that the experience is authentic. We look at each other at these moments, reading those little boxes as containing a real person from another time and space, not even suspecting that they might not in fact be there.

4

If You See Something
Say Something

Nick Drnaso's *Sabrina*

Sabrina is missing.

Her name is on the cover of Nick Drnaso's book, as is her face. Yet, it is her absence that defines the experience of reading Drnaso's critically acclaimed 2018 graphic novel, *Sabrina*. *Sabrina* was praised by the author Zadie Smith, who effused on the back cover, "Sabrina is the best book—in any medium—I have read about our current moment. It is a masterpiece. . . . It scared me. I loved it."[1] As the first comic to be acknowledged alongside novels with its nomination to the Man Booker Prize longlist, it further cements the expansion of what constitutes and how we define literature.[2] Drnaso's book is by no means the first comic to grapple with weighty issues, to wield complex narrative structures, or to demonstrate the extraordinary capacities of the text image form. But it does stand out as an exemplar in a field that has been steadily growing over the past decades. Drnaso's book is novelistic in its ambition and achievement. It is an extraordinary book even among the many extraordinary books that have emerged in the past decade of this flourishing field, nurtured by small publishers whose investment in these works of art have yielded a number of paradigm-shifting works. *Sabrina* is concerned with the disappearance of the title character, who vanishes without a trace instead of returning from work one day. The beginning of the book introduces us to Sabrina shortly before her disappearance, doing mundane things like brushing her teeth, sleeping in her childhood bedroom as she housesits for her parents, chatting with her sister over a crossword puzzle, and washing dishes at the sink. The reader's only direct experience of Sabrina while she is alive appears in the first ten pages of the two-hundred-page book. *Sabrina* pivots after those pages, and for the remainder of the book it follows the people who are left behind to look for her, to wait for her return, or to contemplate her absence. The idea of Sabrina is thus present throughout the book, but her actual corporeal presence is largely deferred or else afforded space in other characters' memories or reactions.

The bulk of the book follows Sabrina's sister Sandra and Sabrina's boyfriend Teddy and explores the multiple ways that the bereft cope with Sabrina's absence. Teddy leaves Illinois to stay with a friend, a member of the U.S. Air Force named Calvin who is stationed in Colorado Springs. Sandra stays at home, supporting her parents, helping with the investigation, and waiting for news of her sister. About a third of the way into the book, a series of duplicate videotapes arrive at various news outlets, depicting an execution-style video. While the reader is spared a direct representation of images from the video, we do see the reactions of those who view the VHS and, later, those who watch the leaked video that has been reproduced and disseminated online. There is no doubt—though we do not see it—that the video shows Sabrina's murder. She has been kidnapped and killed by a stranger, a neighbor named Timmy Yancey, who has subsequently killed himself. Upon the release of the video and the increased exposure of the story as one among many stories of disaster, loss, and violence, Sabrina becomes increasingly the property of media news cycles and, consequently, the subject of discussion among well-meaning strangers, conspiracy theorists, internet sites, and talk radio hosts. Ironically, her absence generates her proliferation in the minds and imaginations of so many others, in what Elisabeth Bronfen would describe as an example of "how a woman, by virtue of dying, materializes earlier aesthetic renditions."[3]

Sabrina serves also to remind us that such aesthetic imaginings are capable of obviating the horrible violence that is done to a physical body when such aesthetic imaginings occur. Drnaso is keenly sensitive to these issues, and his book seems determined to examine the violence of the processes of interpretation rather than the violent details of Sabrina's abduction and subsequent murder. Just as much as it examines our appraisals of recordings and reproductions of violence, Drnaso's book carefully articulates the ways that readers are all too ready to fill in the blanks based on expectations of what will—and should—happen. This careful attention infuses his storytelling throughout the book, from the composition of the narrative to the faded and desaturated color palette of its rigidly arranged and uniform grids.

This chapter explores how *Sabrina* articulates an ethics of surface reading that calls upon the reader to contemplate how and why we need to be better readers. Examples coalesce around ideas of the frame, and how graphic narratives highlight the framed and necessarily fragmented compositions that we, like the characters in *Sabrina*, have grown dangerously accustomed to reading as the full picture. This analysis focuses on the development of a reader's frame preferences: it shows us how we are trained to read framed narratives through exposure, and then reward ourselves for reading according to those preferences. This effect is visualized through the behaviors and activities of the characters in the book, but it is also enacted through the behaviors and activities that it draws from us, the readers of the book *Sabrina*. In this way, the *Sabrina* text theorizes itself by insisting that we interrogate our own reading and interpretive practices as they are revealed in our critique of the characters in the book.

This chapter and the next are concerned specifically with books that use the perfect copies of mechanical reproduction to examine the hazards of believing in and relying on perfect copies. It asks whether we have become too accustomed to accepting versions of ourselves and others in these flat and reproduced forms, thinking of them as interchangeable with the original and then proceeding accordingly. The first three chapters examined the intensely handmade, materially complicated books that announced the unique hand and mind that manufactured the comic. Those kinds of books, even though they are produced as reproduced copies, have found formal ways to maintain an individuality that resists and, to a great degree, overcomes the flattening of the reproduction process. This chapter and the following chapter on Evens intone a cautionary note on the impulse to allocate too much power to the effects of the "primal immediacy of the hand-drawn to reemerge as a form of witness."[4] To be sure, the drawn line can often create "an enveloping, idiosyncratic world of expression that can be powerful for witness."[5] If we concede its exceptional power, we must also acknowledge that the hand-drawn line that can "forge a personal connection with readers" can just as easily be used to deceive and manipulate.[6]

As *Sabrina* shows, the anonymously delivered file, and the audio and video recording, even tempered with the knowledge that it may have been manipulated via computer, has an equal power to move, inspire, and perhaps even control other minds. As legal scholar Danielle Keats Citron wrote about *Sabrina*,

> When video and audio content surfaces online . . . it may go viral. Cognitive biases help explain why certain content grabs our attention. We have a visceral reaction to audio and visual recordings. Audio and video allow us to become firsthand witnesses to events, eliminating the need to trust what others say happened. Their accuracy is self-evident—we trust our eyes and ears to tell us the truth. People will be especially likely to like, link, and share video and audio content if it is provocative and salacious. Human beings are naturally attractive to negative and novel information. Researchers have found that online hoaxes spread ten times faster than accurate stories because they are more novel than real news. According to the study, people—not bots—were responsible for sharing the fake news.[7]

These observations do not appear particularly controversial to anyone with an internet connection and any kind of news feed, social media or otherwise. They do serve to temper an impulse to assume that the hand-drawn or handmade is somehow more sincere or capable of generating a greater degree of empathic commitment from its reader.

As much as we valorize the agency given to a reader who has the liberty to make meaning in the gaps and gutters between panels, to conjure into being that which is not visibly there, we must remain aware of those equally hazardous counterparts of seeing things that are not there. This is especially troubled territory when we make claims about meaning in diametric opposition to fill in a silence or elision too hastily, or even maliciously. As George Butte puts it, "Representation claims to recover *presence*, while confessing to its artificiality as a kind of absence. The representation of subjectivities especially makes claims to presence because subjects, even in texts, famously have a way of desiring, of *intending*, and of focusing action and thought on the future. Hence the ease with which readers, in what has been seen as a kind of naïveté, discuss 'characters' as if they were more than marks on the page, with histories, a subconscious, sometimes even a sequel."[8] In the case of *Sabrina*, where the subject is not only a fictional character but also a character who, within the space of the graphic novel, is wholly absent from the story, due to her disappearance, this question of the subject who must be found acquires a great deal of weight.

Missing Persons

The wordless opening of *Sabrina* immediately engages the reader in the familiar perspective of the voyeur. The top half of the page shows Sabrina viewed from the front, which the reader assumes, upon looking at the bottom half of the page, must be the view from the window, as the next frame directly beneath the half-page image shows her standing at the window at the sink. This view is already troubling, as the voyeurism involved is double. The paratextual reading practice is embedded in our understanding of the surface reader, who brings an unpredictably particular nexus of knowledge to the text. Describing readers of Proust's *In Search of Lost Time*, Genette argues that "most readers of *A la recherche du Temps perdu* are aware of the two biographical facts of Proust's part-Jewish ancestry and his homosexuality. Knowledge of those two facts inevitably serves as a paratext to the pages of Proust's work that deal with those two subjects. I am not saying that people must know those facts; I am saying only that people who do know them read Proust's work differently from people who do not and that anyone who denies the difference is pulling our leg."[9] There are certain paratextual conclusions that may be tentatively taken for granted with *Sabrina*. This includes the reader's awareness that something bad awaits Sabrina, even if it may not yet be clear what that might be or when it might occur, from having heard about the text, from reading reviews, or even from the fact that the cover of the book features a large billboard-sized image of a young woman with the silhou-ettes of human figures in the foreground, gathered as if for an outdoor movie viewing, and the title bearing only a first name.

The opening pages prompt a reaction of suspenseful anxiety formed by the paratextual visual elements commonly associated with ominous scenes in the genre of horror films. We are primed by this visual history, so that our anxi-ety is activated when encountering a view from behind of a young woman alone in a house at night (Figure 4.1). The subsequent image of the woman looking down an empty hallway and then followed, again from behind, into ill-lit rooms only enhances the foreboding mood inherent in the scene. Sabrina walks from room to room, looking for something or someone, and these movements increase the tension from frame to frame. The panels show her alternately look-ing behind a shower curtain, in a closet, and under the bed. It is therefore a great relief to the reader to find that, after Sabrina explores the typical clichéd hiding places of monsters and other predators, there is no monster under the bed. As Drnaso soon reveals, she is not in fact the quarry, but the hunter. She has only been looking for the cat. This relief is almost immediately undermined by Sabrina's surprise—a figure suddenly appears in the window.[10] Again, this is a false alarm: it is only Sabrina's sister Sandra. This series of switches, in per-spective, in tension, and in suspicion, is a neat and formally based introduction to the themes of *Sabrina*, which largely center on the ways that we produce our knowledge and our sense of plausibility by combining surface details with structural frameworks that we have previously developed and stored in our memory.

That process of interpretation is sometimes described as a "frame preference." The frame preference is similar to the "confirmation bias" that, in psychological terms, describes subjects' inclination to accept, and subsequently proceed in accord with, information consistent with their already held views. The frame as an abstract system of fixed structures into which smaller items may be inter-changed or successfully substituted is most succinctly defined by the computer and cognitive scientist Marvin Minsky, who wrote "A Framework for Represent-ing Knowledge." Minsky explains,

When one encounters a new situation . . . one selects from memory a structure called a *Frame*. This is a remembered framework to be adapted to fit reality by changing details as necessary. A *frame* is a data-structure for representing a stereotyped situation, like being in a certain kind of living room, or going to a child's birthday party. Attached to each frame are several kinds of informa-tion. Some of this information is about how to use the frame. Some is about what one can expect to happen next. Some is about what to do if these expectations are not confirmed. We can think of a frame as a network of nodes and relations. The "top levels" of a frame are fixed, and represent things that are always true about the supposed situation. The lower levels have many

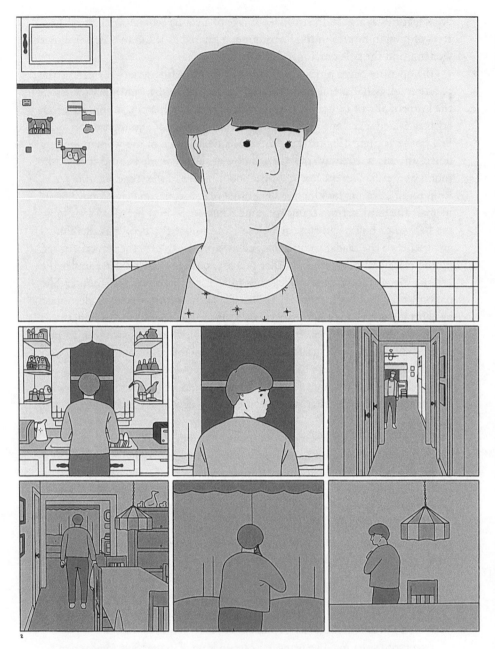

FIGURE 4.1 Kitchen. Nick Drnaso, *Sabrina* (Montreal: Drawn & Quarterly, 2016), 3. Copyright © Nick Drnaso. (Used with permission from Drawn & Quarterly.)

terminals—"slots" that must be filled by specific instances or data. Each terminal can specify conditions its assignments must meet. . . . Much of the phenomenological power of the theory hinges on the inclusion of expectations and other kinds of presumptions. A frame's terminals are normally already filled with "default" assignments.[11]

We take in new information and process it according to already-established frames in our memories and adjust them according to their characteristics. In much the same way, *Sabrina* can be understood as training readers by showing them a system of frames from which to proceed, and, having installed them, guiding the reader within the limited possibilities that they define.[12] As readers, we may strain against these structures, posing alternate interpretations or possibilities; but we do not tend to reject the structures themselves and work within them instead. This means that such texts make us alert to shifts that might affirm the meaning we expect to find, and we take pains to pay attention to subtle shifts in perspective and to the parallelisms that become crucial ways of sourcing information through the book's pages.

Manfred Jahn proposes borrowing this frame-centered model for narratological interpretation, pointing out that Minsky's frame theory had potential application to the study of literature. As for the use of frame theory for narrative situations, he nonetheless turns to an example from visual culture to make the point. Jahn introduces an optical trick, called the "Necker cube," that causes the reader to fluctuate between two different understandings of a drawn shape, which may appear as either an incomplete rectangular shape or a "solid" version of the shape in a different orientation. Resembling the "duck or rabbit" optical illusion, the cube is not simultaneously the two images in its viewer's attention: one interpretation holds until it switches to the other in the viewer's mind. Jahn points to this example as analogous to the ways that a reader interprets data and reaches conclusions after navigating the existing information. Jahn discusses the "working of primacy and recency preferences on an ambiguous (multifunctional, protean) data sequence."[13] The development of frame preferences can provide a descriptive vocabulary for the "moment of sudden reversal when the mind switches from one interpretation to another."[14]

Jahn's meticulous analysis brings together the work of narratologists and the frame preference model borrowed from Minsky to assert that it is typically "almost impossible to pinpoint the exact spot where the switch toward the figural orientation occurs."[15] Putting a point on this switch of perception is relevant to Jahn because it prioritizes the analysis of "the cognitive mechanics of reading."[16] He concludes that "despite the fact that recourse to readers, readers' intuitions, and reading plays an important role in narratological argument, the contribution of mainstream narratology to a dedicated cognitive approach is meager and often counterproductive. In the light of cognitive frames and preferences, much of mainstream narratology is preoccupied with bottom-up analyses."[17] *Sabrina* offers a reading experience that concerns precisely that interplay between the frame-determined and data-driven cognition in the plotting of its narrative and, consequently, its reader's experience. Cognitive preferences that are shaped and managed by recognized frames are of course an efficient structure for relaying information. Because *Sabrina* offers its own commentary on the ubiquity of framed narratives in its plot and in its formal structures, it offers a series of beguiling moments where the way that data are read can be pinpointed to mark such moments of reversal in interpretation. The drawn page enhances the reader's intuition that everything in the frame is there for a reason. There is intentionality behind the drawn line—unlike the photograph or film, which captures everything within its frame—and it purports to represent a collusion of intentionality between the artist's eye, the artist's hand, and the surface of the page. The reader's progress through the book demonstrates the illocutionary power of the text: following the characters as they make their way through the proliferation of data that define them as both interpreting subjects and interpretable objects.

Boundary Technicians

Toward the end of the book, the character Calvin Wrobel walks through a bank of computer servers at his place of work, through a vertiginously presented series of vertical towers that stretch into seeming infinity, accentuated by the regular ceiling tiles that proceed overhead. The very reproducibility of the identical ceiling tiles and lights become the frames among which we may find "readable" information. When we do pay attention to these identical ceiling tiles and lights, we notice that their repetitions are broken up by small anomalous shapes. These are the tiny squares of surveillance cameras occurring at intervals in the upper edges. As a result of this discovery, and alongside our knowledge that where one spot is under surveillance surely there are many others, we begin to look for other cameras (Figure 4.2).[18] The alertness to surveillance, to which we were previously unconscious, now becomes one of our frame preferences. We may behave differently, knowing that we are being watched, than when we proceeded through our lives unaware of the possibility of the watchful eye of cameras. Surveillance, like the earlier iterations that began with the opening pages (Figure 4.1), is the central conceit of my reading of *Sabrina*. We as readers are rewarded for noticing the anomalous detail that attracts our attention because of its anomaly, and that alertness shapes the way that we proceed through the text. That alertness to seeing things, sparked by the disruption of the ordinary that begins with Sabrina's disappearance, makes detectives of everyone, including the readers of the book. The reader is initiated, through the reading process, into a competency of reading that is cultivated by practices that are rewarded in the reading, such as finding the differences between like things and reading patterns that occur amid repetitions and empty spaces.[19]

Calvin's job at Peterson Air Force Base is as a "boundary technician." As he explains to Teddy, his job involves protecting virtual walls, potential security breaches, and weaknesses in the system. The two share a booth in a restaurant, and Calvin explains, "We have our networks, right? You know, sensitive information is being exchanged electronically across the globe. I look for weaknesses in the system, update firewalls, investigate possible security breaches."[20] The majority of the panels on this page depict the dialogue between Calvin and

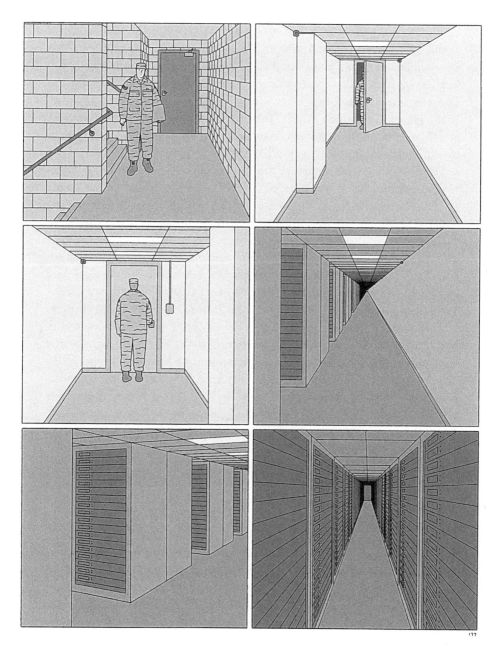

FIGURE 4.2 "There's a problem with a server." Nick Drnaso, *Sabrina* (Montreal: Drawn & Quarterly, 2016), 177. Copyright © Nick Drnaso. (Used with permission from Drawn & Quarterly.)

Teddy, following a shot-reverse-shot style that supplements the back-and-forth of the dialogue. Interspersed between these are panels that show the television screen mounted on the wall behind Calvin's seat. The reader is directed to follow Teddy's glances at the screen during pauses in the conversation. The screen transitions from advertising "Black Friday Deals" to a news story about a vote in Congress and cuts in spending.[21] These panels no doubt give information, too, and the quiet transitions between them signify the ways that information comes to us through various pathways just like these, which we may pause on for brief moments until we determine that the data contained within them is not relevant or necessary to the story at hand. Does a "Black Friday" sign tell us any more than the fact that it is late November? Are these news reports freighted with meaning, or are they simply the background noise of our everyday reality?

The answer to these questions is, of course, that we do not know until after the fact. We wait for that important piece of data that creates that shift in knowledge, that shift in perception that may bring it into sensibility. As Gary Saul Morson has written, real life and certain works of narrative recognize these shifts as happening in real time in our lives, and the "future is experienced and the present possesses real presentness, in which the weight of chance and choice may lead to many different outcomes."[22] Morson calls this sideshadowing, a term that "conveys the sense that actual events might just as well not have happened. In an open universe, the illusion is inevitability itself. Alternatives always abound, and, more often than not, what exists need not have existed. Something else was possible, and sideshadowing is used to create a sense of that 'something else.'"[23] *Sabrina* engages insistently with the sense of the sideshadow, reminding us that we must, to some degree, allow these moments to simply be background noise, lest we allow ourselves to become overwhelmed with information of all kinds of relative value in our efforts toward anticipation and foreshadowing.

The previous chapters have focused on reproductions that, even if unusual or radical in form, follow a progression of causality that is temporally consistent. There is an "original" and, after it, there are reproductions. The case of the boundary technician and, indeed, the case of the retrospective explanations of Sabrina's disappearance and death have more to do with a kind of anticipatory reproduction, a reproduction of knowledge that is not based on an original, because the original does not exist, or, according to adherents of this logic, has not yet come to be. To have a career as a boundary technician is to spend one's days waiting for what is not yet there to begin to manifest, and to put a stop to it before it does. The actual daily practice of cultivating this preparedness is repetitive and dull. The men spend their time staring at the screens on the computers in their cubicles or arrayed on a wall. When they aren't working, they are still staring at screens playing video games with each other, or they are scanning social media feeds and their full complement of advertisements and clickbait news stories.

When Calvin invites Teddy to live with him following Sabrina's disappearance, he points out Cheyenne Mountain on their way to his house from the airport: "That's where they built the NORAD complex in the sixties. There's a bunker deep under there with a cafeteria, convenience store, gym, and chapel that can withstand a full-blown nuclear attack."[24] Calvin works at the Peterson Base nearby, from Monday to Friday, from four until midnight.[25] One of the first things that the men have to do is complete a survey upon arriving at work. The survey asks the men to answer questions that include how many hours of sleep they received the night before, how many alcoholic beverages they consumed, and whether they are experiencing depression or thoughts of suicide. They are asked to rate their overall mood and stress level on a scale of one to five and to elaborate on anything in their personal lives that may affect their duty, and whether they would like to speak with a clinical psychologist.[26] While Calvin logs average responses in the first survey seen by the reader, on September 11, the survey logged the day after Teddy's first night in his home shows tentative movements toward heightened stress and lowered mood.[27] By the time we see another of these surveys, Sabrina's death has been confirmed and her murderer's execution and confession video has been discovered and leaked on to the internet.[28] The November 8 survey reflects answers at the extremes of the range.[29] The numbers begin to approach neutral data points a few days later, when a new story begins to trend, usurping the stories and speculative chatter about Sabrina's murder.[30] In the final evaluation survey shown in *Sabrina*, logged a month after the most extreme survey of November 8, the more optimistic Calvin marks an average night's sleep, the highest possible score for mood, and the lowest possible score for stress.

Taken all together like this, the collected surveys become data points that tell a narrative over a three-month period beginning in early September and ending in early December. The variations and the changes are what make the plot notable, and the impulse—from the government as well as for the reader—to weave a narrative from these data points is at work here. This impulse is what Jacques Derrida described pointedly as "a demand for narrative, a violent putting-to-the-question, an instrument of torture working to wring the narrative out of one as if it were a terrible secret, in ways that can go from the most archaic police methods to refinements for making (and even letting) one talk that are unsurpassed in neutrality and politeness, that are most respectfully medical, psychiatric, and even psychoanalytic."[31] The imbrication of violence and torture with the clinical detachment of the scientific, under the authoritative cause of medical, psychiatric, and psychoanalytic analysis, is apposite. These are the methods of governments and other apparatuses of social control, which shroud their activities in the name of protection and care, to the extent that any methods for wringing out the sought narrative can be tolerated. Drnaso's book lingers on the toll that these systems take. Living as they are in the shadow of 9/11, the government employees perpetrating these acts of watchful surveillance equally submit themselves as subjects of surveillance in a prolonged state of exception that has become the status quo. They submit themselves to the anonymous gaze of little cameras mounted at intervals in the ceiling where they work, and they submit themselves to psychiatric surveys that assess their level of "risk" to themselves and to others. As the book painstakingly shows, these same patterns adhere to all social relations. In their solitude, scrolling through webpages, individuals are not just consumers of information but become data: their patterns of activity are collected and interpreted, and repackaged and served up to them to attract even more of their attention. Online activity produces aggregate data based on views, and attention, good or bad, is monetizable.

An anticipator of things that may go wrong, Calvin keeps a weapon and emergency aid kits locked away in a neighborhood of identical homes filled with people who are all equally and tirelessly preparing for what cannot be prepared for. Even though Calvin had claimed earlier that it was odd that the United States maintains this vast bunker hidden beneath a mountain, he too has his own version of emergency preparedness, if not on as large a scale. On Teddy's first night in his house, Calvin shows him his guns. As he explains, "I only bought them to protect my family. If anything ever happens in the house, come get me and I'll take care of it."[32] On his first night in Calvin's apartment, Teddy has told him that if he finds Sabrina's murderer he will kill him. He continues, "And if he's dead . . . and she's dead, I'm just going to kill myself. That's the truth."[33] Following the news of Sabrina's murder and the leak of the video online, although Calvin assures the detectives who interview him that he does not think that Teddy is a threat to himself or to others, he still attempts preventative measures.

Back in his home, Calvin tries to prevent Teddy from self-harm by taking away potential weapons—even a child's scissors—and the radio that Teddy has been using to obsessively listen to a right-wing talk radio host. When Teddy notices that the radio is missing, he searches the house. Finding the radio in an attic storage space, he also notices a backpack. Opening the bag, he finds that it is packed with items like a flashlight and an emergency preparedness kit. He opens a sealed cardboard box that contains a gas mask. Wearing only underwear and carrying the radio and a kitchen knife, he ventures into the street. The rows of identical homes in identical formations of garage doors, entryways, and upstairs windows acquire an ominous quality in their regularity. In a storage room inside an identical unit, suggesting many other storage rooms inside many other townhouses, Teddy looks around, still armed with only his kitchen knife and radio. He seems stunned to find himself surrounded by floor-to-ceiling shelves stockpiled with food, water, and other supplies in an orderly arrangement. Dozens of cans of tomatoes and black beans are arranged on the shelves, along with bulk packages of toilet paper, and large plastic bottles of water, and white plastic buckets labeled "Food prep, 305 Servings, 1 month."[34] Looking at these items, Teddy is not calmed but is only perplexed: preparedness leads not to a sense of security but only to the desire for even more preparedness.

As Sandra tells Sabrina at the beginning of the book, the "wild animals stay in hotels."[35] The book both highlights and raises the sense of ambient anxiety, extending that sense to the reader of this text, with characters so sparely drawn, so almost indistinguishable, that their uniformity projects a constant awareness of potential threat. The reader's task is then to become precisely like Calvin, the boundary technician, looking for the slightest difference in like things for the purpose of making meaning out of absence and presence, presumably in order to prevent another calamitous harm. The solution that seems to be in operation, from the surveillance of as much as possible to the accumulation of as many stores of items as possible, all rely on an ethos of proliferation, surplus, and excess, as if aiming for extra may well crowd out the potential for damage. This narrative exposes how the proliferation of the identical becomes itself a cause for concern. People are read as indistinguishable from the personas that they present to the world, the habits of looking and buying that they freely give access to. Their reproductions in avatars of video games, in video recordings viewed on tiny screens, photographs cropped or magnified, measured with biometric detail, are all taken as if interchangeable with the real living body that serves as the "original."

Drnaso's book lingers on questions of presence and absence. It also lingers on how our ability to access photographic, audio, and video reproductions of precise moments in time, which we can share and scrutinize in private and at any time, makes claims not only to our attentions but also to our sense of ethical and moral purpose. Teddy's arrival in Colorado coincides with the anniversary of 9/11, but for the men on the Air Force base, the anniversary goes by unnoted. Instead, Calvin's friend Dahlman reads to him a "funny" news story from one of the many screens in front of him in his cubicle. The news that Dahlman chooses to share is one he has found over the weekend, about a product placement conspiracy theory involving an adult film star who takes on the role of whistleblower to expose the fact that pornographic films have been accepting money from various sponsors to place products in the background of their video shoots. The "story" with its combination of the lurid and the promise of exposing the "truth" adeptly describes what constitutes news in the twenty-first century. On television that night, Calvin and Teddy watch the news, which offers a "special edition of nightly news" commemorating "the sixteenth anniversary of the 9-1-1 attacks." In a story about the memorial, a spokesperson explains, "Behind this wall is a repository housing some 8000 unidentified human remains. . . . Our goal is to pay tribute to the ones that were lost that day. . . . We want guests to leave with an increased sense of the value of a human life, that each one is important and won't be forgotten."[36] Again the theme of missing persons is explored in this moment, and again the characters waver between a wholehearted agreement with the expression of the value of individual human lives and a suspicion that these kinds of ritualistic memorial ceremonies and attendant news stories filled with platitudes do little to complement the expressed values.

Headline news stories, conspiracy theories, advertisements, personal photographs, video conferencing conversations, work documents, and video games all exist fleetingly on the same screen. After going to bed, Calvin opens his laptop and joins Dahlman for a short conversation within the world of a role-playing game. As they type to each other as their avatars "Bestbuddy89" and

"Sinistercd89," they exchange banalities about the game while aimlessly shoot-ing at other people's avatars. The irony of soldiers role-playing as soldiers while talking about getting ready for bed is pointed, pricking at an aspect of con-temporary life that we often take for granted. The men take each other's avatars as straightforward representatives of each other, but they are also able to disso-ciate the things that happen to each other within the game from the actual breathing person who controls them. This is a small point, but it is one that raises questions about whether this ability to suspend both possibilities of existence might not have something to do with the ways that the rapacious audiences of strangers who comment on Sabrina's murder or send threatening letters to Cal-vin and Sandra are able to feel simultaneously invested in these "people" while also thinking of them as not quite people.

One must also consider the material facts of the technological tools that assist in these reproductively enhanced dissociations. It is often the case that the many interactions discussed here, which represent interactions of all kinds, take place on the same material object, whether the device is a work computer, a smartphone, or a laptop computer. The next morning, Calvin uses the same laptop that he uses to read news stories and to play his video game with Dahl-man to make a video conferencing call. He calls his estranged wife, Jackie, who has moved with their daughter Cici, to stay with her parents in Florida. His conversation with Cici, who makes faces and plays with her teeth throughout their talk, suggests that she is more interested in seeing her face on the com-puter as much as she is in having a conversation with her father. In contrast to the flexible modes of interaction and communication offered by the computer, Drnaso also demonstrates the impact of more anachronistic technology. Fol-lowing the arrival of Sabrina's bus pass in the mail, Sabrina's fate is finally revealed through the outmoded technology of a VHS tape. The tape has been sent in the mail to a small regional newspaper called the *Standard Journal*, where the breaking news typically involves items such as the mayor's intention to announce land annexation, and the office conversation involves dentist appointments and shortbread recipes. The reader later learns that similar tapes were sent to news outlets around the country, but in these pages the reader sees only the two journalists looking at the screen and then reacting to it.[37] Com-pared to the mix tapes that Calvin has saved from his childhood, and the VHS tape that Terry finds when he digs out the VCR from the storage room to watch this anachronous mail delivery, the internet supplies stories that branch out-ward, suggesting other stories in a swarm of hashtags, links, and images.

When Calvin is alone with his computer, he too succumbs to typing in the name of Sabrina's murderer, Timmy Yancey, into a search engine. A series of images appear, so that reproductions of Yancey fill the entire window of his screen. The images look different from each other, but they are just differently cropped versions of the same two photographs. This idea of generating not only reproduction but reproduction with a false sense of representing something new emphasizes how difference may be generated for novel effect, for calling our attention. Calvin reads the story marked as "Most Popular," and we are shown the different artifacts of internet reproduction, from the cursor arrow over photographs to the "Trending Now" box that intersperses the sought-after detail—"#TimmyYancey," "#SabrinaGallo"—with equally trendy searches like "#Playoffs," "#SalmonRecall," and "#TheAvengers."[38] As Calvin scrolls through a story about Sabrina's disappearance, he finds himself clicking on an adjacent feel-good story with the headline "Teen surprises mom and toddler with good deed at mall" (Figure 4.3).[39]

Calvin, whose concerns about his own toddler child weigh on his mind, even before the unexpectedly gruesome events that befell Sabrina, displays his preference for this attractive news story, which in its patterns could be read as analogous for the way that it also reports a story about a young man who commits a random act. This time, of course, the random act is one of kindness. The shift demonstrates the equivalence of attention that Calvin gives to a grotesque and disturbing story directly related to someone he knows, and then immediately to a heartwarming and feel-good story about someone he has never met, and likely will never meet. The sequence speaks to the superficial and high-speed ways that the news industry engages us with delivered information. It speaks to the way that Calvin needs to balance disturbing facts of Sabrina's abduction and murder with the palliative words and pink hues of the "good deed story." And, most of all, it speaks to the way that the peaks and valleys of individual emotional reactions, despair, catharsis, are so often brokered privately, and separately, without an ounce of physical human contact, and only through impenetrable computer screens.

In the postscript to her 2020 book *The Force of Nonviolence*, Judith Butler meditated on the question of the vulnerable, and the dangers of grouping the vulnerable under such a designation as "the vulnerable" at the risk of denying their ability to resist:

> In exposing their bodies in the context of demonstration, they let it be known which bodies are at risk of detention, deportation, or death. For embodied performance brings that specific historical exposure to violence to the fore; it makes the wager and the demand with its own performative and embodied persistence.... It is not the immediacy of the body that makes this demand, but rather the body as socially regulated and abandoned, the body as persisting and resisting that very regulation, asserting its existence within readable terms. It acts as its own *deixis,* a pointing to, or enacting of, the body that implies its situation: *this* body, *these* bodies; *these* are the ones exposed to violence, resisting disappearance. These bodies exist still, which is to say that they persist under conditions in which their very power to persist is systematically undermined.[40]

To expand Butler's reading to the characters in Drnaso's book, who have been subjected to trauma and continue to be drawn into a news cycle that thrives on

what happens next will shock you

You don't want to know what this economist predicts for 2018

Teen surprises mom and toddler with good deed at mall

A Northwest-Indiana teen is being praised on social media after his random act of kindness went viral.

It all began when Beth Russell, a resident of Portage, was birthday shopping with her youngest daughter, Paige.

As the two-year-old scanned the aisles of toys, her eyes fixed on a blonde doll, the last one on the shelf.

Before she could show her mom the doll, a young man walked over and asked if it was her favorite. She told the stranger that her birthday was approaching, and that she really loved the doll.

The teen laughed, grabbed the doll and left the aisle.

A few minutes later, the young man returned to the aisle with a bag under his arm. He handed Paige's mom a receipt, took the doll out of the bag and wished Paige a happy birthday.

Russell was at a loss for words. After a moment, she managed to thank him for the gift. The teen nodded, smiled and walked off. Before he was out of sight, Russell ushered him back to take a photo with Paige.

That night, Russell shared the story with her friends on Facebook, posting the photo of Paige with the young man, hoping that someone would be able to identify him.

After thousands of shares, someone recognized the teen as Centell Rodgers III, a senior football player at Horace Mann High School.

Russell thanked him again, for showing her daughter that hope is not lost on society as a whole.

Her hope is that sharing this story will inspire others to do good in the community.

"This extraordinary young man has taught Paige a meaningful life lesson. I'm so grateful for that."

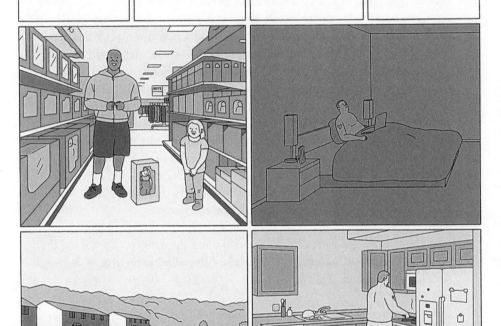

82

FIGURE 4.3 "Teen surprises mom." Nick Drnaso, *Sabrina* (Montreal: Drawn & Quarterly, 2016), 82. Copyright © Nick Drnaso. (Used with permission from Drawn & Quarterly.)

the repetitive renewal of trauma with ever more stories of violence and hate, these are people whose strain to simply just continue living is already heroic. It is significant that there are only a few times in the over two hundred pages of *Sabrina* that we see characters touching each other. To a great degree, the bodies of these characters, defeated though they may be by their circumstances, do also "persist under conditions in which their very power to persist is systematically undermined." On page 4 Sabrina rubs Sandra's sore shoulder, and on page 10 they hug goodbye, and those actions are mimicked in reverse later when Sandra's friend Anna comes to comfort her, greeting her with a hug and then attempting to talk her through a relaxation breathing exercise, sitting behind her, and massaging her shoulders.[41]

Moments of actual physical contact between Calvin and Teddy occur largely when Calvin helps Teddy to bed, or when he rushes to calm him when he is tormented with nightmares. In these moments, in tender acts of care, the bodies of the precarious and vulnerable resist these acts with verbal or physical violence; but even in their resistance they show that they are precisely the bodies that need the most support. As Butler writes, "It is not just that this or that body is bound up in a network of relations, but that the boundary both contains and relates; the body, perhaps precisely by virtue of its boundaries, is differentiated from and exposed to a material and social world that makes its own life and action possible. When the infrastructural conditions of life are imperiled, so too is life, since life requires infrastructure, not simply as an external support, but as an immanent feature of life itself. This is a materialist point we deny only at our own peril."[42] One of the lasting effects of *Sabrina*, with its solitary characters embarking into the world knowing full well that peril is never far away, is that the thing that makes this necessary independent movement bearable may well be a knowledge that such an infrastructure, bearing the possibility of care between the "I" and the "you," does exist. The touch of care from a supporting friend may be terrifying, but it also brings with it a sense of affirmation that makes continuing to live possible. It signifies possibility. This possibility stands in stark contrast to the limitless possibilities of the reproduced but impassive versions of selves—whether in photo reproductions or in narrative reproductions—that flow endlessly through the various media portals that occupy these characters' lives.

The Rest Is Silence

As details of Sabrina's murder are revealed, the strangers invested in the chatter about her disappearance are inversely less willing to find closure in the revelation that she has been murdered. Instead, they become preoccupied with more and more absurd scenarios, exceeding in unimaginability the already absurd reality. The fact that she has been kidnapped and murdered by a stranger who has sought to cement his posthumous celebrity by recording the crime on videotape is absurd enough. This is precisely the paradox that preoccupies *Sabrina*, which questions the tenuous ways that people become attached to certain plots and explanations even as they are quick to be distracted in other directions. This desire to do so stems from an essential loneliness and the fear that comes with it, which is starkly emphasized by the internet chatter that emerges seemingly from a void, floating on the surface until it is overtaken by even more chatter.

When Calvin receives a phone call from Sandra with the first news of Sabrina since her disappearance, it is to report that her parents received a letter in the mail containing Sabrina's bus pass. Calvin finds Teddy sitting on a playground swing, dressed in Calvin's fatigues. The page contains a series of orderly panels, interrupted with the brightness of Calvin's mental health survey at the bottom left corner. There is dialogue on the page, in six panels, but it is represented by straight horizontal lines. It is nonetheless clear that Calvin has told Teddy the news about the bus pass and that Teddy has collapsed and been helped back to bed by Calvin, who goes to work where he sits in distracted silence.[43] In contrast, the endless chatter of the news cycle, facilitated by the internet, is on full display here. The news feeds that Calvin accesses through a search engine promptly produce a seemingly endless supply of variations on the same image and story. It is also clear, from fragments of these stories shown to the reader, that the killer himself was involved with a fair amount of reading and writing online: "Yancey was active on various message boards ranging from body-building and men's rights to theoretical physics and organic farming. Apparently he was banned from several online groups for dominating the discussions with long, vitriolic rants." Another fragment of an online story depicted in *Sabrina* suggests that journalists sought to make sense of Yancey's intentions. The fragment reads: "unable to find a clearly marked suicide note, but what seems to be his last message board post, appearing hours before his estimated time of death, is a list of his fifty favorite movies, ending with the sign-off 'Bye for now.'"[44] Drnaso's details of such postmortem news stories capture the inchoate meanderings of this kind of reportage as well as the fragmentary nature of reading online, where all kinds of details are included with no sign of any meaningful red thread, or through-line, to connect them. The additional detail may be the one point that distinguishes this news story from the others, so it is left in, suggesting something wholly new even though it may introduce only a single increment of change. Instead, the various subjects of Yancey's message board interests are listed, providing data points that array themselves to facilitate future algorithmic keyword searches.

The stochastic potential hastened by the algorithms of the internet are shown in full force when Calvin checks his phone the night after he has been ambushed by reporters following the leak of Sabrina's murder video. In that encounter, he mistakenly refers to Sabrina by her sister Sandra's name, which immediately becomes fodder for the amateur detectives who gather online. When Calvin looks himself up, the search engine provides the most popular words to search with his name, including "fake," "actor," "exposed," "teddy king," "interview," "facebook," "air force," "timmy," and "youtube." He opens a story on "Iron Truth Report" to read a story with the headline "Chicago Execution Lies Unfurl—Actor Flubs Line." The story "exposes" Calvin as a hired actor involved in a "false flag" conspiracy plot.[45] Mistakes and slips of the tongue are themselves misrepresented as invested with meaning. In a news story that Calvin reads on his phone at a restaurant, he reads,

> The problem with these theories is that they can't be reasoned with. Any fact that doesn't fit the alternative explanation is dismissed as a lie or disinformation. Any avoidance is tacit confirmation. Anyone close to the victim is an actor or being paid to remain silent. The most troubling detail of the Timmy Yancey story is that he seemed to be a proponent of such radical conspiracy theories. We now know that he listened to the Albert Douglas radio show every day, and frequently wrote on the show's message board, showing support for the ideas espoused by the host.[46]

This inescapable feedback loop shows itself in the hundreds of emails that flood Calvin's and Sandra's email inboxes. Sitting in his car, Calvin reads an ominous email from a stranger that includes the names and address of Cici and Jackie in Tampa and the warning that "I must insist that you join us in the good fight. Expose the conspiracy before it's too late. You're going to die anyway, someday. Why not be the greatest American hero who ever lived."[47]

At a coffee shop open mic event, Sandra reads aloud from similar emails that she received. She reads aloud a message from someone who has been sending her death threats: "Your address is online. People in our community are waking up to the truth. I'm armed and protected. See what happens if they try to test me. I don't buy this story. I don't really believe anything I'm told from so-called verified sources. . . . Why should we believe your story? This whole thing is fake. It's a f-cking lie. It doesn't make any sense. Where is she?"[48] This rhetoric is especially difficult to manage because no one actually disagrees with the singular fact of the mindlessness of Sabrina's murder: "It doesn't make any sense." The difference here is that the reaction to and interpretation of that senselessness is so disparate. This is precisely the problem described by the article that Calvin reads on false flags: ignoring the rant suggests acknowledgment. Engaging in an argument only confirms the speculators' beliefs.

Words such as "truth" and "real" acquire a troubled state of ambiguity, becoming floating signifiers where they once were used with a sense of confidence that speaker and listener agreed on their meaning. During all of this, Teddy has been taking comfort in the soporific tones of the fictional Albert Douglas, whose similarity to "America's leading conspiracy theorist" Alex Jones is obvious. The voice on the radio, unlike the speech bubbles with their white backgrounds, hover transparently over the background, filling Teddy's environment with the comforting words that senseless acts of the world can in fact be blamed on a malicious "someone" who is at fault and against whom we can take up arms to protect ourselves. As Teddy lies on the bed, with his head pressed into a pillow, the words wash over him: "Someone is at fault, someone is scheming and capitalizing big time. To untangle the wires, to get to the heart of the matter and expose the conspirators for the thieving murderers they are; that is my vocation. It is my life's work. I have been targeted for voicing what amounts to perfectly legal and acceptable free speech."[49] Later on, this faceless voice continues to muse, "If you're willing to believe the official story, that an archetypal loner with no resources abducted and slaughtered a total stranger in his small apartment for no reason, by all means, pull that wool a little bit tighter. There is something more complicated at work, you can be sure of that."[50] The desire to make meaning out of absurd situations, absurd situations that occur one after another, is palpable. How does one make sense of airplanes flying into buildings, neighbors who kidnap and murder neighbors, "supremely gifted" people who livestream themselves murdering children in a day care center on Facebook? What reading apparatus can we turn to in the face of this absurdity? It feels more urgent than ever that we learn how to read properly, and that we acknowledge that part of reading properly is knowing the limits of our capacity to understand things that escape understanding.

Seeing and Believing

Let us return to the small detail of a star on a bag. On his way home from work on Teddy's second night in Colorado, Calvin stops at a restaurant to pick up dinner. The final panel on the bottom right of the page shows an outdoor scene at night, with the gray color broken with small yellow shapes that convey the illumination that comes from the moon, street lamps, a sign, and the lighted interior of a fast food restaurant.[51] The reader has seen a similar panel twenty pages earlier, the first night that Calvin returns from work, and in the neutral landscape depicted in these frames we have come to rely on specific details that can provide meaning and connection between the panels. In this case, the star with a smiling face on the illuminated sign becomes the icon that delivers meaning. When it shows up on the paper bag that Calvin holds, saying "Hungry?" on the next page, the reader is able to make the connection between the sign on the panel on the previous page and its reproduction on the paper bag on this one.[52] Without any explanation, the recurrence of the star, from the context of a large illuminated sign to the print on a paper bag, communicates provenance as competent branding is meant to do. Yet, star and moon shapes appear all over the image on the facing page. The top half of the page is an image of what we learn is Cici's favorite book, a book that Teddy spends time reading. In the image teeming with images of children engaged in various activities, with regularly placed stripes on flags and T-shirts, and multicolored bricks and shapes littering the surface, the book shows precisely the kind of drawing that attracts the pattern-making mind (Figure 4.4). There are, in fact, several yellow stars in this picture as well, and our eyes are drawn to these familiar shapes on the walls and in the artwork posted on the bulletin

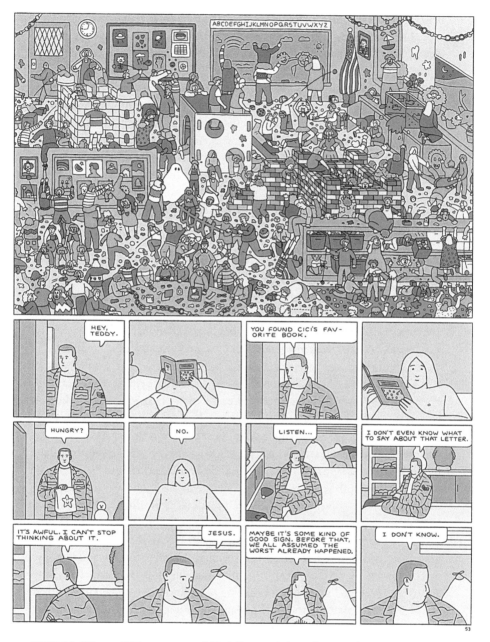

FIGURE 4.4 "Hungry?" Two-page spread. Nick Drnaso, *Sabrina* (Montreal: Drawn & Quarterly, 2016), 53. Copyright © Nick Drnaso. (Used with permission from Drawn & Quarterly.)

board. We notice these images because of their appearance in the immediately preceding panel, suggesting how proximity generates a preparedness for making connections. Significantly, most readers would not conclude that there might be a hidden meaning between the child's book and its surrounding pages.

Although Sabrina is gone after the first ten pages of the book, her afterimage remains, in the memories of both Teddy and Sandra, demonstrating the sequence of frame preferences at work in the text. A color can thus summon for each of them a snapshot memory of Sabrina that, in their primary colorways, recalls the most colorful pages in *Sabrina*. In a wordless sequence, Teddy sits alone in Cici's room and picks up one of her dolls, swathed in red fabric. The next panel shows Sabrina, in the image that also appears on the cover of the book. She is in three-quarter profile, looking at the reader from a red and unornamented background that matches the color of the doll's clothing, and wearing a shirt in a slightly colder tone of the same red as the background.[53] Later in the book, Sandra is shown, also in a wordless sequence. She goes out alone, waits for a bus, rides it, watches a movie, and then has a meal alone in a restaurant. Afterward, she walks past a store with illuminated windows, and passes a yellow evening gown in the display. The next panel shows Sabrina smiling in a yellow shirt against a yellow background. The page ends with Sandra in bed with her hands covering her face.[54]

This attention to faces imagined, obscured, and reproduced is highlighted in the following six-panel page, where we see Sandra represented six times without ever seeing her face. She is seen doubled in the first panel because she is cleaning a mirror. Her hand wipes the mirror at the level of her face, so that both the Sandras in the panel are faceless. In the next panel we see her sideways as she walks through the rain. Her hood is up, covering her face. The next two panels show her from behind: in one she is alone in her kitchen, and in the next she mops the floor. In the fifth panel, Sandra sits with her head down and tucked into her collar, and we see the faint outline of her nose. Five enormous heads loom behind her on the walls of the bus stop shelter, large reproductions of smiling and happy faces (Figure 4.5).[55] In composition, these faces are not at all unlike the red and yellow images of Sabrina that we have seen on previous pages. These are faces that we have developed an ability to interpret as inconsequential to the plot and to belong to people that we need not "care" about. Visual acuity is an essential skill that allows for speed and efficiency for reading of all kinds, but those same skills of close reading and pattern finding can result in chillingly perverse conclusions.

It feels potent that a story about a missing person will settle as it does on a book that, in its busy overflowing images and its "spot the difference" activities, underscores the didactic goals of teaching children how to make meaning and order out of the given. The half-page spreads from this book resemble the "Where's Waldo" books popular in the late eighties and nineties, in which a man wearing blue pants and a red and white striped shirt is hidden in a crowded scene and the reader is challenged to find him and other objects within the crowded image.[56] Those books are an innocent version of what Teddy, Sandra, the police,

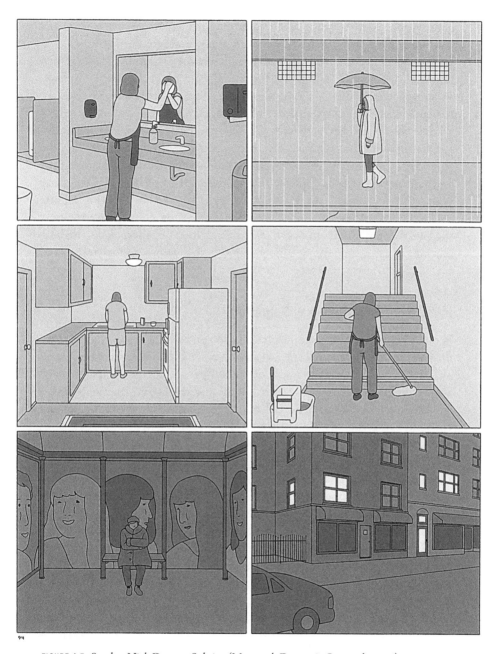

FIGURE 4.5 Sandra. Nick Drnaso, *Sabrina* (Montreal: Drawn & Quarterly, 2016), 94.
Copyright © Nick Drnaso. (Used with permission from Drawn & Quarterly.)

and a crowd of strangers are doing, too: searching for the missing person. The message is quite plain: look closely enough, and you will find what you are looking for. In the innocence of the schoolroom and the playground scenes shown on these pages there is also an urgency to find a specific person amid the chaos. Drnaso gives over a full two-page spread to Cici's activity book (Figure 4.6). In the book, the alphabet is illustrated with images that correspond to the letters. A "Spot the Differences" activity rewards the child who can find the twenty differences between two otherwise identical photographs. The book teaches the reader that the aberrant detail can and will be found, that order exists, that tigers and squirrels are friends. There is an ethos operating here that is particularly familiar to close readers of texts. *Sabrina* emphasizes the way that this impulse to find meaning from the stochastic is also primary to our cognitive needs. It suggests that our minds are drawn to the recognition of pattern and to making meaning of those patterns, as a mental process that we rely on for survival and that may be precisely why we read fiction in all its forms.

If You See Something Say Something

What is this image from a child's activity book if not a microcosm of what we do when we look at pictures or texts, and when we look at the world around us? While we valorize close attention to detail, Drnaso's book cautions that we must also become equally alert to the ways that those same impulses may follow existing frame references that we, as readers, bring to a narrative that will completely change the direction of its interpretation. As the interest in Sabrina's case gains momentum, the conspiracy theory speculating on Calvin's involvement in Sabrina's disappearance develops rapidly. A surprising number of people believe that the murder has been an invention to distract the population from eerie forms of government control and surveillance. The fact that Calvin is a member of the military, that he accidentally refers to Sabrina by Sandra's name, and his vague resemblance to an obscure television actor now all become crucial pieces of evidence for these conspiracy theories. They seem particularly truthful to those who feel that they were the first to notice these resemblances. The same reward centers in our minds activated by finding the differences in two nearly identical pictures are the reward centers activated every time a solitary investigator alone on his computer makes what he thinks is a new discovery. It is easy to find these small clues to sustain a narrative that Calvin facilitated Sabrina's removal to an atoll somewhere in the South Pacific in a vast government conspiracy. It is even easier, it seems, to read his denials as further proof that he has something to hide.

At the beginning of the book, we saw Sabrina as she walked around her parents' house, looking for their missing cat. Near the end of the book, Teddy realizes that he has not seen Calvin's cat Randy around the house for quite some time as well, and he goes out in search for it. Thirty pages before that, shortly after Calvin receives a disturbing email from a stranger detailing the theory of Calvin's part in a Sabrina cover-up, we see Calvin fueling his car at a gas station. A

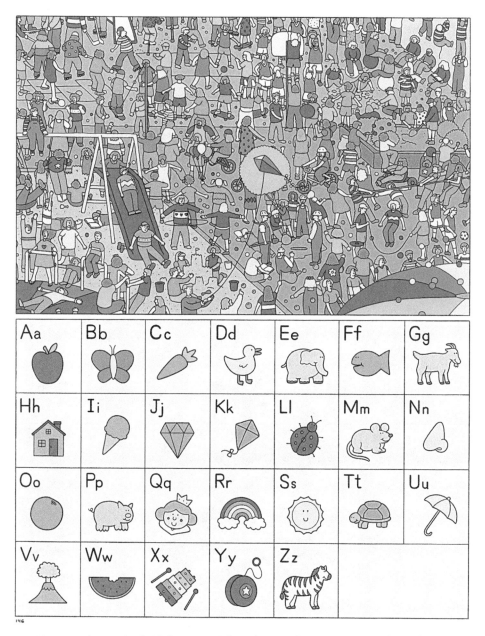

FIGURE 4.6. Activity book. Nick Drnaso, *Sabrina* (Montreal: Drawn & Quarterly, 2016), 146. Copyright © Nick Drnaso. (Used with permission from Drawn & Quarterly.)

man in a dark jacket with a white pickup truck appears to be watching him.[57] Perhaps he is simply someone who is also fueling his car. The pages do not give us any more information than the man's presence: why would he be there unless there is some significance? Are we conceding to the same paranoia of the conspiracy theorists in the previous pages? Thirty pages later, this same man

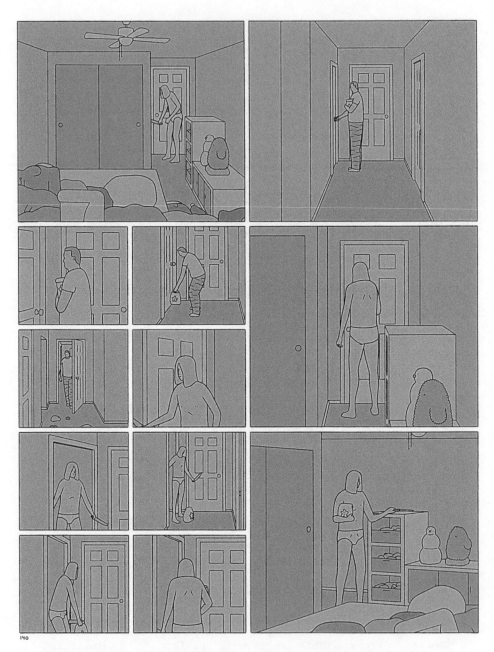

140

FIGURE 4.7 Door. Nick Drnaso, *Sabrina* (Montreal: Drawn & Quarterly, 2016), 139.
Copyright © Nick Drnaso. (Used with permission from Drawn & Quarterly.)

reappears, this time offering to help Teddy look for the missing cat. He drives Teddy to the animal shelter, and then offers to wait in the car while Teddy inquires about the cat. He then drives Teddy back to Calvin's home, asking Teddy to identify where he lives. The reader worries when Teddy identifies the house as Calvin's, but is this, too, a product of our undue anxiety? How can we tell the good neighbor from the diabolical murderer? How do we know that the person offering to help us look for our cat is not the person sending anonymous letters that have become increasingly threatening as they remain unanswered?

Mistaken identity corresponds to mistaken intentions; everything is invested with meaning in these spare pages. The first three chapters of *Perfect Copies* were occupied with moments of intentional interruptions between sight and touch. This book operates on the firm belief that learning to read carefully helps us make better sense of the world, better sense of the ways that the surface of the reader brushes and presses against the surface of the text. This and the next chapter continue to hold on to that belief, but they also serve as reminders and demonstrations of the inherent dangers of close reading, of believing that there is an answer for everything, that for every abhorrent act there is an evil that can be isolated and treated, and that hyper-vigilance guarantees our safety. Books like Drnaso's, and like Evens's in the next chapter, suggest otherwise. While Teddy seeks to be completely alone in Calvin's home, listening to the radio in his underwear, eating cheeseburgers that Calvin periodically leaves outside his bedroom door, he also becomes increasingly para-noid. An indelible image in this book is presented through the dimmed and faded colors of Calvin's apartment at night. Teddy, clad in his underwear, a knife-wielding guest, prepared to murder his host if he tries to enter the room. Calvin the bound-ary technician, carrying nothing but a bag of cheeseburgers that he patiently deliv-ers as a show of care to his suffering friend. Each stand on opposite sides of the door, trying desperately to understand everything they have encountered, to read the signs, to prepare accordingly (Figure 4.7).[58]

After 9/11 the visual landscapes of public gathering spaces, especially the non-spaces of train stations and airports, were filled with large signs reminding every individual that they could be the one who prevents the next atrocity. The signs contain a direct address: "If you see something, say something." Everything around them could be a potentially dangerous object, and everyone held respon-sible for doing their part to notice things. Shoes could be weapons. Luggage could contain bombs. Liquids were measured and displayed in clear plastic bags. Photographs were scrutinized and reasons for entry challenged. We were on the lookout to see something. And once we saw them, we were meant to act. What were the things we were to look for? The kinds of things that would only mean with the hindsight of a retrospective gaze, of course. Bags left unattended. An anxious-looking person. A cell phone. A person who seemed to be watching us. A large, unoccupied, idling van. Seeing was not enough; reporting it was the right thing to do. "If you see something, say something." But we do not know what we have seen. And we do not know what to say.

5

There Is a Monster
in My Closet

Brecht Evens's *Panther*

We all know a story that goes something like this. A little boy is punished for
being naughty. A little girl is angry at her parents. She runs away because of a
harsh scolding. He is sent to his room without his supper. A brother and sister
go to live with an old uncle because of some trouble at home. There was a sick
parent. There was an attack by tigers. There was the scarlet fever. The children
discover a secret room. They open a hidden door. Suddenly, out of thin air, a
creature appears. Only the child can see this creature. The creature is usually
an animal, and has some of the animal's mannerisms, but it also wears clothes
or has other human properties, the most common one being the ability to
speak. The little girl indulges her "animal" self, or the little boy gains the power
he lacks at home, perhaps she gives in to excessive cravings, or perhaps he
indulges in an unalloyed bliss of the kind that adults simply cannot access. The
children spend the night in a mysterious forest. The boy betrays his siblings for
a delicious sticky sweet with a name that suggests exotic origins. There are
adventures. There are tests. There is heroism. Then, at story's end, he returns to
the world of the father, she puts back on the mantle of civilization, and the
children return to being ordinary children safe in their bedrooms once again.
The animal friend has played his part, and now it is time for him to leave. The
only animals the child knows are once again the nonverbal family pet or
beloved toy.

The children's story may be a curious way to mark the final chapter of a book about the complications of technological and biological reproduction. It is curious to liken Brecht Evens's *Panther* to a children's story, anyway. I do so because this story contains a warning akin to the images from the children's book that Teddy explored in the previous chapter. In *Sabrina*, readers were reminded of how familiarity itself has taken on an implacable aura of potential threat, that in fact that which was most familiar still contained little details, tiny differences, that would betray it. The proliferation of reproductions in *Sabrina* put on stark display how readily we accept reproductions, and how heedless we have come to be about the existence of an original. In this chapter, the facts of reproduction are pushed to their limits. Whereas in the previous chapter the prevailing conceit was of the children's activity book that challenged children to find which things were not like the other in two seemingly identical reproductions, *Panther* offers the obverse. It asks how far we allow ourselves to accept some things as the same, even when the variances that differentiate them would seem to be stark. How far, in short, are we willing to follow our frame preferences, until the moment of sudden reversal to a different interpretation?

Panther was published in 2014 in Dutch and French and then, with a few additions and amendments, two years later in German and English.[1] To the casual viewer who picks up the 2016 English-language book printed by Drawn & Quarterly, it appears as if it follows in the tradition of the children's picture book. Though somewhat thicker and heavier, it projects the material qualities of the illustrated children's book, down to its shape, its bright primary colors, and its promise of suspended reality. Like the majority of the texts analyzed in *Perfect Copies*, it is stocked with and sold alongside comics and graphic novels, but it eschews frames and panels and is drawn in vivid watercolors. First suggesting that it is a children's book, and then upending those expectations, *Panther* achieves an unnerving and unforgettable effect that strikes equal parts horror and shame in the reader. Not only can the titular Panther appear and disappear as if by magic, but he is visually different each time we see him, taking advantage of the "sequential irregularity" facilitated as a matter of course by the comics form.[2] From the way that rooms lose their firmness and balance in response to the emotions of the depicted characters, to pronounced shifts in perspective resulting in an overwhelming sense of instability, Evens's artwork cites a sensibility that is inspired by artists of the Berlin expressionist movement, artists like George Grosz,[3] who redefined "realism" by eliding caricature with precise details: producing teeming and teetering masses brimming over with anxiety and fear. Spareness, variation, and pattern create the visual texture of this physically beautiful book's aesthetic, but also communicate its meaning. In its purposeful manipulation of the reader's interpretive investment in reading, *Panther* continues to theorize itself. It highlights the complex epistemic challenges of the reading process that in turn reinforce the themes of ambiguity and double entendre on which its plot turns.

The contemporaneous book *Beautiful Darkness* (*Jolies Ténèbres*) by Fabien Vehlmann and Kerascoët presents a similarly disquieting fantastical storyworld as alternate reality, using the simplistic and cartoonish to interrogate the darker horrors from which they are nourished and eventually emerge.[4] The cover of the book already puts this contradiction in stark display. Under the pretty cursive of the title and against a background of watery green foliage, a charming little blond figure with bare feet peeks out. She has giant eyes and little round circles on her cheeks, and wears a full skirted dress with blue polka dots. A closer look reveals that she is peeking out from behind a hand that is bent—we must surmise—in rigor mortis and decomposition, as it is the same shades of green as the foliage around them. The little fairy-tale creature bears the same name as the body from whose dripping orifices she has clambered out, and she has been expelled from the midst of a Prince Charming dream that she has been acting out into the real world survival in the forest now that her host is most decidedly dead. The book imaginatively follows Aurora and a whole group of archetypal cartoon heroes, heroines, and their antagonists, after they have been expelled from the head where they resided prior to the host child's death.

Roaming the forest, they now contend with other woodland creatures, including insects, birds, and the mysterious giant who lives in a cottage in the woods. In their aspect and their behaviors, these characters resemble the archetypes of children's books and fairy tales, the kinds of innocent bromides of good boys and girls, the unexamined brutality of villains who are ultimately vanquished in such stories, but perhaps not when they have been released from their typical fastenings. As the body continues to decompose, the little characters also lose the thread of their original innocent expectations and their incipient plots are allowed to play out according to their new contexts. By the end of the book, the fairy-sized Aurora has taken shelter in the cottage of the giant in the woods. The debris in his cottage, and the several encounters that the creatures—and the corpse—have with him strongly suggest that he is the reason that the girl-sized Aurora lies decaying in the woods. Her alter ego, wide eyes even more widened by her experiences, concludes the book with an ending that is troublingly in line with the generic conventions from which she is born. She manages to manipulate the evil queen and her minions into walking directly into the oven where they are locked in, just like the evil witch in "Hansel and Gretel." But instead of resisting the true sovereign power that has most assuredly murdered her host girl and sent her into the cruelties of the real world, she looks at those structures that he represents to define her safety and success. In the last pages of the book, she gazes out from her perch in a cuckoo clock, hands propping up her chin. She thinks to herself, "I'll need to rebuild my little nest . . . it's all right, I've got plenty of time. That meal you're making for us smells good. My sweet prince."[5]

The structure of such inherited narratives, and consequently the sovereign powers that invent these structures, can and should be explored as the pernicious structures that they are. This chapter analyzes the intermedial narrative structure of *Panther* and how it guides its readers through those philosophical provocations by exploiting some of the narrative structures of the comic form. In most comics, there is a certain degree of regularity in sequences that generate enough familiarity to secure the reader's sense of continuity. Individual characters, even though they change position or expression, have to remain recognizable as consistent in person. Equally, differences between items in sequence transmit knowledge about shifts in mood, activity, and so on. This is a familiar structure that balances repetitions that rely on the reproduction of characters, and a sequential way of proceeding through those reproductions by comparing an image to its preceding image. The reader is able to follow along in the comic even when significant differences are introduced from panel to panel, whether through a change in color, representation of a character, or even a change in action.[6]

The cartoon form allows for quite radical shifts that still may not cause a reader to lose the thread. *Panther* playfully, and then not so playfully, shows what can go wrong when the balance is slightly off, and how rapidly minor adjustments can cause major and devastating shifts. In the book, especially early on in the book, minor shifts are depicted with changes in aspect, form, expression, and color that at first allow the reader to continue to account for consistency of person or location despite striking alterations. As the plot progresses, the book begins to assert what might happen with major shifts, as well. Among the distinctions that the book deconstructs are those between man and animal, and between local and outsider, distinctions that not only rely heavily on, but actively produce, difference. To that end, this graphic narrative challenges those distinctions by training its focus on boundaries.

Panther exploits the fact of being an animal, a fact that is particularly notable in the history of comics, which harbors a rich tradition of funny animals in comics that have been integrated now into an equally rich history of tragic animals in comics. The animal in the comic is already a way of foregrounding allegorical thinking. Unlike their real-world counterparts, animals in comics possess the qualities that Derrida designates as proper, and by proper he means unique, to man, such as dress, speech and reason, the *logos*, history, laughing, mourning, the gift.[7] Animals in comics possess these qualities, and they possess them in such ways as to undermine purely allegorical ways of reading.[8] Comics historians like Joseph Witek suggest that the traditional animal allegory typical of, for example, Aesop's fables is undone by the figure of the funny animal in comics, where the comic overturns those conventions.[9] The allegorical suggestiveness of creating types through the mechanism of animal traits is accommodated in the *Animal Farm*–style metaphorical readings of the classic graphic novel *Maus*, about which Orvell remarks, "The reader comes to forget that these are cats, mice, pigs, and soon begins to view them instead as human types."[10] The animal form, or rather the human-animal hybrids of *Maus* in which the characters are human in body and dress and have animal faces, create avatars that facilitate the storytelling shorthand in cat and mouse distinctions. The animals serve as allegorical commentaries, and the reader keeps the epistemological separations in suspension while reading: we see frogs, mice, and pigs on the page and read them as people.

Similarly, animals are used to different effect in comics such as Gene Yang's *American Born Chinese*. Michael Chaney has argued that Yang's comic complicates the simple distinctions that take place on the allegorical level, where animal stands in for human, by taking the animal-human distinction and making it a meaning-making part of the story. In Yang's exploration of the immigrant hybrid identity-making of self-erasure and projection in the protagonist Jin Wang, the animal in the book turns out to be not an allegorical avatar or storytelling convention but an incarnation of the legendary monkey king from Chinese tradition, an already transtextually anthropomorphized animal. Chaney sees in comics like Yang's a specter, suggested when "social norms of anatomical and emotional proximity" are replaced by more microscopic shifts in human animal relationships.[11] More importantly, the animal in the comic challenges either-or binaries that are highlighted by attempts to distinguish the human from the animal. In the comic narrative, this distinction is blurred, and allowing the animal to act human is precisely the mechanism upon which Evens's narrative turns. *Panther* is a narrative of suggestiveness. The panther arrives at different times of day. Every time he slinks into view, his appearance is different. Every time we see him, we nevertheless accept that he is "Panther." We do this in the same way that we allow ourselves to easily slip into thinking of the vast variety of other lives—lives as distinct from each other as sea anemones and giant pandas—as members all grouped together within the same category of "animal." We use terms like "animal" as if the only important distinction is that they are not like us, the human.

Of course, the predator's cunning is precisely that of suggestiveness, and one of the ways that the problem of distinguishing like things comes into prominence is the way that meaning too can be doubled. From a linguistic and literary perspective, wordplay productively engages in keeping meaning as an active process of committed making: "Wordplay invites to and is expressive of metalinguistic reflection. It directs the hearer's/reader's attention to the message and the language itself, as it often functions as a riddle that has to be solved, and, in order to be solved, requires the hearer's reflection about the meanings and ambiguities involved as well as about the structures of language that are playfully manipulated."[12] The manipulation of meaning can be playful and humorous, but it also allows for a certain distance from responsibility from the speaker. Due to the scalar nature of wordplay, Panther can use strategies of indirectness to speak, expecting the listener to pick up on his meaning when desired and, if they take umbrage, to be able to retreat from those insinuations. As with metafictional devices in general, its power is twofold and comes from the combination of "linguistic and narrative structures . . . [and] the role of the reader."[13]

Critics and scholars have pointed to the quality of the comics form that makes it the essential writerly text described by Barthes, the kind of text that enlists the reader into the production of its meaning.[14] Perhaps the most theorized convention of the comics form is the gutter, as the site where narrative "closure" is produced,[15] or, in Groensteen's analysis, as "the site of a semantic articulation, a logical conversion, that of a series of utterables (the panels) in a statement that is unique and coherent (the story)."[16] The gutters, the spaces that divide panels from each other, create discreet units that are read individually, but the discreet units do not necessarily represent a completed action. Units of time or action may emerge from considering units in contiguity: narratives are indicated through the exercise of difference and repetition. Groensteen's interpretation of this narrative strategy, what he calls its "arthrology," analyzes the way that a graphic narrative focalizes the narrative through its redundancies.[17]

The sense of a narrative thus coheres not simply from the transition from one panel to the next, but around a perception of clustered repetitions. For example, an identical subject against changing backgrounds indicates the passage of time or travel in space. Similarly, it could indicate the obverse: changing postures or appearances of a subject against static backgrounds. The idea of a unit of completed action should thus be defined not only by the relationships between adjacent individual panels, but by a range of different parameters—a splash page, a cluster of panels, a series of actions within a single panel, a sequence of panels across several pages—that are functionally variable in their combinations. *Panther* does not indicate its gutters by drawing black lines that frame panels, opting instead to indicate them through absences. This sense of absence will be used to the same effect in the construction of its narrative, where the unspoken and unseen are crucial elements for the determination of what has happened. The construction of meaning across related but variant units is essential to *Panther*'s problems of identification: in terms of both subject and meaning. Likewise, the way that specific units or actions are "thought together" relays the complex processes of witnessing and interpretation that attach to perceptions formed in their reading.

Panther exercises the simultaneous presentation afforded by the sequential narrative form. Typically noncontiguous elements are easily broadcasted in the comics form: outsides and insides, objects within and without borders, good and evil are no longer unequivocally static categories. The graphic narrative allows for a kind of continuity achieved by the serial: where proximity is an essential aspect of the production of meaning. The repetitions, or redundancies, work in service of producing narrative continuity, but as Groensteen warns, "*continuity* is assured by the *contiguity* of images, but this side-by-side is not necessarily an end-to-end of narrative instances structured according to a univocal and mechanical logic of repetition and difference. We must guard ourselves here against dogmatic conclusions. Comics admit all sorts of narrative strategies."[18] Postema also notes the way that comics urge the viewer to complete narratives through a notion of lack, critiquing Arnheim's drawing distinctions between a pictorial image as a whole, in contrast to the literary image that allows for "stepwise change." She suggests that impressions of wholeness are inaccurate: "The 'wholeness' that Arnheim ascribes to the pictorial image is in fact problematic at two levels. When he says the image resents itself in 'simultaneity,' this implies it can be taken in all at once, which is not the case. Pictorial images are scanned and require reading, just as literary images do. Furthermore, the image often implies other, unrepresented, moments. Thus again, the image is not whole, at least not in the sense of being complete."[19]

The mechanisms of reading the spaces between and of comprehending sequence based on a certain capaciousness of the imagination turn out to be urgently necessary when seen through epistemological as well as political readings of *Panther*. Games of cat and mouse, predator and prey, initially seem to hinge upon the utter lack of alertness or surveillance that could perhaps prevent its disturbing ending. As the book unfolds, however, it becomes eminently clear that no amount of alertness or surveillance would have a preventative effect within a system defined as it is by a notional understanding of molar entities. The players initially suggest a triangulation: a girl, a father, and a panther who has the ability to change his shape from moment to moment while maintaining a consistency of identity. In his body, the panther enacts not only the narrative contiguity outlined by Groensteen, but a contiguity of person where "Panther" coheres into a single unit in spite of continuous variations in his appearance throughout the text. This idea of multiple "molecular" identities cohering into a molar one also brings to mind the moment of assemblage that takes place in the "becoming-animal." Outlined in the tenth stave of Deleuze and Guattari's *A Thousand Plateaus*, the process of becoming is a state that dissolves borders of identity, where the dominant molar identity of "man" becomes, in their terms, molecular in a zone of proximity, and therefore indiscernible.[20] This becoming is meant to activate a recalibration of hierarchies between human and animal identities, creating a space for the ethical considerations of animal lives, or to show how critics cling to "an imperialistic view of the world and of nature that is accompanied by a series of transcendent values [that Deleuze and Guattari] seek to deconstruct."[21]

Positive analyses of Deleuze and Guattari's model of becoming point out the ways that becoming-animal can help articulate a means for minority identities to elude the grasp of authorities that manipulate or exploit them. To that end, the emphasis is on the liberatory promise of this formulation, which allows for "escape routes—the becoming ahuman of Man. If we humans are the problem with the world then attempts to treat nonhuman animals well or differently within this world is trying to force an eternal victim into an unresolvable problem. Better to unravel the problem itself."[22] There are other benefits to unraveling the problem itself. This final chapter reads *Panther* as a way of highlighting the dangers that can easily attach to ignoring the possibilities of becoming. *Panther* is a case study that visualizes continuous processes of becoming, and the hazards of refusing to observe that reality. This is especially true when actual boundaries are nowhere near where they are imagined to exist.

While the interest in *Panther* is thus less motivated by care for the animal, it also exposes the tendency to oversimplify the animal or vulnerable other as definable and therefore controllable. It presents a profound reminder of the blind spots that are created by identification systems that depend on reified identities. The reader of *Panther* relies heavily on visual and linguistic clues not only to sort out the developments in plot but to aid in identifying its players. We are thus forced into confronting our epistemic limits, a productive position that encourages us to look closer rather than to look away. If the panther, seemingly *one* panther, can assume so many contiguous and yet continuous identities, and if we so easily accept each vastly different visual iteration as equal to the same panther, what categories of judgment have we relied on to assign Panther his identity? Where are the limits of contiguity, that allow us to tell him apart with certainty from, for example, Christine's father?

Although this chapter is concerned primarily with the question of form itself—the form that the book *Panther* takes, and the forms that the character Panther takes—it also looks outward beyond the aesthetic and formal puzzles to see what it might mean to apply these structures to ethics beyond the text. For *Panther* is not only about the interpersonal triangulations between these three characters. The distress that it inspires in the reader may indeed generate questions about how the vulnerable and unsuspecting may be preyed upon, and how they may be protected from coming to harm. This kind of concern maps on to contemporary rhetoric about the stranger and pollution that is used to justify suspicions about immigrants and all kinds of newcomers in general. By inextricably linking form and content, *Panther* explores the ways that we constantly rely on surface detail for meaning and patterns, to try to tell one thing from another. The book asks what happens when our very sense of safety and security is tied to our belief in our ability to maintain control of borders of all kinds. *Panther* takes the problem of our resistance to ambiguity as its central premise. As readers think that they have overcome that resistance to visual ambiguity, they find themselves pushed to grapple with questions of narrative ambiguity. It is in this most surprising of twists that *Panther* ingeniously elides the two processes, using a momentous page turn to show how the sovereign father is deeply implicated in maintaining everyone's blindness to this state of affairs. *Panther* thus poses an investigation of two kinds of domestic terror, both overseen by the father. Using the threat of the domestic terror of incestuous sexual abuse, Evens suggests its consonance in the rhetoric used to describe the threat of the domestic terrorist lurking within the borders of the home state.

The family home becomes a metonym for the home state, dominated by vigilance against terrorist attacks that come from beyond borders yet unwilling to acknowledge the equally present terror of the predator within its borders, where seemingly ordinary citizens deploy seemingly ordinary objects as weapons of mass destruction. The answer to the question of "How did the stranger get into the house?" is that he was not a stranger in the first place. Evens's work questions the value of responses that emphasize border control to the detriment of overreliance on inflexible terms. Borders, like the subjects they are meant to control, are in constant states of becoming, changing and repositioning. It is clear that the apparatus of border control maintained by the sovereign father does not adequately acknowledge the flaws inherent in such protections, and *Panther* points to the equal dangers of the false sense of security bolstered by restrictions and the gathering of biometric data, that pretends that fences and boundary technicians of any kind are capable of keeping evil out. Evens asks us to acknowledge the unnerving fact that structures as firm as walls and as finely detailed as biometrics cannot fully account for the stranger within. The problem, he suggests, is not one of porous borders or weakly constructed ones; the problem, instead, is that the danger already lies within the borders, and that those structures not only fail to keep the evil out but indeed create harbors that protect the evils within. The problem is not that the sovereign father is negligent or ignorant, but that in fact he depends on these false and failing structures to maintain his power.

If we insist on believing that we can divide out the evil from the safe, we allow those variations to remain unaccounted, and our mechanisms for sorting, including, and excluding fail the protections that we intend to supply. What *Panther* suggests is a greater sensitivity to not only the structures that allow for these predations, but a greater sensitivity to how those structures are created and insinuated in their maintenance. The use of spots and patterning in *Panther* is both an aesthetic and ethical gesture: what is the panther's body if not a model of the molecular form, the body that coheres from a formal arrangement of dots? *Panther*, cat-like, playfully overturns systems of deducing meaning from images, reducing the separations to show how the outsider is already inside, how the animal is also the human. His take on proximities elides the proximity of sequential reading; the proximity of Christine, Panther, and father; and, ultimately, the proximity of the reader and the text.

The Panther

Illustrated in gem-like watercolors, *Panther* centers around a little girl named Christine, who lives alone in a large and vertiginously balanced house with her father. It is unclear what has caused her mother's departure from the home, but the longing for her seems palpable. The memory of the missing mother has cast a pall over the household, leaving the daughter and father behind in a home that is muted on multiple levels. The first chapter is titled Lucy, and the first full-page pictorial spread is painted in reds, blues, and blacks. We learn that Lucy is an emaciated cat, skulking along with a dragging leg. The primary colors of blue and red are muted and shadowy. On the wall there is a featureless portrait of a woman in profile, and a little girl pours cat food into a bowl from a box with an abstractly drawn cat face. She says simply, "Here, Lucy!" In the background, a man washes dishes at the sink, and although he is illuminated by an overhead light, we only catch a glimpse of his receding hairline and the bald patch developing on the top of his head. We see more of his features, which mirror the limited features of the cat face on the box of cat food, in his reflection in the reflective surface behind the sink. On a ledge between the sink and the reflective surface there sits a vase filled with flowers, and on the surface of the vase we can see the spotted tail and back half of a leopard—or panther—body.[23]

The next page of the comic is divided into six panels. In the top half of the page, three panels show the girl coaxing the cat to eat while the cat refuses. The bottom half of the page shows two adjacent panels that mark the transition from night to day, and in the final panel the girl addresses her cat in its carrier: "I have to go to school now but Daddy's going to take you to the vet and then you'll feel much better." After being dropped off from school by a friend's mother, she returns to find her father sitting at the table. He begins to explain when she inquires about the cat: "Well, you know Lucy was in a lot of pain. . . ."[24] The next page shows Christine running up the stairs as her father calls "Christine!" behind her (Figure 5.1). On the wall downstairs is a family portrait in which father and daughter are shown with little blue dots showing features, and again the featureless woman seated behind. In the foreground on a pedestal sits a statue of a cat-like figure resembling a Balinese mask. So the book begins, with the kinds of fictions that parents tell their children to explain away sudden disappearances from their lives. Perhaps there are other fictions that children are told—or tell themselves—to make sense of sudden appearances in their lives as well.

After Lucy's death, Christine mourns alone in her room until one day she magically finds a replacement companion in the form of a Panther, who emerges from the bottom drawer of the dresser in her room. He explains that the drawer is a portal to his home, Pantherland (or Panthésia, which sounds like "fantasia"), an exotic place full of lively, fantastical, and colorful stories and elements. The book also begins with the bottom compartment of another container, the freezer where Christine's father is keeping her dead cat's corpse while they wait to bury it in the right spot. The formal similarity of one cat going into a bottom compartment while another cat pops out from another suggests a symbolic resurrection: it is from the loss of this first cat that the new cat is summoned. The world of Christine's everyday life is initially depicted only in sedate washes of reds and blues. When Panther arrives, he introduces yellow into the pages

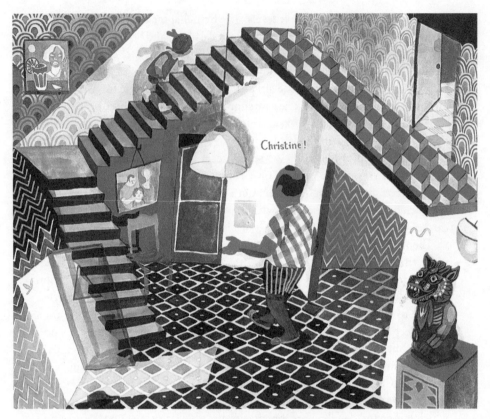

FIGURE 5.1 "Christine!" Brecht Evens, *Panther* (Montreal: Drawn & Quarterly, 2016), n.p. Copyright © Brecht Evens. (Used with permission from Drawn & Quarterly.)

of her world, which allows for mixing with the other primary colors to make the gem like tones that fill Christine's life with lively and fantastical sights. Panther and his name may call to mind a pantheon of diverse cartoon panther-like characters such as the unspotted Pink Panther and Bagheera and Marvel's Black Panther, or the yellow-spotted Marsupilami. It even suggests the tiger-striped Hobbes of *Calvin and Hobbes* in the jubilant early interactions between Christine and Panther when he dances with her and swings her around the room. The panther thus first appears as the pretend companion or imaginary playmate that one might expect in such a nursery room context. However, he is a master of deception who can hide his more frightening face most of the time, a face that is sourced, like most objects of the imagination, from real objects in Christine's house. The home that she lives in is decorated with exotic items where many objects and ornamentations resemble the panther. Most of all this Panther is the patterned kind of panther; he is covered in spots, a characteristic that complements the visual design of the book, and which will have profound significance in our understanding of the text at the end of the book. The panther's ability to look completely different every time is matched only by his ability to change his storytelling according to Christine's prompting, and initially, his intrusion into her life is a welcome addition. It literally brings color and liveliness to the depressed blues and reds that accompany the world of her life at home with her father.

The transgressiveness of the friendship between Christine and Panther moves from playful to increasingly suspicious, threatening, and dangerous quite rapidly over the course of the book. This transformation occurs all the while showing the uneasily framed borders between those states. From the moment of clarity that follows after the book is closed, one wonders exactly when things started to go wrong. The reader wonders whether this imaginary companion has been devised as a coping mechanism, what psychologists have pointed to as "the adaptive nature of imaginary companions as a means for coping with psychopathology or with life traumas such as . . . childhood abuse."[25] Through our retrospective gaze, the warning signs are clearly there, and were there from the very beginning. In interviews, Evens has described the Panther's behavior as explicitly that of the pedophile. He emphasizes the way that the Panther grooms Christine while separating her from those to whom she is closest: "He tries to be her ideal friend, following all of her cues to avoid shock or concern. Later, he seeks information from her, thus making himself gentle and tameable in the manner of the pedophile who gains the confidence of his future victim, isolating her from her potential protectors."[26] In this particular case, Panther makes quite easy work of it. The mother is gone. Friends barely register in the background, with the exception of the casual car-pool exchanges. Even the cat is dead. Her father appears to have retreated into a haze of muted interactions.

Upon his arrival, Panther does indeed gradually separate Christine from her other fantastical friends, the toys in her room, including a small stuffed dog named Bonzo, by being the most exciting and charismatic figure in her life. He tells her fantastic stories about his homeland, Pantherland. It is a world he conjures up to suit her specific tastes, changing according to what he anticipates are her own frame preferences. He reads her responses, and then makes adjustments to his descriptions so that it accords exactly with what she wants to hear. For example, when she asks him to tell her about Pantherland, they have an exchange that shifts repeatedly as it develops:

"We Panthers are natural-born acrobats! Every year we have a. . . ."
"And horses! You have horses!"
"Horses, of course. . . . To play chess with!"
"Chess?"
"Yes, because don't tell anyone, Christine—horses are really bad at chess. So we Panthers always win."

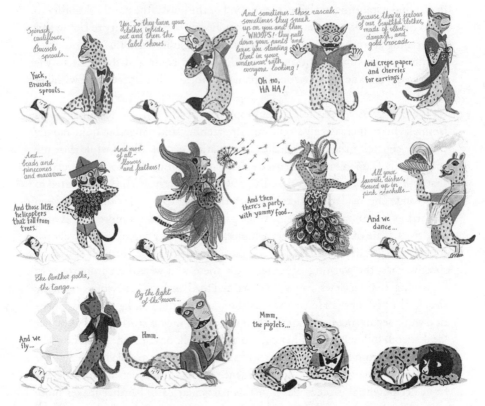

FIGURE 5.2 "Yuck, Brussels sprouts." Brecht Evens, *Panther* (Montreal: Drawn & Quarterly, 2016), n.p. Copyright © Brecht Evens. (Used with permission from Drawn & Quarterly.)

"Horses aren't dumb!"

"Of course not. Horses excel at geography and languages. Not so much at algebra. But you know who's really dumb?"

"Dogs!"

"Dogs, yes. We Panthers have a great joke. . . . We pretend we're throwing a stick. . . . But there is no stick!"[27]

When Panther describes the dinner parties, he quickly takes Christine's cue to relate her desires to the fantastic world he describes. While he describes the panthers' clothes as made of "velvet, damask, and gold brocade," Christine suggests "crepe paper and cherries for earrings." In the next picture, Panther has shed his top coat and bow tie for a paper hat and cherries for earrings, and continues in her tone: "And . . . beads and pinecones and macaroni" (Figure 5.2).[28] The frivolity of their conversation begins to take on an increasingly uncomfortable, then sinister, tone, and the chapter ends with a wordless full-page painting of Christine under the covers with the Panther's body encircling hers on the bed. Later when she is playing with Panther and he is tickling her, he "accidentally" bites her too hard, and when she tells him she is hurt he replies, "Oh, I'm sorry. That's how we Panthers always play." When he claims that panthers never lie and she asks him to prove it, he says "One need only consult the Great Panther Book. It's all there in black and white!"[29]

Chapter 3 begins with an image of Christine in bed with her father saying, "Good morning, Christine." Where has Panther gone? Eventually, Christine summons Panther and he tells her more about Panther behavior. While the reader might assume an elision between Panther and Christine's father, early in the book they appear as two distinct entities. Indeed, Panther is the imaginary friend that Christine hides from her father. While they enjoy a tea party together with Bonzo, who is "just sitting there, quiet as a mouse," her father knocks on the door and Christine quickly tells Panther to hide. The yellow tones are drained from the room with the entrance of her father, who tells her to brush her teeth and go to bed. When he offers to read her a bedtime story, she claims that she is too tired for a story. After her father leaves and she closes her door, she searches for Panther. The spots on the wall behind her slowly cohere into a form and Panther reemerges from the spots as he claims, "The spots on our Panther coats aren't just there to look pretty. They're also for camouflage. . . . A real Panther can always blend into his surroundings." When she begs him to teach her, he is all too happy to comply, and we next see Christine only in her underwear and painted with spots. Panther confides in her, "That was a close shave just now, eh? When your dad came in? Your mother . . . she's not around?"

There are in fact ominous warning signs that alert us to the danger that Panther poses to Christine's safety, in both color and in black-and-white. Among her companions, at least one appears to sense danger; but, lacking the ability to speak, does not appear to know how to protect her. The other toys' fear of Panther is palpable and, it turns out, justifiably so. Bonzo tries to sneak away from the panther's watchful eye to warn Christine of imminent danger. He begins to write a message of warning to Christine on the wall, but he is only able to write "watch out for pa" before he is caught by Panther, who surprises him from the bottom drawer and gobbles him up.[30] When Christine comes upon him from behind and pulls on his tail, he whirls around with a roar but quickly dissembles, explaining away why his tongue is furry. When Christine asks after Bonzo, Panther explains that he has gone off to "have an adventure. . . . See the whole wide world!"[31] Christine and Panther play an uncomfortably intimate game of Twister, and Panther tells her that he is so hot that he must undress. Christine tells him that her father will not give her a key to her room: "I'm too young and it wouldn't be safe if anything happened." Panther consolingly tells her, "Your father doesn't see what I see. That you're not his little girl anymore."[32]

When Panther reintroduces a replacement Bonzo, with the excuse that Bonzo has just returned from his travels to Pantherland, the new visitor is more than slightly changed by his experience abroad. Unlike the various forms of Panther, Bonzo has been from the very start more or less visually consistent throughout the book. Like Christine and her father, his aspect visibly changes between panels, but only in the ways that are natural to comics, with position or expression, expressing "the relational play of a plurality of interdependent images."[33] When Bonzo comes back from his trip to Pantherland, however, his physical change is drastic: it is not posture or expression that marks difference, but facial characteristics. Bonzo returns with a leering face that bares sharp teeth and, more significantly, he now has the surprising ability to speak. Adding to the strangeness of this new persona, Bonzo's speech is not colloquial; it is contextually jarring, and unambiguously sinister to the reader, but both tone and content are almost incomprehensible to Christine. Although uncertain that he is the "same Bonzo," Christine accepts Panther's explanation of his transformation. Indeed, she readily accepts all of the animals and animated toys that arrive from the portal to Pantherland, who arrive from her dresser drawer for her birthday party. On her birthday, she comes home from school and announces to her father that she is exhausted and wants to take a nap. In fact, she is rushing to her room to attend a surprise party hosted by Panther.

With his entrance into Christine's world, Panther was already a decontextualized figure, one who arrives from the fantasy world of children's fantasy fiction but who turns out to have actually come from the fantasy (or is it realistic?) world of adult horror. The predator cunningly turns responsibility away from himself and on to his victim. Wordplay has an "(anti-)social function in that it may create a gap between various groups of hearers, e.g. between hearers who appreciate a certain playful use of language and others who do not, between hearers who participate in the social practice and master it, and others who do not, or at a more basic level, between hearers who understand . . . the wordplay and others who fail to do so."[34] *Panther* plays on the multiple meanings that can adhere to the ludic approach to language with semiotic systems both visual and verbal. Different hearers may be distinguished from each other based on their levels of understanding, and this may result in the creation of an alienating distance between them. As Maik Goth has written, "Hearer-induced wordplay underscores the hearer's verbal dexterity, when the *double entendre* depends on his creative ability to generate unexpected and surprising disambiguations for an unequivocal speech act. . . . It can also stress a hearer's narrow-mindedness when he sees a *double entendre* where there is none."[35] The decontextualization inherent in the double entendre protects Panther from blame. If the hearer accuses him of being lewd, it allows him to shift the shame to us: how in the world did we come to construe this meaning? He can not only deny that such a meaning was intended but also suggest instead that we are the ones with dirty minds as to have come up with such conclusions.

Panther works his way into Christine's life with ease, and the facts of his being playful and cat-like call into the foreground an unavoidable reality. This very consistency undoes the possibility of binary distinctions, because it is not possible to say that the panther transforms into the monstrous. We are asked instead to consider the fact that monstrosity is very much within the continuum of reasonable behavior of this predator who takes many forms, who contains the capacity for violent attack just as much as he contains the capacity for gentle tenderness. By the time Christine has been swept into the party brought from Pantherland into her room for her birthday, it seems that interventions are far too late. Yet, what is this after-ness that makes something too late? What does it follow from if we recognize that the danger has always been present, and not a new manifestation? Panther's latent efforts at protecting Christine, during the party scene gone awry, lack credibility. When Bonzo more than suggestively asks her to stroke Giraffe, who "changes shape as you stroke it,"[36] are we still to think in terms of ambiguities, of warning signs that make sense only in hindsight? We are left to parse the tone and meaning of his statement, and the double entendre that floats between the text and the reader reminds us of all the other assumptions we make about things that we do not have to see in order to believe. At the party, the visitors from Pantherland separate Christine from Panther, and they drug her. Then they proceed, though it is not shown, to rape her. This vacancy in the sequence, following a frenetic and crowded series of images, is the most suggestive of all. As discussed earlier, it is frequently the vacancies and the white spaces that hold the greatest power of meaning making in the comics text. In a comic about our insecurities of reading too much or too little into things, we do not know what to do.

As the animals crowd around her, the drawing style abruptly changes once again. The picture world shifts dramatically and the images appears to be seen from Christine's point of view. Color and figurative representation are absent. The successive pages play out in a series of flat black-and-white images that are composed of black spots on a white page, the kind one would expect from a diagnostic eye exam. Gone are the fluid and colorful images that we have become accustomed to in the pages so far.[37] The transition from the fluid, the transparent, and the varied into the stark world of black-and-white conjures up the kinds of associations we make when using these words metaphorically. The questions of what really happened, allegations of testimony, are materialized in the sequence. The series of full-page spreads go from the leering face of Bonzo to the vague outlines of circles where spots are clustered together and to a sequential diagram that slowly transforms that circle and its nucleus into view again as the face of the Panther (Figure 5.3). The images in this sequence

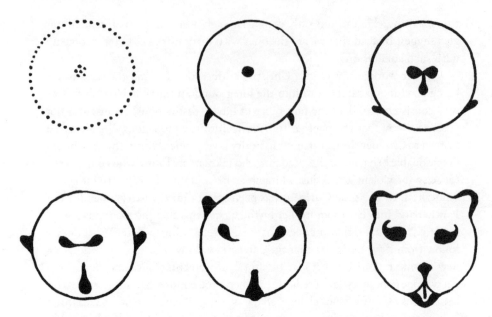

FIGURE 5.3 Black-and-white spots. Brecht Evens, *Panther* (Montreal: Drawn & Quarterly, 2016), n.p. Copyright © Brecht Evens. (Used with permission from Drawn & Quarterly.)

ask the reader: do you need to see something to know what happened? How closely must the atoms be arranged for them to become recognizable as assemblages?

The Girl

During the days leading up to the birthday party attack, Christine has been having nightmares. Her father sits quietly next to her on the edge of her bed. We make these assumptions based on the way that the figures are drawn and from their relative positions. She tells him about the dreams that she has been having. Christine tells him that he was in her dream, that he was angry at her, "like an animal," she says. He tenderly puts his hand on her knee. At the end of the sequence, he suggests that she sleep with her windows open. "Ugh. I feel weird," she says, and tells him that she needs to scream (Figure 5.4).[38] In the book so far, the father has seemed to us affectionate, if at times distant. He has seemed kind and tender, if sometimes strangely absent. We sense the precariousness of Christine's situation, and we see the way that the panther's grasp has become tighter and more inevitable. We wonder why the father has not been present, why he hasn't noticed how withdrawn she has become, why he

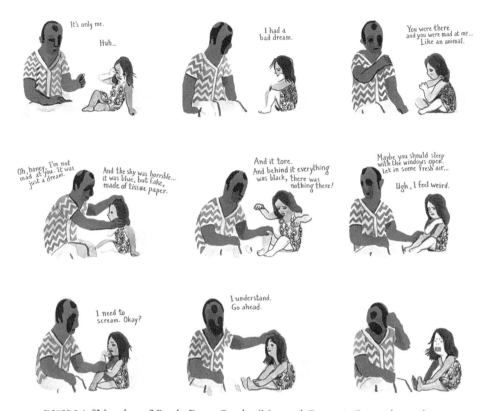

FIGURE 5.4 "It's only me." Brecht Evens, *Panther* (Montreal: Drawn & Quarterly, 2016), n.p. Copyright © Brecht Evens. (Used with permission from Drawn & Quarterly.)

hasn't sensed the imminent danger. We wonder why hasn't he stepped in to protect her.

But a new question also begins to take form. Is the problem not a problem of his being absent, but that he actually has been present all along? After the diabolical birthday party, a scene plays out between Christine and Panther that looks remarkably similar (Figure 5.5). Indeed, it almost exactly reproduces the earlier scene between Christine and her father. This time it is Panther who sits on her bed. Instead of a rumpled nightgown, she is naked under the sheets. This time it is Panther who soothingly tells her not to be frightened. He, too, pets her tenderly. He, too, demonstrates concern. She tells him, "Aah, I don't feel right." He tells her that he is Panther, *her* Panther.[39] What do these two tender scenes have to do with each other? And what is it about the text that nudges us to hold these two scenes against each other and to compare their patterns? The ambiguities of the book force the reader to try to determine whether the father is so negligent that he has failed to protect his daughter from falling to the predations of the bad elements who wait for vulnerable subjects, or if the father is

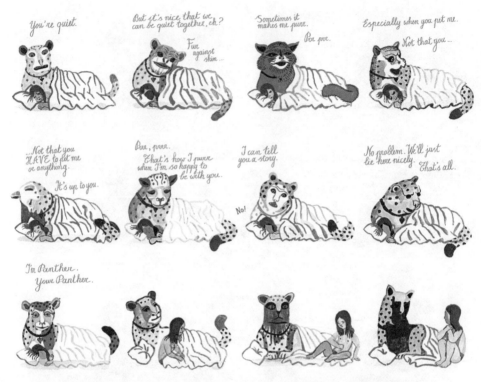

FIGURE 5.5 "I'm Panther." Brecht Evens, *Panther* (Montreal: Drawn & Quarterly, 2016), n.p. Copyright © Brecht Evens. (Used with permission from Drawn & Quarterly.)

the predatory bad element itself. Yet both of these potentialities redound to the same conclusion: that what happens to Christine happens to her because of the father.

It is at this point that we return to a consideration of the patterns that we see in the spots that litter the pages of the book. Jacques Derrida used an encounter with his cat, or rather his awareness of his cat's encounter with his naked body, as the premise for "The Animal That Therefore I Am." In his bathroom, beheld by his cat, he contemplates the way that humans are capable of being naked, whereas the cat that beholds him cannot. This knowledge is what humans use to claim themselves sovereign over "the animal," referring to animals as a singular unit in spite of the surplus of forms of life that are grouped under that single word. In the naming of the animal as something from which humans have emerged, there is the blindness of what Lawlor attributes to human auto-affection.[40] In the self-designation "human" as separate from animal, we see only that though we come from animal, are still animal, we claim that human is what animal is *not*. Not only does the surplus of meaning that attaches to the word "animal" reveal our unwillingness to accept multiplicities in others, it reveals the unspoken fact that humans are still in fact the animal. What Evens's book exposes more than anything else are our attempts and failures to sublimate the panther inside us.

"I'm panther. Your panther." After everything that has transpired by the time we reach this moment, these words sound differently to us. The truth that Evens's book points to is that precautions that seek to do away with panthers, or to do away with the animal, falsely equate security with singularity, as if preventing the passage of the animal is all that it takes to prevent the child from harm. What is clear from this book is that while it may be possible to do away with what we *call* the animal, we cannot do away with the animal that we are unwilling to recognize in ourselves. This panther is spotted, and *Panther* asks the reader to think through what these spots can suggest. It asks the reader to literally connect the dots. There are patterns that decorate the pages, and there are patterns of repeated motifs in the book, from the spots on the panther to the spots on the Twister mat, to the black-and-white spots at the scene of Christine's assault. There are patterns in the visual cues, and patterns in the language. There are suggestions left unspoken but still there at the surface, waiting to be read.

Panther gazes at Christine as she sits bewildered on her bed. Her father is in his bedroom, getting ready to take her out to dinner to celebrate her birthday. They have been planning for and looking forward to this night out. He looks in the mirror as he adjusts his tie, and whistles happily to himself. The panther has taken many shapes throughout the course of the book, but in the last panel of twelve, his face is cast over with shadows that obscure his eyes and mouth. It is hauntingly familiar, actually exactly the same, when we see it next, reflected in the mirror in the father's bedroom. The father is reproduced in aspect and manner, and the cast of those shadows as he stands before his bedroom mirror unravel the mysteries of the circles of black-and-white that Christine saw resolving earlier into Panther's face. These patches of black oozing in and out of focus, resolving into the spotty organization of a panther's features are uncannily those of the father's patterns of baldness as his hair recedes from his forehead (Figure 5.6).

There are other, retrospective, connections. Not just notable, but impossible to avoid in our newfound clarity, is the introduction of yellow into the representation of Christine's father's room. Evens has trained us to see color, and its absence, as a tool freighted with meaning over the course of the book. Up until this point, Christine and her father's world was exclusively shown in washes of reds, blues, and blacks. Only the intrusions from Pantherland were accompanied by shades of yellow. The black figures against multicolored geometric shapes have been reserved only for scenes that bear the presence of the panther, literally marked by the prowling cat. Yet now we see the colors, now we see the shadowy figure, and we search for the panther in the room. And we

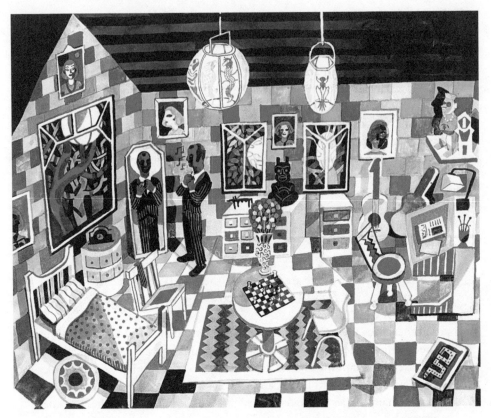

FIGURE 5.6 Getting ready. Brecht Evens, *Panther* (Montreal: Drawn & Quarterly, 2016), n.p. Copyright © Brecht Evens. (Used with permission from Drawn & Quarterly.)

don't see him. Or perhaps we do. He may be there, looking out at us, directly from the borders of the mirror. Why is it that we are unwilling to believe that we see it now, before our eyes? I made a point earlier that the Panther resembled an everyday object in the father's house, the statuette of a cat in the foyer of the house. But perhaps the actual everyday object is Christine's father himself.

There are other patterns. The father has been depicted throughout this narrative wearing short-sleeved T-shirts, bedroom slippers, shorts or underwear. In the earlier pages of this book, this seems only like signs of his depression. His dishabille is not notable until it is contrasted with the preening father standing before the mirror and admiring himself in suit and tie. It calls to mind Panther himself, who brightens everything with his cheerful yellow tones. It calls to mind the strangeness of those funny cartoon animals whose nakedness is made stranger when they wear only shirts, and are shown naked from waist down. Now suddenly we see warning signs where before we only saw ordinary conventions. Now we see the monster in the mirror and wonder how long we have known that he was there. By the end of the book, it becomes abundantly clear that the problem is not that there is an anthropomorphic—animal with human form—panther, whose possession of language has allowed him his access to Christine; instead, we are confronted by the much more troubling possibility that it is Christine's father who is therianthropic—human cast into animal form[41]—and that he has always, always, always had access to Christine. "I'm panther. Your panther." Though the power of the book comes from the very fact that Evens leaves open the question of whether Panther and Pater are one and the same, the pattern is unmistakable. The father, the panther, and the literal structures around her are united, and Christine does not stand a chance. Bonzo warned to watch out for "Pa." What separates the panther, *Panter* in the original Dutch, from the father, the *pater*, only requires the slightest adjustment of a few letters of the alphabet.

The Wardrobe

Panther serves as a reminder that we often believe that the stranger is a new arrival from other shores. He has come without the necessary papers. The prevailing narrative is that he is an intruder who has snuck across the border, an uninvited guest who comes with the intent of harm. This is a belief that strengthens confidence in making assertions that if only borders can be secured, and the appropriate forms and papers assigned and produced, the realm of sovereign power can and will be maintained. The vocabulary of inside and outside extends to here and there, to us and them; and the security of the borders becomes the security of that which we keep within. But the events in *Panther* interrogate this assertion. The reader is reminded that it is more often the case that the predator is undocumented because he did not need documentation to enter in the first place: he was already on the inside. The comics elision of the animal and the father in the figure of the Panther makes this point without needing to delve into the questions of allegory or metaphor. By its very nature of allowing for the multiple iterations of form that fall within the convention of the comics narrative, *Panther* does not allow for easy gestures toward difference and identity. The panther has appeared in remarkably varied forms, but we have accepted him throughout the book as if he is a singular, individual entity. Similarly, the safeguards we take against abstract threats from unknown entities are made in the name of the singular (the outsider, the terrorist, the undocumented, the radicalized) as well, even though we know that in such terms any number of entities can be signified. Evens's Panther has been construed as a possible creation throughout the novel, he has been plausibly understood only as a fantasy companion or an imaginary friend. The reader has been led to believe that this act of creation was the result of Christine's imagination, whether because of past or ongoing trauma.

As the book develops, however, the reader discovers the stunning fact that Panther may in fact be a mutually constituted character, and that his

persona may well be the creation of Christine's father, an allegorical construction of animal-like id as separate from the mutely caring and shadowy
father. He thus invokes the so-called inclusive exclusion, the bare life, that is
the central self-producing activity of the sovereign father. It is this bare life
that precisely forms that "zone of indistinction and continuous transition
between man and beast, nature and culture."[42] Giorgio Agamben's sustained
interrogation of "bare life" (*la nuda vita*) is "the element that, in the exception, finds itself in the most intimate relation with sovereignty."[43] Agamben
explains his use of the term as originating from "an obscure figure of archaic
Roman law"[44] as a man who is to be punished for a crime but cannot be sacrificed according to the law, yet who also may be killed without the killing
being designated as a murder. This structure creates a simultaneous insider-
outsider hybrid figure who serves as the "bearer of sovereignty."[45] This is the
bare life that is created by and for the sovereign. As *Panther* suggests, it is
the sovereign father, the creator of the *homo sacer* in the form of the Panther,
who has been the greatest threat all along. It may be that the more shocking
conclusion of *Panther*, however, is that a sovereign father can knowingly
manipulate and exploit the very model of the imaginary figure of the Panther itself in his predations. He can be simultaneously sovereign father and
outsider Panther, and the disposability of the latter guarantees the former's
predominance. The comic makes it plain that if father and panther are one
and the same, the only inevitability that we can reliably assume is that *his*
presence is truly and wholly inescapable.

Apart from the political implications of this reading of *Panther*, we might
read *Panther* as a critique of the proliferation of identities that are accepted as
singular. This is reinforced by the mechanical reproduction processes that
assure us that every version of *Panther* the book is identical to each other.
Evens's book was created using watercolors and the layers of paint and the white
spaces untouched by the medium are no longer traceable on the reproduced
pages of the book. What remains are the metaphorical layers, where earlier versions of the panther and earlier versions of the father are animated by the reader's memory rather than actual physical interactions with the printed page.
Here, too, the text recalls for us the role of the imaginative act. Whereas the
imagination may be accused as being overactive by the predator, the text itself
reminds us of the importance of those very faculties. The spaces between what
is shown on the page cannot be wholly supplanted by a single forceful interpretation if the reader has been vigilant. All the more reason for the reader to be
vigilant.

There is a mistake to attributing singularity to groups of others. There are no
protective precautions that can be taken against singulars meant to define
everything that we are not. The animal. The foreigner. We simply cannot prepare for and identify threats that we cannot distinguish from the ordinary. The
problems of dealing with Panthers of all sorts are thus related to a false faith in

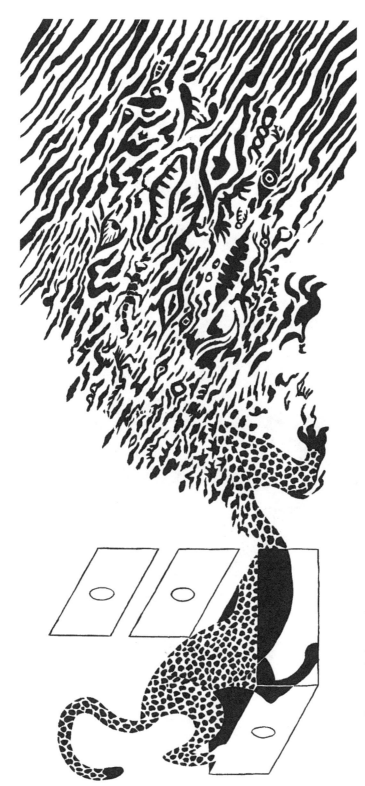

FIGURE 5.7 Back into wardrobe. Brecht Evens, *Panther* (Montreal: Drawn & Quarterly, 2016), n.p. Copyright © Brecht Evens. (Used with permission from Drawn & Quarterly.)

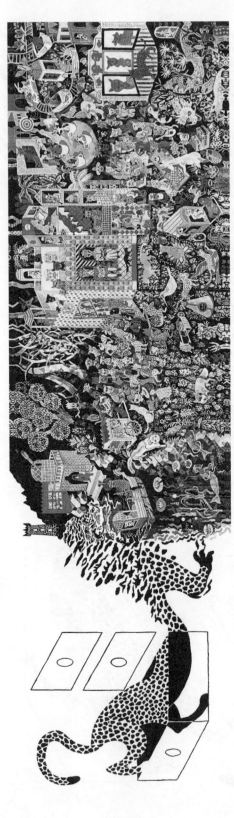

FIGURE 5.8 Panthesia. Brecht Evens, *Panther* (Montreal: Drawn & Quarterly, 2016), n.p. Copyright © Brecht Evens. (Used with permission from Drawn & Quarterly.)

our biopolitical apparatuses, created based on how things appear. Our methods are those depending on anticipation and control, in service of risk management. Forms of security are expressed as border policing, technologies of surveillance, the gathering of biometric data, the tracking system of visas and immigration laws, the patterns of movement. They are expressed as travel bans. They are expressed as alerts for the unusual, without articulating what constitutes the unusual. Borders in Evens's book are configured so that they flicker back and forth between the bare life and the sovereign-sanctioned life; sometimes the panther, sometimes the father. Always the panther, always the father. This provocation asks us to think about the other ways that we fail with our biopolitical assertions of borders maintained in purely spatial and territorial terms. Because just as much as biopolitical apparatuses have become increasingly mobile and invisible, so are their objects mobile and invisible. Flickering on the atomic level, on the level of little spots that cohere into meaning only after it is too late, they reside within. They have always already been there. And we are responsible for them.

The belief that dangerous elements can be reduced out, isolated, and contained, is too often the belief at the heart of our mechanisms of security. Keeping our children away from animals may protect us from *those* animals, those that we define ourselves against. But what do we do about the fact that we, too, are animals? We see in the spatial territory of the wardrobe the embodiment of this paradox. The wardrobe is the border, the portal between Christine's world and Pantherland (or its more evocative "Panthésia"). But the wardrobe is both exterior and interior, both container and contained. Closing the border may keep out what we think are the outsiders from our borders, but this will not solve the fact that we are all outsiders to each other. It is undeniable that the violence against Christine began once the Panther was invited into her room, but the fact remains that he emerged from her bureau drawer. The bureau drawer that was already inside the room. He was always already there.

The last page of the book is a surprise; a black-and-white page continues into the endpapers with the image of the panther skulking off the page back into the wardrobe (Figure 5.7). In fact, the book presents its final illusion: the wardrobe contains a secret passage, a foldout page that transforms into the technicolor magical dreamscape world of Panthésia, or Pantherland, unfolding seductively into an illustration of Panther's exotic land (Figure 5.8). In this final action, Evens literally forces the reader's hand, making her carry out the border crossing that cannot be passive, active because we all play a part in assuming the impassability of a border. The problem of access, of closed doors, of who holds the keys, are simply distractions. The danger is already here, inside all of our homes. We are blind to its power, and so long as we remain blind, so long as we remain complacent to it, it threatens to consume us. Each and every one.

Conclusion

Perfect Copies has explored the especially revelatory effects of material and mechanical reproduction that the comics form brings to our ways of thinking about the printed book. The specific cases discussed in these chapters have proceeded from the assumption that the comic mixes the material and the spiritual, and that this form facilitates an animistic medium that encases the meeting of multiple surfaces: the reader, the reproduced word-image text, and the author. Each of these surfaces—person, text, person—contains its own particular histories and material properties. At the meeting of these surfaces, we encounter opportunities of wonder, incurred with a sense of communion that heightens the reader's sense of what is missing. Over the course of these five chapters, I argue that reading comics with a focus on the multiple related interpretations of "reproduction" addresses a certain ambivalence about our current moment, reflecting a range of reactions to an insurmountable proliferation of information. That such information is all delivered on the same material platforms that take the form of the illuminated window—screens on digital readers, monitors, tablets, laptops, and smartphones—lends only an exigence that makes it all the harder to shed a sense of the tethers that inhere. They cannot be broken because they cannot be touched. We want to touch things, and these books offer a kind of respite, but also their own new problems. One of those problems is the problem of reproduction: these are materials that deny the authority of materiality. They remind us that we are touching something, but also not touching the something that was originally created.

The material forms that bear and communicate the information we consume no longer convey the authority that may have come with the specificity of paratextual hints about how to receive them, such as book covers or ornately carved frames. One can argue that this ambivalence about one's age, one where the sense of assault by information and mutability is ever-present, may well bespeak an ambivalence shared by every age. I myself harbor that conviction. I have also harbored the conviction that this anxiety about reproduction, in all the ways I have meant it in this book, may well be the most enduring and profound anxiety of being human. I have no doubt that my own forays into motherhood may play more than its share in shaping this conviction. But what stronger evidence can be made than to watch another person, who starts out as just another insensate sac of stuff; another part of one's body, really; part of one's own physical, material, biological person; emerge, separate, and then grow, and then transform as if by magic from day to day. It may be that they resemble us physically—a like copy—and yet behave as an unpredictable and unknowable stranger; or it may be the other way around, and they physically do not resemble us at all, but share in our habits or tone or voice or reactions in unmistakably like ways. So: reproductions. As I wrote in the introduction, reproduction is a particularly rich conceit for thinking about narratives because of the ways that it is explicitly temporal: it expresses ideas of past, present, and future inextricably in concert. Formally speaking, it is also a mode for focusing our attentions to the ways that writerly texts, like the image-text books I have chosen to write about, can do. I would like to close this book with a consideration of a final instance in which the idea of likeness takes on its sonority through a series of performances of likeness itself.

E.A. Bethea's *Francis Bacon* is sixty pages of "kinda poetic comics" that is clearly the inheritor of many traditions and also most assuredly a form that is its own.[1] I first encountered Bethea's short stories in her 2017 *Book of Daze*, and the story "Vigée le Brun" (Figure C.1), which staggered through a narrative of loss and temporality in twelve panels across three pages of newsprint. The pages of my copy are smeared with my finger-width smudges made by my hands as I held the comic, perhaps too tightly. The ink on the page is fugitive, and marks one's fingers in a way that makes them complicit with the surface of the page as well. "Vigée le Brun" is also marked by a kind of stuttering passage between moments in time that is characteristic of Bethea's work; the narrative "I" jumps around in time between panels unpredictably, so that a first panel might introduce the titular painter, and then immediately shift to a consideration of a library book: "I turn the page in the library book to find a single sheet of toilet paper serving as a bookmark."[2] This shifts, too, to the memory of a childhood friend who disappeared, in the middle of an everyday activity: "The iron was left on. She was ironing her shirt for work. She was a hostess at Brennan's. . . . This was before irons turned themselves off automatically. This was before I had an email address." The "befores" of the events, and the implied "afters," of the writing are embedded in the text, insisting on an accounting of chronology. The second panel on the third and final page of the story is a reproduction of a photograph—not a drawing—of Daphne, "still missing and missed by many."[3] The poor quality of the reproduction makes it almost impossible to see any of

NEW YORK WAS JUST A MIRAGE, A LONE CYPRESS IN A LAGOON, A TRICK COIN, HEADS EVERY TIME, AN ORANGE SUNSET, CREAMY TURTLE SOUP SERVED FROM A VERMILLION TUREEN, INTO A GOLDEN BOWL. OH NO, I'M LOSING THE THREAD...

HOW CAN I TELL YOU ABOUT DAPHNE JONES AND KEEP THE THREAD. SHE IS STILL MISSING AND MISSED BY MANY. SHE WAS SMART AND PRETTY. I CAN NOT TELL HER STORY FOR MANY REASONS. THIS WAS SUPPOSED TO BE ABOUT LOUISE ÉLISABETH VIGÉE LE BRUN, WHO PAINTED A REVILED QUEEN HOLDING RIBBON-ENTWINED ROSES, BABIES, AND BOOKS, OVER AND OVER AND OVER AGAIN.

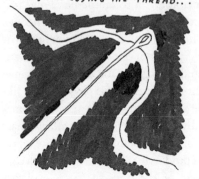

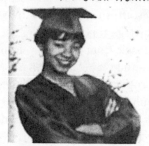

I AM JUST TRYING TO KEEP THE CAN MOVING. I AM PASSING IT FROM FOOT TO FOOT. THE IRON IS ON AND WILL NOT SHUT ITSELF OFF. WE WILL KEEP GOING. I WILL KEEP KICKING THE CAN. THE CAN WILL NOT MOVE WITHOUT ME. YOU CAN KICK THE CAN, TOO.

KEEP IT MOVING...
IF WE KEEP IT MOVING
IT NEVER
STOPS.

WHAT ELSE IS THERE TO DO, ON THIS FEBRUARY AFTERNOON, AT THE EDGE OF THE CITY, BETWEEN THE OCEAN AND BAY, IN FAR ROCKAWAY, QUEENS, NEW YORK, USA, BUT TO DRAW A ROSE FOR DAPHNE IN MARIE ANTOINETTE'S HAND, IN THE STYLE OF VIGÉE LE BRUN, IN MY OWN POOR HAND? I AM DREAMING OF SALTWATER SPRAY IN MAY AND BROKEN HEARTS MENDED ON THIS COLD AND FUCKING MISERABLE DAY, AND I AM WARMED.

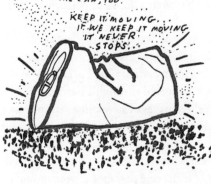

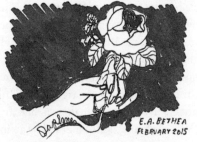

E.A. BETHEA
FEBRUARY 2015

FIGURE C.1 "How can I tell you about Daphne Jones." E. A. Bethea, *Book of Daze* (New York: Domino Books, 2017), n.p. Copyright © E. A. Bethea.

Daphne's features. The high school graduation cap, the trace of an earring, the white spots on the cheeks that insinuate a smile, the V-shaped neckline of a graduation gown just a grade less shaded, the tops of a few fingers of crossed arms, and the darkened crease of a page held to a photocopier are all that I can make out of Daphne Jones. The text intones, "She was smart and pretty. I can not tell her story for many reasons."[4] And indeed, Bethea cannot allow herself to draw her friend, either, choosing instead to offer this shadowy copy of a photograph, which withholds clarity in the same way that the narrative—and the disinterest of the news that failed to cover the disappearance—did to Daphne.

This is a story about the failure of "the news" that is told in newsprint. It is a story about the disappearance of a person, and how that person's disappearance goes unnoted in "the news" because she is Black, and who is now in this time of "afterness," obscured in a copy of a photograph, which is itself only a copy of a missing person, who is irretrievable in space and time.

The threads that connect these panels together are not just invisible: they are deliberately subtended, like the bracts that embrace the flower from beneath, allowing it to open outward on the page. The suspension in which we hold these thoughts is articulated by Bethea in the final panel: "What else is there to do . . . but to draw a rose for Daphne in Marie Antoinette's hand, in the style of Vigée le Brun, in my own poor hand?"[5] The hand of the author, the hands of the subjects of the story, and the reader's own stained hands are activated through this interaction that exceeds the figurative. There is a union brokered in these texts, a union that desires and demands our communion with others and that allows us to share in an ether that is by its very nature temporary and impossible to reproduce in exactly the same way. In Bethea's case, they stain us lest we begin to forget.

Francis Bacon continues the detailed explorations of loss and disconnect that haunt Bethea's earlier short works. The book announces its preoccupation with likenesses in its playfully constructed table of contents on the inside cover. Along the left side of the page are four equally sized photographs that show, from top to bottom, E. A. Bethea, Francis Bacon, Bethea's father, and "Mike Hammer." The first page announces its motif—"My friend Joey Davis told me I look like the painter Francis Bacon but I think I'm better looking"—with the first of a series of similes that press the use of "like" through all sorts of forms until resting at an ending that refers to where it began (Figure C.2). In its final pages, a journey is invoked that returns the reader to the beginning: "Joey chainsmoked Marlboro lights, like the teen girls of my youth to whom, being frozen stiff in worriment over my buttonfly-donning tendencies, I could never express my amatory devotion. How far I have come. Searching my face for some time Joey opined that I bore semblance to the Irish painter Francis Bacon, who I seemed to recall looked a wee bit deranged."[6] The comic moves furtively between the states of "I am" (better looking, just pretty average, emotional perpetrator) to "I am not" (the chocolate bunny, George Dyer, Francis Bacon) and in between there are the "I have been," "I'd," and "I'll"s of states of being that are suspended there, too, in the liquid states that I have tried to show are promises of possibilities and disappointments alike. In its elegiac tone, Bethea's comic indulges these questions of the ways that likeness may be tried and tested through her estranged biological father ("he knew every bookie in town and never met a stranger, except perhaps for me") and the strangers who mean as much ("the poets and painters, hornblowers, ivory ticklers, and blind candlestick makers . . . peddling light through the direst of hours").[7] It is an easy act of the imagination to see Bethea's hand streak the page, making uneven marks and scratches that resemble the

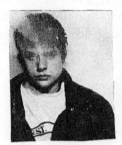

E.A. BETHEA

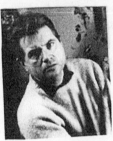

FRANCIS BACON

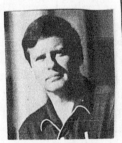

MY DAD

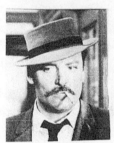

MIKE HAMMER

E.A. BETHEA'S
francis bacon

VOL. 1, NO. 1   2021
PUBLISHED BY DOMINO BOOKS
© E.A. BETHEA ALL RIGHTS RESERVED ETC.

ON NEWSSTANDS AND IN
BOOKSTORES THROUGHOUT THE WORLD
EVERY OTHER THURSDAY.
READERS IN 77 COUNTRIES.

CONTENTS

HOT HOMEMADE WINE RECIPES	VARIOUS
INTERVIEW WITH FLO CAPP	E.A. BETHEA
HORTENSE BEVERIDGE, FILM EDITOR EXTRAORDINAIRE	E.A. BETHEA
POETRY: "SIPPING YOO-HOO ON THE BEACH WITH YOU"	E.A. BETHEA
FICTION: "ARPEGGIOS FOR A SAVAGE FLU"	GERARD SMITH
ON THE SCENE: PARTY DISPATCHES AND MORE	THE EDITORS
REVIEW: "THE GARFIED CHRISTMAS SPECIAL KNOCKS IT OUT THE PARK"	E.A. BETHEA

DEPARTMENTS

COMINGS & GOINGS	THE CURRENT CRISIS
FEAST OR FAMINE	WHAT PRICE FAME?
PUZZLE ZONE	SHIT YOU DON'T NEED

ON THE COVER

MR. SKRIBBLES IS A CHIHUAHUA DACHSHUND MIX
LOOKING FOR A GOOD HOME AND AVAILABLE IMMEDIATE-
LY FOR ADOPTION. MR. SKRIBBLES ENJOYS HER RUBBER
SQUEAKY NEWSPAPER TOY AND WOULD PAIR WELL
WITH SEAFOOD. WHATEVER YOU DO, DO NOT TOUCH
HER EARS OR SHE'LL BITE YOU. SHE'S REALLY SENSI-
TIVE ABOUT HER EARS. SHE ALSO LOVES TO SNIFF
THE BUTT OF A CERTAIN PUG AT THE DOG PARK, AND
DANCING AT TOPS, THE PREMIERE NIGHT CLUB LOCATED IN
THE LOVE TOWER (NOW LEASING OFFICE SPACE & STUDIO APTS).

FIGURE C.2 Front inside cover and first page. E. A. Bethea, *Francis Bacon* (New York: Domino Comics, 2021), n.p. Copyright © E.A. Bethea.

MY FRIEND JOEY DAVIS TOLD
ME I LOOK LIKE THE PAINTER
FRANCIS BACON BUT I THINK
I'M BETTER LOOKING —

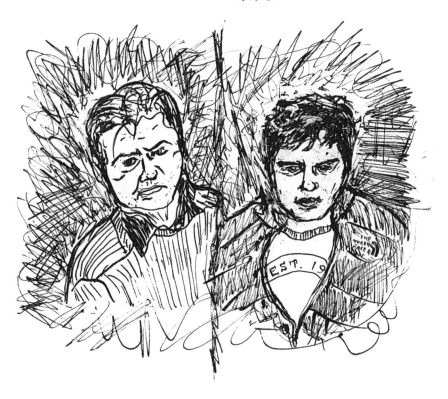

FIGURE C.2 (*Continued*)

kinds of lines made by sputtering pen tips in their own final throes. These scratchy lines and the accompanying clots of white correction fluid adhere to the page, asserting their visual residue of presence and absence that confirm that some-one was there, and still is.

In the pages of the books discussed here in *Perfect Copies*, we are invited to keep these feelings in suspension, too. We are invited to want to feel the pages as they look to us and that abrade our fingers on the textures of the paper they are printed on, even though we know that—newsprint ink excepted—the dis-tance between the hand creating the pages and our own cannot be broached. We see the textures and suspect the overs and the unders that their aspects imply, but we cannot feel them no matter how hard we try. We are invited instead to imagine a union forged from a series of paths. This is a series of paths that merge and cross in ways that we don't always understand at first encounter, or even at second or third encounter. Indeed, it is the case that we may not ever understand these crossings, either because we cannot or will not. I think that the uncertainty that they articulate is the point they are trying to make. These texts allow us to imagine a communion between eyes and hands that is divided by time and space, and that nonetheless communes. The fact that they never forget the incommen-surateness of this task and yet continue onward is the very thing that keeps them alive, future looking, and ready. Because of them, we will be ready, too.

Acknowledgments

I wish to extend a big thank you to the wonderful people who have directly and indirectly influenced and encouraged me in the writing of this book: Maaheen Ahmed, Shar'-Lin Anderson, Gabrielle Bell, Dori Broudy, Nicole Capobianco, Leela Corman, Brannon Costello, Brian Cremins, Allison Felus, Marnie Galloway, Emile Holmewood, Emma Hunsinger, Shing Yin Khor, Annie Koyama, MariNaomi, Tamar Norquist, Dan Nott, Laura Park, Ben Passmore, Keiler Roberts, James Sturm, Julianne Viscardo, and Tillie Walden. As always, my friends at work have given me advice, strength, and encouragement along the way, especially Kim Cassidy, Oliva Cardona, Yvonne Chireau, Rad Edmonds, Susanna Fioratta, Michelle Francl, Ignacio Gallup-Díaz, Hank Glassman, Tim Harte, Pat Healy, Ken Koltun-Fromm, Yan Kung, Agnès Peysson-Zeiss, Adrienne Prettyman, Erin Schoneveld, Marc Schulz, Maja Šešelj, Gina Siesing, Sarah Theobald, Kate Thomas, and Alicia Walker. Penny Armstrong kindly invited me to participate in a panel, which struck the spark for the chapter on *Sabrina*. Even this many years after graduate school, it is his approval I covet the most: my mentor Wilt Idema kindly suppressed an eyeroll, and indeed congratulated me, when I once again delayed completion of another project in favor of this book.

Many thanks to the good people of Fantagraphics, Drawn & Quarterly, Breakdown Press, Domino Comics, Kuš! Comics, and Myriad Editions. They consistently make incredible choices about work to publish, circulate, and promote, and their efforts have changed the landscape of reading for the better. Thank you to Eric Reynolds at Fantagraphics and Francine Yulo at Drawn & Quarterly. I would like to especially thank E. A. Bethea, Gareth Brookes, Nick Drnaso, Brecht Evens, Emil Ferris, Jerry Moriarty, Frank Santoro, and Conor Stechschulte, for whom my enthusiasm and gratitude are eternal. Thanks to Emile Holmewood for the cover art and for the many conversations that this project occasioned. Elizabeth, Gareth, Emil, Brecht, and Conor, thank you for the extra words of encouragement at so many steps of the way and also for the treats, both material and spiritual, that you have shared with me over the years. You truly make this world a better place to live in.

I am grateful to the Bryn Mawr Provost's Office and the Bryn Mawr College Faculty Research Awards Committee for supporting my participation in lectures and academic conferences where much of the work of this book was originally presented. These include the Seventh Biennial Congress in Comparative Literature in 2017 in Helsinki; the Biennial Conference of the Society for Multi-Ethnic Studies (MESEA) in 2018 in Graz, Austria; the International Comics Arts Forum Conference (ICAF) in 2019 in Davenport, Iowa; the University of Ghent in 2019; and two conferences that gracefully pivoted in a pandemic to a virtual format in 2021: Northeast Modern Languages Association (NEMLA) in Buffalo, and "Der Text und seine (Re)Produktion" in Wuppertal, Germany.

Thank you to Nicole Solano for your enthusiastic support of this book from proposal to finish. I thank the anonymous readers of the manuscript, whose suggestions shaped and informed this book. More importantly, their generosity and encouragement renewed my faith in academia and in people, in general, and kept my spirits up when they were down. I have always thought about reading as answering the question of what one does when one meets a stranger, and these readers have been exemplary models.

Parts of chapter 1 appeared in "The People Upstairs: Space, Memory, and the Queered Family in *My Favorite Thing Is Monsters* by Emil Ferris," in *The Routledge Companion to Gender and Sexuality in Comic Book Studies*, edited by Frederick Aldama (Abingdon: Routledge, 2021), 469–482, and parts of chapter 5 appeared in "The Panther, the Girl, and the Wardrobe: Borderlessness and Domestic Terror in Brecht Evens' *Panther*," in *Strong Bonds: Relationships between Children and Animals in Comics*, edited by Maaheen Ahmed (Liège: University of Liège Press, 2020), 165–179. Parts of my discussion on surface appeared in "Surface," in *The Oxford Encyclopedia of Literary Theory*, edited by John Frow (Oxford: Oxford University Press 2022), which was also published online as "Surface." *Oxford Research Encyclopedia of Literature* (Oxford University Press, 2020). I thank Routledge Press, University of Liège Press, and Oxford University Press for permission to reprint them here, and I thank the respective editors, Frederick Aldama, Maaheen Ahmed, and John Frow, who have been such wonderful interlocutors.

As always, I wish to thank my family, Shialing and Stephen Powell, Lucy and Boo Hoe Kwa, and Daniel and Helene Roses. Most of all, Robert, Ben, and Elly Roses: your good humor, tolerance, patience, and encouragement dispel all bad dreams, making me feel as if queen of infinite space. Everything I start and everything I finish is because of you.

Notes

Introduction

1 Adorno, "Essay as Form," 33.
2 Hirsch, *Family Frames*, 10.
3 Hirsch, *Family Frames*, 11.
4 Spiegelman, *Complete Maus*.
5 Bechdel, *Fun Home*.
6 Satrapi, The Complete Persepolis.
7 Dash Shaw's *Bottomless Bellybutton*, discussed later in this book, and Olivier Schrauwen's *Arsène Schrauwen* come to mind. Crucifix and Meesters, "Medium Is the Message."
8 Szép, *Comics and the Body*, 5.
9 Crary, *24/7*, 25.
10 Danto, "Artworld," 574.
11 Danto, "Artworld," 580.
12 Gardner, *Projections*.
13 Beaty, *Comics versus Art*, 163.
14 Crucifix, "Drawing from the Archives."
15 Kashtan, *Between Pen and Pixel*.
16 Bredehoft, *Visible Text*, 17.
17 Kwa, *Regarding Frames*.
18 McCloud, *Understanding Comics*, 68.
19 Marx and Engels, *Capital*, 133.
20 Marx and Engels, *Capital*, 133–134.
21 Bourdieu, *Distinction*; Bourdieu, *Logic of Practice*.
22 Horkheimer and Adorno, *Dialectic of Enlightenment*, 94.
23 Horkheimer and Adorno, *Dialectic of Enlightenment*, 95.
24 Horkheimer and Adorno, *Dialectic of Enlightenment*, 95–96.
25 Horkheimer and Adorno, *Dialectic of Enlightenment*, 100.
26 Prosser, "Introduction," 1.
27 Adorno, "Culture Industry Reconsidered."
28 Benjamin, *Walter Benjamin and Art*, 1.

29 Benjamin, "Work of Art in the Age of Mechanical Reproduction," 220.
30 Benjamin, "Work of Art in the Age of Mechanical Reproduction," 224.
31 Deleuze, *Difference and Repetition*, 209.
32 Benjamin, "What Is Epic Theater?," 151.
33 Jarvis, *Adorno*, 39.
34 Adorno, "Essay as Form," 34.
35 Danto, "Artworld," 581.
36 Foucault, *This Is Not a Pipe*, 23–24.
37 I have written extensively on the subject of surface theory elsewhere, in, for example, Kwa, *Regarding Frames*; Kwa, "Comics at the Surface"; Kwa, "Surface."
38 Hay, "Passage of the Other," 66.
39 Love, "Close but Not Deep."
40 Culler, *Structuralist Poetics*; Iser, *Implied Reader*.
41 Milutis, *Ether*.
42 Mitchell, "Commitment to Form," 324.
43 Fish, *Surprised by Sin*; Fish, *Is There a Text in This Class?*
44 Brown, "Thing Theory," 3–4.
45 Ingawanij, "Animism and the Performative Realist Cinema," 92.
46 Hatfield, *Alternative Comics*, 36.
47 Pizzino, *Arresting Development*; Heimermann and Tullis, *Picturing Childhood*; Ahmed, "Children in Graphic Novels"; Ahmed, *Strong Bonds*.
48 Machosky, "Comics Creator Frank Santoro."
49 Novak, "Experiments in Life-Writing," 3.

Chapter 1   The People Upstairs

1 As we write in our article on this book, Ferris's maximalist attitude is precisely what gives life to this fantastical storyworld and suggests a generous path forward in our readings of it and other books like it. Ahmed and Kwa, "Kill the Monster!"
2 Jenkins, *Comics and Stuff*, 195.
3 Ingawanij, "Animism and the Performative Realist Cinema," 91.
4 Szép, *Comics and the Body*, 5.
5 Ferris, *My Favorite Thing Is Monsters*, n.p.
6 Ferris, *My Favorite Thing Is Monsters*, n.p.
7 Ferris, *My Favorite Thing Is Monsters*, n.p.
8 Ferris, *My Favorite Thing Is Monsters*, n.p.
9 Ferris, *My Favorite Thing Is Monsters*, n.p.
10 Moncion, "Time Frames," 199; see also Chaney, *Reading Lessons in Seeing*, 178–179.
11 Groensteen, "Le Réseau et Le Lieu."
12 Landsberg, *Prosthetic Memory*, 2.
13 Landsberg, *Engaging the Past*, 19.
14 Hirsch, *Generation of Postmemory*, 33.
15 Hirsch, *Generation of Postmemory*, 21.
16 Hirsch, *Generation of Postmemory*, 36.
17 Ahmed, *Queer Phenomenology*, 178.
18 Ahmed, *Queer Phenomenology*, 90.
19 Ferris, *My Favorite Thing Is Monsters*, n.p.
20 Ferris, *My Favorite Thing Is Monsters*, n.p.
21 My translation from Groensteen, "Le Réseau et Le Lieu," 118; Groensteen, *System of Comics*, 22.

22 Groensteen, *System of Comics*, 10.
23 For a short discussion of the pervasiveness of monster culture during the 1960s, see Jenkins, *Comics and Stuff*, 196–201.
24 Johnson, "My Monster/My Self," 16.
25 Ferris, "Bite That Changed My Life."
26 Ferris, *My Favorite Thing Is Monsters*, n.p.
27 Bachelard, *Poetics of Space*, 17–18.
28 Bachelard, *Poetics of Space*, 25–26.
29 Ferris, *My Favorite Thing Is Monsters*, n.p.
30 Ferris, *My Favorite Thing Is Monsters*, n.p.
31 Ferris, *My Favorite Thing Is Monsters*, n.p.
32 Ferris, *My Favorite Thing Is Monsters*, n.p.
33 Ahmed, *Monstrous Imaginaries*, 172.
34 Ferris, *My Favorite Thing Is Monsters*, n.p.
35 Ferris, "Bite That Changed My Life."
36 For a study of the influence of this and other graphic novels of "social engagement" on Ferris, see Hassler-Forest, "My Favorite Thing Is Monsters."
37 Spiegelman, *MetaMaus*, 16.
38 Spiegelman, *Complete Maus*, 101–105.
39 Hirsch, "Generation of Postmemory," 108.

Chapter 2   Reach Out and Touch Someone

1 "Comics is a site-specific medium; it can't be re-flowed, re-jiggered on the page; hence, it is spatially located on the page the way that poetry often must be." Chute, "Secret Labor by Hillary Chute."
2 Brookes, "No Strings."
3 Brookes, "No Strings," 127–128.
4 This is a realization that is made even more stark in the case of digital reproductions of a book, in which each "page" does indeed become its own discrete entity.
5 Brookes, "No Strings," 134.
6 Fish, *Surprised by Sin*, 26–27.
7 "[The reader's] inability to read the poem with any confidence in his own perception is its focus." Fish, *Surprised by Sin*, 4.
8 Derrida, *Writing and Difference*, 27.
9 For my earlier survey of the different disciplinary dialogues that have informed surface literary theory, see Kwa, "Surface."
10 Kwa, "Surface."
11 Bruno, *Surface*.
12 In addition to Bruno, see also Hay, "Passage of the Other," 62–69; Hay, *Sensuous Surfaces*.
13 Sankovitch, "Structure/Ornament and the Modern Figuration of Architecture."
14 Derrida, *On Touching*, 6.
15 Friedberg, *Virtual Window*.
16 Merleau-Ponty, *Phenomenology of Perception*, 106.
17 Brown, "Thing Theory," 4.
18 Parker, *Subversive Stitch*, xix.
19 As with all kinds of media, there will be exceptions. For a discussion of a particularly compelling case from 1830 England, see Flower, "Wilful Design." For another example of the flourishing of embroidered objects in late Qing dynasty China, see

Silberstein, *Fashionable Century*. A recent and profound book-length exploration of an embroidered material object is Miles, *All That She Carried*.

20 The Finnish artist uses a variety of media including embroidery to represent stories. Moisseinen, *Setit Ja Partituurit*.

21 Brookes, *Black Project* (Myriad Editions, 2009), n.p.

22 Brookes, *Black Project*, n.p.

23 Brookes, *Black Project*, n.p.

24 Brookes, *Black Project*, n.p.

25 Brookes, *Black Project*, afterword.

26 Brookes, *Black Project*, afterword.

27 Brookes, *Black Project*, n.p.

28 Brookes, *Black Project*, n.p.

29 Brookes, *Black Project*, n.p.

30 Brookes, *Black Project*, n.p.

31 Brookes, *Black Project*, n.p.

32 Brookes, *Thousand Coloured Castles*.

33 Brookes, *Dancing Plague*.

34 I have written on this phenomenon in the work of Emile (BloodBros) Holmewood, "Speech Bubble." See Kwa, "In Box."

35 Brookes, *Threadbare*.

Chapter 3   Phantom Threads

1 See chapter 3 on Dash Shaw in Kwa, *Regarding Frames*.

2 Pizzino, *Arresting Development*, 48.

3 Stechschulte, *Generous Impression*.

4 Readers who have acquired these books directly from the author may be happily surprised by one of these pieces of tracing paper tucked between the pages, as I have been.

5 Kane, *High-Tech Trash*, 48.

6 Kane, *High-Tech Trash*, 9.

7 Michel Foucault in his introduction to Canguilhem, *Normal and the Pathological*, 21–22.

8 Bechdel, *Fun Home*, 6.

9 Bechdel, *Fun Home*, 100–101.

10 Bechdel, *Fun Home*, 101.

11 Bechdel, *Fun Home*, 100.

12 Stechschulte, *Christmas in Prison*, n.p.

13 Stechschulte, *Christmas in Prison*.

14 Stechschulte, *Christmas in Prison*.

15 Stechschulte, *Amateurs*.

16 Stechschulte, *Amateurs*.

17 Stechschulte, *Amateurs*.

18 Stechschulte, *Amateurs*.

19 Stechschulte, *Amateurs*.

20 Flescher, "Language of Nonsese in Alice," 129.

21 Lecercle, *Philosophy of Nonsense*, 2.

22 Stechschulte, *Generous Bosom*.

23 Stechschulte, *Ultrasound*. Readers are directed to this now more easily available collected volume, but this chapter refers to the original risoprinted issues of the *Generous Bosom* series throughout.

24 Stechschulte, *Generous Bosom: A Dry Spell Ended*, 1:4.

25 Stechschulte, *Generous Bosom: A Dry Spell Ended*, 1:51.

26 Stechschulte, *Generous Bosom: A Dry Spell Ended*, 1:65.

27 Stechschulte, *Generous Bosom: Ears Rung*.

28 Brown, "Thing Theory," 4.

29 Benjamin, "Work of Art in the Age of Mechanical Reproduction."

30 Stechschulte, *Generous Bosom: The Human Element*.

31 Stechschulte, *Generous Bosom: A Dry Spell Ended*, 1:32.

32 Stechschulte, *Generous Bosom: The Human Element*, 2:49–50.

33 Stechschulte, *Generous Bosom: Ears Rung*, 3:30–31.

34 Stechschulte, *Generous Bosom: Ears Rung*, 3:46.

35 Stechschulte, *Generous Bosom*.

36 Stechschulte, *Generous Bosom: The Human Element*, 2:12–18.

37 Stechschulte, *Generous Bosom*.

Chapter 4   If You See Something Say Something

1 Drnaso, *Sabrina*, back cover.

2 The book was reviewed widely including in Terrien, "Sabrina"; Smith, "Nick Drnaso's 'Sabrina' and Affronts to Truth"; "Sabrina"; Park, "Graphic Content"; Yo Zushi, "Dystopia Now"; Winslow-Yost, "Savage Torpor"; Saler, "Boundary Technician."

3 Bronfen, *Over Her Dead Body*, 59.

4 Chute, *Disaster Drawn*, 67.

5 Chute, *Disaster Drawn*, 168.

6 Keats Citron, "Cyber Mobs, Disinformation, and Death Videos," 1073.

7 Keats Citron, "Cyber Mobs, Disinformation, and Death Videos," 1081.

8 Butte, *I Know That You Know That I Know*, 9.

9 Genette, Lewin, and Macksey, *Paratexts*, 8.

10 Drnaso, *Sabrina*, 2–3.

11 Minsky, "Framework for Representing Knowledge," n.p.

12 The way that such contextualizing frames shape everyday experience was the subject of sociologist Erving Goffman's influential study in 1974. Goffman, *Frame Analysis*.

13 Jahn, "Frames, Preferences, and the Reading of Third-Person Narratives," 459.

14 Jahn, "Frames, Preferences, and the Reading of Third-Person Narratives," 461.

15 Jahn, "Frames, Preferences, and the Reading of Third-Person Narratives," 461.

16 Jahn, "Frames, Preferences, and the Reading of Third-Person Narratives," 464.

17 Jahn, "Frames, Preferences, and the Reading of Third-Person Narratives," 465.

18 Drnaso, *Sabrina*, 177.

19 On the competent reader, see Culler, *Structuralist Poetics*.

20 Drnaso, *Sabrina*, 104.

21 Drnaso, *Sabrina*, 104–105.

22 Morson, "Sideshadowing and Tempics," 600. These ideas are also developed in Morson's book *Narrative and Freedom*.

23 Morson, "Sideshadowing and Tempics," 601.

24 Drnaso, *Sabrina*, 15.

25 The base was renamed Peterson Space Force Base in 2021.

26 Drnaso, *Sabrina*, 23.

27 Drnaso, *Sabrina*, 23, 52.

28 See Figure 4.

29 Drnaso, *Sabrina*, 115.
30 Drnaso, *Sabrina*, 144.
31 Derrida, "Living On," 78.
32 Drnaso, *Sabrina*, 20.
33 Drnaso, *Sabrina*, 37.
34 Drnaso, *Sabrina*, 136.
35 Drnaso, *Sabrina*, 9.
36 Drnaso, *Sabrina*, 38–39.
37 Drnaso, *Sabrina*, 66–69.
38 Drnaso, *Sabrina*, 81.
39 Drnaso, *Sabrina*, 82.
40 Butler, *Force of Nonviolence*, 196–197.
41 Drnaso, *Sabrina*, 57–64.
42 Butler, *Force of Nonviolence*, 197–198.
43 Drnaso, *Sabrina*, 52.
44 Drnaso, *Sabrina*, 81.
45 Drnaso, *Sabrina*, 119–121.
46 Drnaso, *Sabrina*, 121.
47 Drnaso, *Sabrina*, 122.
48 Drnaso, *Sabrina*, 155.
49 Drnaso, *Sabrina*, 89.
50 Drnaso, *Sabrina*, 108.
51 Drnaso, *Sabrina*, 52.
52 Drnaso, *Sabrina*, 53.
53 Drnaso, *Sabrina*, 87.
54 Drnaso, *Sabrina*, 93.
55 Drnaso, *Sabrina*, 94.
56 Drnaso, *Sabrina*, 53, 146.
57 Drnaso, *Sabrina*, 137.
58 Drnaso, *Sabrina*, 139–140.

Chapter 5   There Is a Monster in My Closet

1 The editions are, respectively, Evens, *Panter*; Evens, *Panthère*; Evens and Kluitmann, *Panter*; Evens, *Panther*.
2 Chaney, "Animal Subjects of the Graphic Novel," 130.
3 Brown, "Brecht Evens on Crafting Horror."
4 Kerascoët is the pen name used by the artist collaborators Marie Pommepuy and Sébastien Cosset. They are the illustrators of the book and the story was written by Marie Pommepuy with Fabien Vehlmann.
5 Vehlmann, Kerascoët, and Pommepuy, *Beautiful Darkness*, 94–95.
6 McCloud details a taxonomy of the kinds of shifts between panels in *Understanding Comics*.
7 Derrida and Wills, "Animal That Therefore I Am," 373.
8 Cremins, "Funny Animals."
9 Witek, *Comic Books as History*, 110.
10 Orvell, "Writing Posthistorically," 119.
11 Chaney, "Animal Subjects of the Graphic Novel," 130.
12 Zirker and Winter-Froemel, *Wordplay and Metalinguistic/Metadiscursive Reflection*, 8.
13 Hutcheon, *Narcissistic Narrative*, 6.

14 Barthes, *S/Z*.
15 McCloud, *Understanding Comics*.
16 Groensteen, *System of Comics*, 114.
17 Groensteen, *System of Comics*, 98–100.
18 Groensteen, *System of Comics*, 117.
19 Postema, *Narrative Structure in Comics*, 14.
20 Deleuze and Guattari, *Thousand Plateaus*.
21 Beaulieu, "Status of Animality in Deleuze's Thought," 85.
22 Gardner and MacCormack, *Deleuze and the Animal*, 5.
23 Evens, *Panther*, n.p.
24 Evens, *Panther*, n.p.
25 Klausen and Passman, "Pretend Companions (Imaginary Playmates)," 357.
26 Le Saux and Evens, "La Bédéthèque Idéale #75."
27 Evens, *Panther*, n.p.
28 Evens, *Panther*, n.p.
29 Evens, *Panther*, n.p.
30 Ominously, "watch out for Pa" could be suggestively read as a warning about Christine's father.
31 Evens, *Panther*, n.p.
32 Evens, *Panther*.
33 Groensteen, *System of Comics*, 22.
34 Zirker and Winter-Froemel, *Wordplay and Metalinguistic/Metadiscursive Reflection*, 14.
35 Goth, "Double Entendre in Restoration and Early Eighteenth-Century Comedy," 79–80.
36 Evens, *Panther*, n.p.
37 Evens, *Panther*, n.p.
38 Evens, *Panther*, n.p.
39 Evens, *Panther*, n.p.
40 Lawlor, "Following the Rats," 169.
41 Baker, *Picturing the Beast*, 108.
42 Agamben, *Homo Sacer*, 109.
43 Agamben, *Homo Sacer*, 67.
44 Agamben, *Homo Sacer*, 8.
45 Agamben, *Homo Sacer*, 128.

Conclusion

1 Bethea, *Francis Bacon*. In a private email conversation with me, Bethea reluctantly supplied the term "kinda poetic comics" as an unsatisfactory but currently adequate descriptor for these graphic narratives.
2 Bethea, *Book of Daze*.
3 Bethea, *Book of Daze*, n.p.
4 Bethea, *Book of Daze*, n.p.
5 Bethea, *Book of Daze*, n.p.
6 Bethea, *Francis Bacon*, n.p.
7 Bethea, *Francis Bacon*, n.p.

Bibliography

Adorno, Theodor. "The Culture Industry Reconsidered." *New German Critique* 6 (1975): 12–19.

———. "The Essay as Form." In *Notes to Literature*, edited by Rolf Tiedemann, translated by Shierry Weber Nicholsen, 29–47. New York: Columbia University Press, 2019.

Agamben, Giorgio. *Homo Sacer: Sovereign Power and Bare Life*. Translated by Daniel Heller-Roazen. Stanford, CA: Stanford University Press, 1998.

Ahmed, Maaheen. "Children in Graphic Novels: Intermedial Encounters and Mnemonic Layers." *Etudes Francophones* 32 (Spring 2020): 129–148.

———. *Monstrous Imaginaries: The Legacy of Romanticism in Comics*. Jackson: University Press of Mississippi, 2019.

———, ed. *Strong Bonds: Child-Animal Relationships in Comics*. Liège: Presses Universitaires de Liège, 2021.

Ahmed, Maaheen, and Shiamin Kwa. "Kill the Monster! My Favorite Thing Is Monsters and the Big, Ambitious (Graphic) Novel." *Genre* 54, no. 1 (2021): 17–42.

Ahmed, Sara. *Queer Phenomenology: Orientations, Objects, Others*. Durham, NC: Duke University Press Books, 2006.

Bachelard, Gaston. *The Poetics of Space*. Repr. ed. Boston: Beacon, 1994.

Baker, Steve. *Picturing the Beast: Animals, Identity, and Representation*. Urbana: University of Illinois Press, 2001.

Barthes, Roland. *S/Z*. New York: Hill & Wang, 1974.

Beaty, Bart. *Comics Versus Art*. Toronto: Toronto University Press, 2012.

Beaulieu, Alain. "The Status of Animality in Deleuze's Thought." *Journal for Critical Animal Studies* 9, no. 1/2 (2011): 69–88.

Bechdel, Alison. *Fun Home: A Family Tragicomic*. Boston: Houghton Mifflin, 2006.

Benjamin, Andrew E. *Walter Benjamin and Art*. London: Continuum, 2005.

Benjamin, Walter. "What Is Epic Theater?" In *Illuminations*, 147–154. New York: Schocken Books, 1969.

———. "The Work of Art in the Age of Mechanical Reproduction." In *Illuminations*, 217–252. New York: Schocken Books, 1969.

Bethea, E. A. *Book of Daze*. New York: Domino Books, 2017.

———. *Francis Bacon*. New York: Domino Books, 2021.

Bourdieu, Pierre. *Distinction: A Social Critique of the Judgement of Taste*. Cambridge, MA: Harvard University Press, 1984.

———. *The Logic of Practice*. Stanford, CA: Stanford University Press, 1990.

Bredehoft, Thomas A. *The Visible Text: Textual Production and Reproduction from Beowulf to Maus*. Oxford: Oxford University Press, 2014.

Bronfen, Elisabeth. *Over Her Dead Body: Death, Femininity and the Aesthetic*. New York: Routledge, 1992.

Brookes, Gareth. *The Black Project*. Brighton: Myriad Editions, 2009.

———. *The Dancing Plague*. London: SelfMade Hero, 2021.

———. "No Strings." In *BFF*, 27:127–134. Kuš! (Baltic Comics Magazine š!). Latvia: Grafiskie stāsti, 2017.

———. *A Thousand Coloured Castles*. Brighton: Myriad Editions, 2017.

———. *Threadbare*. Self-published, 2019.

Brown, Bill. "Thing Theory." *Critical Inquiry* 28, no. 1 (Autumn 2001): 1–22.

Brown, Hillary. "Brecht Evens on Crafting Horror and Storybook Beauty in Panther." *Paste Magazine*, April 27, 2016. https://www.pastemagazine.com/articles/2016/04/brecht-evens-on-crafting-horrific-storybook-beauty.html.

Bruno, Giuliana. *Surface: Matters of Aesthetics, Materiality, and Media*. Chicago: University Of Chicago Press, 2014.

Butler, Judith. *The Force of Nonviolence: An Ethico-Political Bind*. London: Verso, 2020.

Butte, George. *I Know That You Know That I Know: Narrating Subjects from Moll Flanders to Marnie*. Columbus: Ohio State University Press, 2004.

Canguilhem, Georges. *The Normal and the Pathological*. New York: Zone Books, 1989.

Chaney, Michael A. "Animal Subjects of the Graphic Novel." *College Literature* 38, no. 3 (June 26, 2011): 129–149.

———. *Reading Lessons in Seeing: Mirrors, Masks, and Mazes in the Autobiographical Graphic Novel*. Jackson: University Press of Mississippi, 2017.

Chute, Hillary L. *Disaster Drawn: Visual Witness, Comics, and Documentary Form*. Cambridge, MA: Belknap, 2016.

———. "Secret Labor by Hillary Chute." *Poetry Foundation Magazine*, July 1, 2013. https://www.poetryfoundation.org/poetrymagazine/articles/70022/secret-labor.

Crary, Jonathan. *24/7: Late Capitalism and the Ends of Sleep*. London: Verso, 2014.

Cremins, Brian. "Funny Animals." In *The Routledge Companion to Comics*, edited by Frank Bramlett, Roy T. Cook, and Aaron Meskin, 146–153. New York: Routledge, 2016.

Crucifix, Benoît. "Drawing from the Archives: Comics Memory in the Graphic Novel, Post 2000." UC Louvain, 2020.

Crucifix, Benoît, and Gert Meesters. "The Medium Is the Message: Olivier Schrauwen's Arsène Schrauwen beyond Expectations of Autobiography, Colonial History and the Graphic Novel." *European Comic Art* 9, no. 1 (2016): 24–62. https://doi.org/10.3167/eca.2016.090103.

Culler, Jonathan D. *Structuralist Poetics: Structuralism, Linguistics, and the Study of Literature*. Ithaca, NY: Cornell University Press, 1975.

Danto, Arthur. "The Artworld." *Journal of Philosophy* 61, no. 19 (1964): 571–584.

Deleuze, Gilles. *Difference and Repetition*. Translated by Paul Patton. London: Continuum, 2001.

Deleuze, Gilles, and Félix Guattari. *A Thousand Plateaus: Capitalism and Schizophrenia*. Translated by Brian Massumi. Minneapolis: University of Minnesota Press, 1987.

Derrida, Jacques. "Living On." In *Deconstruction and Criticism*, 62–142. New York: Continuum, 1979.

———. *On Touching, Jean-Luc Nancy*. Stanford, CA: Stanford University Press, 2005.

———. *Writing and Difference*. Chicago: University of Chicago Press, 1978.

Derrida, Jacques, and David Wills. "The Animal That Therefore I Am (More to Follow)." *Critical Inquiry* 28, no. 2 (2002): 369–418.

Dillon, Martin C. *Merleau-Ponty's Ontology*. Evanston, IL: Northwestern University Press, 1997.

Drnaso, Nick. *Sabrina*. Montreal: Drawn & Quarterly, 2018.

Evens, Brecht. *Panter*. Brussels: Uitgeverij Oogachtend, 2014.

———. *Panther*. Translated by Michele Hutchison and Laura Watkinson. New York: Drawn & Quarterly, 2016.

———. *Panthère*. Arles: Actes Sud Editions, 2014.

Evens, Brecht, and Andrea Kluitmann. *Panter*. Berlin: Reprodukt, 2016.

Ferris, Emil. "The Bite That Changed My Life." *Chicago*, February 8, 2017. http://www.chicagomag.com/Chicago-Magazine/February-2017/Emil-Ferris-The-Bite-That-Changed-My-Life/.

———. *My Favorite Thing Is Monsters*. Seattle: Fantagraphics, 2017.

Fish, Stanley. *Is There a Text in This Class? The Authority of Interpretive Communities*. Cambridge, MA: Harvard University Press, 1980.

———. *Surprised by Sin: The Reader in Paradise Lost*. 2nd ed. Cambridge, MA: Harvard University Press, 1998.

Flescher, Jacqueline. "The Language of Nonsense in Alice." *Yale French Studies* 43 (1969): 128–144.

Flower, Chloe. "Wilful Design: The Sampler in Nineteenth-Century Britain." *Journal of Victorian Culture* 21, no. 3 (2016): 301–321.

Foucault, Michel. *This Is Not a Pipe: With Illustrations and Letters by René Magritte*. Translated by James Harkness. Berkeley: University of California Press, 1982.

Friedberg, Anne. *The Virtual Window: From Alberti to Microsoft*. Cambridge, MA: MIT Press, 2006.

Gardner, Colin, and Patricia MacCormack, eds. *Deleuze and the Animal*. Edinburgh: Edinburgh University Press, 2017.

Gardner, Jared. *Projections: Comics and the History of Twenty-First-Century Storytelling*. Stanford, CA: Stanford University Press, 2012.

Genette, Gérard, Jane E. Lewin, and Richard Macksey. *Paratexts: Thresholds of Interpretation*. Cambridge: Cambridge University Press, 1997.

Goffman, Erving. *Frame Analysis: An Essay on the Organization of Experience*. Cambridge, MA: Harvard University Press, 1974.

Goth, Maik. "Double Entendre in Restoration and Early Eighteenth-Century Comedy." In *Wordplay and Metalinguistic/ Metadiscursive Reflection: Authors, Contexts, Techniques, and Meta-Reflection*, edited by Angelika Zirker and Esme Winter-Froemel, 71–94. Berlin: De Gruyter, 2015.

Groensteen, Thierry. "Le Réseau et Le Lieu: Pour Une Analyse Des Procédures de Tressage Iconique." In *Time, Narrative, and the Fixed Image*, 117–129. Amsterdam: Rodopi, 2001.

———. *The System of Comics*. Translated by Bart Beaty and Nick Nguyen. Jackson: University Press of Mississippi, 2009.

Hassler-Forest, Dan. "My Favorite Thing Is Monsters: The Socially Engaged Graphic Novel as a Platform for Intersectional Feminism." In *The Oxford Handbook of Comic Book Studies*, 490–509. New York: Oxford University Press, 2020.

Hatfield, Charles. *Alternative Comics: An Emerging Literature*. Jackson: University Press of Mississippi, 2005.

Hay, Jonathan. "The Passage of the Other: Elements for a Redefinition of Ornament." In *Histories of Ornament: From Global to Local*, edited by Gülru Necipoğlu and Alina Payne, 62–69. Princeton, NJ: Princeton University Press, 2016.

———. *Sensuous Surfaces: The Decorative Object in Early Modern China*. Honolulu: University of Hawaii Press, 2010.

Heimermann, Mark, and Brittany Tullis. *Picturing Childhood: Youth in Transnational Comics*. Austin: University of Texas Press, 2017.

Hirsch, Marianne. *Family Frames: Photography, Narrative, and Postmemory*. Cambridge, MA: Harvard University Press, 1997.

———. "The Generation of Postmemory." *Poetics Today* 29, no. 1 (March 1, 2008): 103–128.

———. *The Generation of Postmemory: Writing and Visual Culture after the Holocaust*. New York: Columbia University Press, 2012.

Holmewood, Emile (BloodBros). "Speech Bubble." In *BFF*, 91–94. Š! 27. Latvia: Kuš Komiksi, 2017.

Horkheimer, Max, and Theodor W. Adorno. *Dialectic of Enlightenment: Philosophical Fragments*. Stanford, CA: Stanford University Press, 2002.

Hutcheon, Linda. *Narcissistic Narrative: The Metafictional Paradox*. Waterloo, Ontario: Wilfrid Laurier University Press, 2013.

Ingawanij, May Adadol. "Animism and the Performative Realist Cinema of Apichatpong Weerasethakul." In *Screening Nature: Cinema beyond the Human*, edited by Anat Pick and Guinevere Narraway, 91–109. New York: Berghahn Books, 2013.

Iser, Wolfgang. *The Implied Reader: Patterns of Communication in Prose Fiction from Bunyan to Beckett*. Baltimore: Johns Hopkins University Press, 1978.

Jahn, Manfred. "Frames, Preferences, and the Reading of Third-Person Narratives: Towards a Cognitive Narratology." *Poetics Today* 18, no. 4 (1997): 441–468.

Jarvis, Simon. *Adorno: A Critical Introduction*. New York: Routledge, 1998.

Jenkins, Henry. *Comics and Stuff*. New York: New York University Press, 2020.

Johnson, Barbara. "My Monster/My Self." *Diacritics* 12 (1992): 2–10.

Kane, Carolyn L. *High-Tech Trash*. Oakland: University of California Press, 2019.

Kashtan, Aaron. *Between Pen and Pixel: Comics, Materiality, and the Book of the Future*. Columbus: Ohio State University Press, 2018.

Keats Citron, Danielle. "Cyber Mobs, Disinformation, and Death Videos: The Internet as It Is (and as It Should Be)." *Michigan Law Review* 118, no. 6 (2020): 1073–1093.

Klausen, Espen, and Richard H Passman. "Pretend Companions (Imaginary Playmates): The Emergence of a Field." *Journal of Genetic Psychology* 167, no. 4 (2006): 349–364.

Kwa, Shiamin. "Comics at the Surface: Michael DeForge's Ant Colony." *Word & Image* 32, no. 4 (October 1, 2016): 340–359.

———. "In Box: Text and the Speech Bubble in the Digital Age." In *The Oxford Handbook of Comic Book Studies*, 36–52. Oxford: Oxford University Press, 2020.

———. *Regarding Frames: Thinking with Comics in the Twenty-First Century*. Rochester, NY: RIT Press, 2020.

———. "Surface." In *The Oxford Encyclopedia of Literary Theory*, edited by John Frow. Oxford: Oxford University Press, 2022.

Landsberg, Alison. *Engaging the Past: Mass Culture and the Production of Historical Knowledge*. New York: Columbia University Press, 2015.

———. *Prosthetic Memory: The Transformation of American Remembrance in the Age of Mass Culture*. New York: Columbia University Press, 2004.

Lawlor, Leonard. "Following the Rats: Becoming-Animal in Deleuze and Guattari." *SubStance* 37.3, no. 117 (2008): 169–187.

Lecercle, Jean-Jacques. *Philosophy of Nonsense: The Intuitions of Victorian Nonsense Literature*. London: Taylor & Francis, 1994.

Le Saux, Laurence, and Brecht Evens. "La Bédéthèque Idéale #75: La Panthère Rosse de Brecht Evens." January 22, 2015. http://www.telerama.fr/livre/la-bedetheque-ideale -75-la-panthere-rosse-de-brecht-evens,121766.php.

Love, Heather. "Close but Not Deep: Literary Ethics and the Descriptive Turn." *New Literary History* 41, no. 2 (2010): 371–391.

Machosky, Michael. "Comics Creator Frank Santoro Explores Growing Up in 'Pittsburgh.'" *Trib Live*, September 20, 2019. https://triblive.com/local/pittsburgh -allegheny/comics-creator-frank-santoro-explores-growing-up-in-pittsburgh/.

Marx, Karl, and Friedrich Engels. *Capital: A Critique of Political Economy*. Translated by Ben. Fowkes. London: Penguin, 1990.

McCloud, Scott. *Understanding Comics: The Invisible Art*. New York: HarperCollins, 1993.

Merleau-Ponty, Maurice. *Phenomenology of Perception*. New York: Psychology Press, 2002.

Miles, Tiya. *All That She Carried: The Journey of Ashley's Sack, a Black Family Keepsake*. New York: Random House, 2021.

Milutis, Joe. *Ether: The Nothing That Connects Everything*. Minneapolis: University of Minnesota Press, 2006.

Minsky, Marvin. "A Framework for Representing Knowledge." June 1974. https:// courses.media.mit.edu/2004spring/mas966/Minsky%201974%20Framework%20 for%20knowledge.pdf.

Mitchell, W. J. T. "The Commitment to Form; or, Still Crazy after All These Years." *PMLA* 118, no. 2 (2003): 321–325.

Moisseinen, Hanneriina. *Setit Ja Partituurit—Häpeällisiä Tarinoita*. Finland: Huuda Huuda, 2010.

Moncion, Laura. "Time Frames: Graphic Narrative and Historiography in Richard McGuire's Here." *Imaginations: Journal of Cross-Cultural Image Studies* 7, no. 2 (2017): 198–213.

Morson, Gary Saul. *Narrative and Freedom: The Shadows of Time*. Rev. ed. New Haven, CT: Yale University Press, 1996.

———. "Sideshadowing and Tempics." *New Literary History* 29, no. 4 (1998): 599–624.

Novak, Julia. "Experiments in Life-Writing: Introduction." In *Experiments in Life-Writing: Intersections of Auto/Biography and Fiction*, edited by Lucia Boldrini and Julia Novak, 1–36. Cham: Springer, 2017.

Orvell, Miles. "Writing Posthistorically: Krazy Kat, Maus, and the Contemporary Fiction Cartoon." *American Literary History* 4, no. 1 (1992): 110–128.

Park, Ed. "Can You Illustrate Emotional Absence? These Graphic Novels Do." *New York Times Book Review,* June 3, 2018, 37.

Parker, Rozsika. *The Subversive Stitch: Embroidery and the Making of the Feminine*. London: Bloomsbury, 2010.

Pizzino, Christopher. *Arresting Development: Comics at the Boundaries of Literature*. Austin: University of Texas Press, 2016.

Postema, Barbara. *Narrative Structure in Comics: Making Sense of Fragments*. Rochester, NY: RIT Press, 2013.

Prosser, Howard. "Introduction." In *Dialectic of Enlightenment in the Anglosphere: Horkheimer and Adorno's Remnants of Freedom*, 1–9. Singapore: Springer, 2020.

"Sabrina." *Publishers Weekly* 265, no. 2 (2018): 48.

Saler, Michael. "Boundary Technician." *Times Literary Supplement*, no. 6004 (2018): 12.

Saltzman, Lisa. *Daguerreotypes: Fugitive Subjects, Contemporary Objects*. Chicago: University of Chicago Press, 2015.

Sankovitch, Anne-Marie. "Structure/Ornament and the Modern Figuration of Architecture." *Art Bulletin* 80, no. 4 (1998): 687–717.

Satrapi, Marjane. *The Complete Persepolis*. New York: Pantheon Books, 2007.

Shaw, Dash. *Bottomless Belly Button*. Seattle: Fantagraphics, 2008.

Silberstein, Rachel. *A Fashionable Century: Textile Artistry and Commerce in the Late Qing*. Seattle: University of Washington Press, 2020.

Smith, Gregory. "Nick Drnaso's 'Sabrina' and Affronts to Truth." *PopMatters*, October 17, 2018.

Spiegelman, Art. *The Complete Maus*. New York: Pantheon, 1996.

———. *MetaMaus: A Look Inside a Modern Classic, Maus*. New York: Pantheon, 2011.

Stechschulte, Conor. *The Amateurs*. Chicago: Crepuscular Archives, 2011.

———. *Christmas in Prison*. Chicago: Crepuscular Archives, 2016.

———. *Generous Bosom*. Vol. 4. London: Breakdown Press, 2021.

———. *Generous Bosom: A Dry Spell Ended*. Vol. 1. London: Breakdown Press, 2014.

———. *Generous Bosom: Ears Rung*. Vol. 3. London: Breakdown Press, 2017.

———. *Generous Bosom: The Human Element*. Vol. 2. London: Breakdown Press, 2015.

———. *Generous Impression*. Chicago: Crepuscular Archives, 2014.

———. *Ultrasound*. Seattle: Fantagraphics, 2022.

Szép, Eszter. *Comics and the Body: Drawing, Reading, and Vulnerability*. Columbus: Ohio State University Press, 2020.

Terrien, David. "Sabrina." *Art Review* 70, no. 5 (2018): 126.

Vehlmann, Fabien, Kerascoët, and Marie Pommepuy. *Beautiful Darkness*. Translated by Helge Dascher. Montreal: Drawn & Quarterly, 2014.

Winslow-Yost, Gabriel. "Savage Torpor: Nick Drnaso's Hypnotically Grim Graphic Novels." *Harper's Magazine* 337, no. 2019 (2018): 70–73.

Witek, Joseph. *Comic Books as History: The Narrative Art of Jack Jackson, Art Spiegelman, and Harvey Pekar*. Jackson: University Press of Mississippi, 1989.

Yo Zushi. "Dystopia Now." *New Statesman* 147, no. 5431 (2018): 52–53.

Zirker, Angelika, and Esme Winter-Froemel. *Wordplay and Metalinguistic/Metadiscursive Reflection: Authors, Contexts, Techniques, and Meta-Reflection*. Berlin: De Gruyter, 2015.

Index

Page numbers in italic indicate illustrations.

About the Author

SHIAMIN KWA teaches at Bryn Mawr College. She is the author of *Regarding Frames: Thinking with Comics in the Twenty-First Century.*